Tony Collins, 34, is execu
Weekly. He began his care
Crawley Advertiser and la national
newspapers, including the *Daily Mail* and *Sunday Mirror*. He has also worked for the BBC and for technical magazines. His articles have appeared in the *Listener* and the *Independent* and he is a regular contributor to radio and TV. In December 1989 he became the UK Technology Press Awards Features Journalist of the Year. He is married with two young children.

Stephen Arkell, 29, was the UK Technology Press Awards News Journalist of the Year 1985. In 1986 he became news editor of *Computer News* and reported for BBC TV's *Micro Live* programme. Since leaving *Computer News* in 1987 he has worked for Thames TV's *City Programme* and is currently a news journalist with ITN.

OPEN VERDICT

An account of 25 mysterious deaths
in the defence industry

by
Tony Collins

Edited by
Stephen Arkell

SPHERE BOOKS LTD

A Sphere Book

First published in Great Britain by Sphere Books Limited 1990

Grateful acknowledgement is made to Peter Watson and Peters, Fraser and Dunlop for permission to include extracts from *War on the Mind: The Military Uses and Abuses of Psychology* by Peter Watson (Hutchinson 1978)

Grateful acknowledgement is also made to William Collins, Sons & Co Ltd and Andrew Lownie 15/17 Heddon Street, London W1R 7LF for permission to include extracts from *Spy* by Richard Deacon with Nigel West (Grafton 1988)

Grateful acknowledgement is also made to Weidenfeld & Nicolson Ltd for permission to include extracts from *GCHQ – The Secret Wireless War* by Nigel West (Coronet Books 1987)

Photoset in North Wales by
Derek Doyle & Associates, Mold, Clwyd
Printed and bound in Great Britain by
Richard Clay Ltd, Bungay, Suffolk

ISBN 07474 0146 2

Sphere Books Ltd
A Division of
Macdonald & Co (Publishers) Ltd
Orbit House
1 New Fetter Lane
London EC4A 1AR
A member of Maxwell Macmillan Pergamon Publishing Corporation

Acknowledgments

Particular thanks are due to the families of the deceased who have made the book possible by supplying information about their loved ones in the hope that my investigation would throw some light on why they died. I hope the book does not disappoint them. I am also grateful to the following for their help in the investigation of the deaths: ABC (*20/20* programme), NBC, Thames Television (*Reporting London*), HTV (*The West This Week*) and Australia's *60 Minutes*. Thanks also to BBC's *Out of Court* programme for help with the Jonathan Wash case. Many journalists, and others, have written articles or supplied information which has proved particularly useful. Some names that spring to mind include Andrew Bell and Gerry Gable of *Time Out*; the Bristol Press and Picture Agency; South West News and Pictures; John Sweeney of the *Independent Magazine*; Madeleine Burton of the *Herts Advertiser*; Tony Tweedie of the *Derby Evening Telegraph*; journalist Brian Inch; defence specialist Ted Hooton; Keith Dovkants of the *Evening Standard*; Shaun Williams of South West Counties Newspapers Ltd; the *Evening Post*, Bristol; June Sparey of the *Camberley News*; Val Tyler of the *Epping Gazette*; Will Bennett of the *Mail on Sunday; New Life Asian Weekly;* the *Sunday Telegraph*; the *Evening Argus*, Brighton; Alan Johnson of the *Evening Advertiser*, Swindon; Colin Pritchard, specialist in social work and suicide statistics at Southampton University, and particularly Antony Preston who advised me on specific aspects of the defence industry.

I am especially indebted to the book's editor Stephen Arkell who has managed not only to smooth over large areas of syntactic imperfections but has been unremittingly supportive since the early days of the investigation by providing useful material and invaluable advice. Thanks also to Ian Cheeseman, my former editor who had the courage to print the original story and to my former editorial director Ron Condon who has been a trusted adviser and whose contact provided the tip-off that prompted the investigation. Finally my thanks or rather my sympathy to my wife Caroline who has coped with being a single parent for the past two years.

Contents

Prologue

The world hopes that warmer relations between East and West could one day make nuclear weapons obsolete. In superpower terms, they already are obsolete. The military, particularly in the West, have been unable to rely upon the political will to use nuclear weapons for the past forty years. Instead, they have commissioned the technocrats to work out ways in which conventional weapons can be used to eliminate more targets. They have used technology, in times of shrinking defence budgets, to give their armies 'more bang per buck'. They have devised methods of making their own ships and planes invisible to the enemy's radar. They have discovered how computers and telecommunications can allow one soldier to do the jobs of ten. They have learnt that a computer chip can just as easily aim and pull the trigger, and that a computer chip does not need to be fed and clothed.

This book is about a new type of war, electronic war. It is not fought on a battlefield with swords and spears, or their modern day equivalents. It is fought in the laboratories of defence research establishments with circuit boards and software. It is not fought by generals and lieutenants but by research students in universities and electronics engineers working for defence contractors. It is not a war that can be declared, it is a war that must be waged constantly during peacetime to maintain the upper hand. It is a war that must be waged in secrecy.

When the initial tip-off came just before Christmas 1986, neither Tony nor myself were aware that the apparent suicides in Bristol of two Asian programmers working for Marconi might be connected with this secret war. At the time, I was news editor and Tony was chief reporter on the weekly business magazine *Computer News*. A City electronics analyst had spoken about the deaths to the magazine's editorial director, Ron Condon. The analyst had also heard that Marconi was being investigated by the fraud squad in connection with allegations made about certain defence contracts. He wondered if there might be a link between the deaths, or whether they had been in some way precipitated by the fraud inquiry. The search for an answer began.

The attitude of the dead workers' families was, for the most part, that no matter how or why their loved ones had died, nothing would bring them back. They did not want to be besieged by the press. Yet as long as serious doubt remained, the wounds of bereavement could never properly begin to heal. Relatives who later shunned worldwide media attention granted the magazine interviews at this stage because of the investigative nature of its approach. Those interviews, and later interviews with the families of others who died, form an important part of this book, although where the information given was particularly sensitive, names have been omitted.

After a lengthy investigation, it became clear that there were definitely unanswered questions about the circumstances surrounding the deaths of the two men, although if murder was involved no motive was apparent. In deciding to print the original story, we got our first glimpse of the paranoia that grips electronics companies who work for the Ministry of Defence. Even before Marconi was asked for a comment on the deaths for inclusion in the story, one of the company's public relations officers rang our offices on several occasions to say that we had received confidential information, and that some of that information had been 'jumbled'. He said that the information Tony had received from talking to employees at the dead men's workplaces 'might be useful to an enemy'. He wanted to meet Tony, take him out to lunch, give him a guided tour of the company's factory. Finally, he spoke to the magazine's editor, Ian Cheeseman, and asked for details of what we intended to publish. When his request was refused on journalistic grounds, his tone became menacing. 'There's an easy or a hard way to go about this,' he said. Marconi eventually gave an official comment.

A different press officer said, 'The dead men were not involved in top secret programmes. They were not working on the same programme. They were at separate sites. There is no link whatsoever.'

The story was published in *Computer News* on Thursday, 5 March 1987. Since then, many other deaths and bizarre incidents involving defence workers have come to light. This book details 28 such cases. That number by no means represents every death or accident involving somebody working in a defence related area. Undoubtedly some have yet to come to light. Our research could not extend to every report of every accident, suicide or murder in every national, regional and local newspaper. Many reports of such incidents contain little or no details of the dead person's work. This is more often than not because of sheer lack of space. Sometimes, however, it is because such details have been suppressed by the authorities. Furthermore, many accidents, suicides and murders go unreported. In 1986, for example, 685 people were murdered in the UK, but only 300 or so were deemed worthy of coverage in the national press. Additionally, a number of other cases, where, for example, there were independent witnesses or definite suicide notes, have been deliberately omitted from this book.

Everybody who has taken an interest in or written about the mystery deaths since the story was printed in 1987 has wanted to know the answer to one question. Are the deaths linked? A link between the scientists' work, or the fact that they were, perhaps, all suffering from chronic stress, might provide the connection. Yet the simplest explanation could be mere coincidence. Statistics show that, among males between the ages of fifteen and fifty-nine, suicide is the third most common cause of death after accidents and cancer. In that age bracket, suicide is also ten times more common than murder. Official figures show that in 1987, 4,500 people, the equivalent of one in every 12,650, killed themselves in the UK. Taking Marconi as an example, we might therefore expect there to have been a minimum of nine and a maximum of twelve suicides among its 47,000 male and female workers during the three years 1986, 1987 and 1988. In fact there were, to the best of our knowledge, only five which resemble suicide. When, however, it is realized that the majority of those who commit suicide are already receiving clinical treatment for a mental illness, and that it is unlikely in the extreme that a defence contractor would knowingly continue to employ someone who was mentally ill, then Marconi's suicide rate is higher than the national average.

In the end, it is unlikely that statistics can be used to either prove or disprove that anything sinister has been taking place. If the number of deaths in the defence industry is lower than average, it does not lessen the likelihood that any one of them is suspicious. Similarly, a higher than average death rate does not make murder more likely. The figures could merely represent a statistical fluke. Only a close examination of each death can yield any clues to the truth. If in just one of the cases there is enough doubt to overturn a previous assumption of accident or suicide, it must surely be a cause for deep concern.

As for a link between the deaths, a work connection might lead to the conclusion that we have stumbled upon a conspiracy. It might, after all, provide a motive if everybody involved had been working on the same project. It might even point a finger at who, if anyone, would wish to murder these people. If, on the other hand, all the dead scientists could be shown to have been suffering from stress, it would lend weight to the theory that an increase in the pressure of defence work, coupled perhaps with the inability to share work problems with family members because of the secrecy involved, caused them to end it all. Obtaining any information, however, about what the defence workers had been employed on has proved extremely difficult. The companies and establishments where they worked are reluctant to give out details of any projects, even those already in the public domain. In addition, there are many other projects, so-called 'black' projects, which these organizations cannot even officially admit to.

The secrecy surrounding the peacetime preparations for a future electronic war ensures that any attempt to prove or disprove a definite work link can be no more than a calculated stab in the dark. When the national press and media followed up the *Computer News* story in 1987, there was much speculation that the scientists had all been involved in various aspects of the US Star Wars project. The theory was that foreign intelligence agents had been targeting Star Wars contractors and civilians working in Ministry of Defence establishments and were now closing the operation down. This seemed as plausible a theory as any on offer at the time. Civilian scientists lead a relatively unrestricted lifestyle compared to their military counterparts. This makes them easier prey for today's spies, who are more likely to be the kind of suited businessmen seen at defence exhibitions than the traditional cloak and dagger types portrayed in thrillers. In May 1989, for example, eleven Russians and four Czechs were expelled from the UK for allegedly trying to obtain highly sensitive information about powerful microchips, radar, laser technology and advanced materials such as titanium and carbon fibres. These agents were reported to have approached the executives of defence contractors in a series of 'cash for secrets' deals.

Another theory which has surfaced occasionally concerns the investigation into alleged fraud at Marconi. Our initial informant, nearly three years ago, proved correct in saying that there was an investigation being carried out by the Ministry of Defence Police into Marconi. This investigation has since resulted in charges being brought, in February 1989, against four individuals and three Marconi companies – the Marconi Company, Marconi Space and Defence Systems and Marconi Secure Radio Systems. The charges are thought to relate to contracts worth £1.2 million. Other contracts are also being investigated and are believed to be in the areas of radar and underwater systems, including Sting Ray. Clearly such allegations could provide a neat tie-up between the dead Marconi employees at least. The dead men may have been involved in fraud in some way and thus either committed suicide to escape the shame of detection, or were silenced before they could blow the whistle, or succumbed to the stress of having secretly blown the whistle. One psychological study of nearly 100 whistleblowers in the US, where the disclosure by employees of corruption in defence contracts is actively encouraged by government agencies, found that nearly 10 per cent had attempted suicide. However, there is not a scrap of hard evidence to suggest that any of the scientists named in the book were involved in fraud. Moreover, the one ex-Marconi employee who is definitely known to have provided information regarding alleged fraud at the company, a Mr Kingsley

Thrower, is alive and well and living in Preston, Lancashire. Mr Thrower is expected to be a key prosecution witness in the forthcoming Marconi fraud trial.

Whether there is a link or not, whether any or all of the cases are suspicious, or whether they are connected by nothing more than coincidence, the deaths and disappearances of 28 defence workers is one of the most bizarre and enigmatic stories of the past decade. The story of the peacetime war and the deadly seriousness with which it is waged is one of the most chilling. This book sets out to tell them both.

Stephen Arkell

CHAPTER ONE

The Funeral

In a cramped chapel at the Breakspear Crematorium in Ruislip, Middlesex the family and friends of 24-year-old computer programmer Vimal Bhagvangi Dajibhai gathered to pay their last respects. But as the coffin slid ceremoniously behind the curtain they were unaware that minutes earlier police had telephoned the crematorium to prevent the body's incineration.

At first the death of Vimal, a talented software engineer in the field of underwater defence, looked like just another suicide. It happened on a Monday in a city which claimed an overworked coroner and one of the highest suicide rates in Britain. With grim regularity the local pathologist performed post mortems on bodies recovered from beneath the Clifton Suspension Bridge. Suicidal people with irreconcilable love problems were often attracted to the bridge by its eerie romanticism and the awesome views across the Avon Gorge. Yet when Vimal fell 245 feet on Monday, 4 August 1986 he would have seen little of the Avon Gorge beforehand. He died late at night.

Nobody saw it happen, although the point at which he fell from the bridge was only yards from the permanently manned tollkeeper's office. One tollkeeper told the police he thought he may have seen an Asian standing on the bridge at about 10 p.m. that Monday night. When he looked ten minutes later the figure in dark casual clothing was gone. There was no positive identification. If the tollkeeper thought a man had jumped his concern was hardly evident.. The body was found the following morning by a passing cyclist.

In daylight a fall from the centre of the bridge, hundreds of feet above the meandering Avon river, might have been indicative of a young man whose love had been unreciprocated and who, disaffected with life, had decided to end it all spectacularly. But the point from which Vimal had fallen was only a few yards from the end of the bridge. He landed on a footpath, nowhere near the water, in the dead of night. It was an ignominious end. But a certain one.

In a small car park a few minutes walk from the bridge was Vimal's Renault 18 estate, a reliable though rusting 'N' registration car he had used every day for the thirty minute drive from his Kenton home to work at Croxley Green near Watford in Hertfordshire. On the front passenger's seat was a bottle of wine. A full bottle of the same wine lay on the rear seat, behind the driver. In the post mortem report traces of alcohol in his blood were recorded. According to his family, Vimal never drank wine but that seems to have mattered little to the Bristol police who in 1986 logged dozens of suicides. On Tuesday morning, only a few hours after the body was found, Vimal's family were invited to formally identify the body and were allowed, to their surprise, to take the Renault home before it had been tested for fingerprints.

'It was as if the police thought it just another suicide,' said Hitesh Shah, one of Vimal's closest friends. He had asked police to do saliva tests on the bottles. They said it was not necessary.

Vimal's death caused as much bewilderment as shock. Although he shied away from outward displays of feelings, his strength of character had often provided a prop for some of his more emotionally fragile friends. Confidants knew him as a man of outstanding talent and temporal ambition. They could think of no reason why he would go to Bristol. He knew nobody in the town. He had never even been to Bristol before. But this seemed inconsequential to the police, who said it looked like a tragic suicide. Apparently a police report did, however, mention, without explanation, that Vimal's trousers were found down below his buttocks. It was also mentioned that there was a tiny puncture mark on Vimal's left buttock.

From the family's point of view the inquest was short and sour. A policeman referred curtly to Vimal as an intelligent young man who did not appear to be depressed.

A desultory reference was made to the trousers and puncture mark and the Bristol coroner, Donald Hawkins, concluded the markedly formal proceedings by announcing an open verdict. He was saying, in effect, that he could not be certain whether it was an accident, suicide or murder. Some of Vimal's friends had already privately ruled out the first two.

The inquest verdict appeared to mark the end of the police investigation. But a few days later someone somewhere decided the computer expert's death warranted a closer examination. Police rang Vimal's widow Nita at her house in a prosperous area of Kenton, North London only to be told that the funeral was already in progress. The call to the crematorium arrived just in time. 'A few minutes later and the cremation would have taken place,' said the Breakspear's superintendent. 'The police told us to hold the cremation. We've never had a request like that before.' As guests mingled outside the chapel, some studying the condolence notes on the dozens of wreaths, the family was informed discreetly that the body was to be retained because the Bristol coroner wanted to reopen the police investigation. A second post mortem was to be carried out. It would be performed not by the local pathologist, as before, but by a top home office pathologist, Professor Bernard Knight. Part of his brief was to examine the mysterious puncture mark.

Professor Knight is no ordinary pathologist. He is chairman of the Board of Examiners of the College of Pathologists. He is also a trustee of a little known organization in London, the Medical Foundation for the Care of Victims of Torture. From its clinic on the second floor of the National Temperance Hospital in London the Foundation carries out its treatment in the utmost secrecy. Neither the victims nor those thought to be responsible for their torture are identified. Many of the victims are found to have suffered psychological torture. It would also emerge that the Foundation has treated at least one UK resident for signs of brainwashing.

Why the police suddenly decided to reopen the file on Vimal Dajibhai is a mystery. They said that it was due to pressure from Vimal's family, friends and work colleagues. But since the inquest there had been no direct pressure. The family's initial anger had subsided. Conceivably, a policeman had spotted a possible link with some previous suspicious death of a computer expert. After all, there were several on file.

The results of Vimal's second post mortem were not made public, though Bristol police offered every assistance to Nita when she telephoned them for further information. A constable told her no drugs were found, the puncture mark was most likely caused by a fragment of bone which jerked upwards and back again on the point of impact. The lowered trousers were to be expected given the concertina effect of a fall on hard ground.

For the police it was another case closed, until, less than three months later, the body of another computer expert from London was found in an Audi 80 car in Bristol. It appeared that 26-year-old Arshad Sharif had tied together four lengths of rope, secured one end to a tree, the other end around his neck and driven off in the car. Police did a short report for coroner Donald Hawkins. In it, they recorded the details of the till receipt from the shop where Arshad had bought one blue tow rope. Where the other three lengths of matching rope were acquired was never disclosed. The police also arranged for a translation of a taped message found in the car, which they later described as 'tantamount' to a suicide note.

In Arshad's desk at work police found some letters but the contents of these were never disclosed. Police also managed to talk to the owner of a guest house where Arshad had spent his last night. But the coroner did not seem satisfied with the police inquiries. He felt he could not be seen to be doing his job properly without asking the police to inquire further into why two computer specialists came to Bristol to commit suicide when they both lived in London. In fact the coroner alluded to a possible 'James Bond' link.

'As James Bond would say, "this is past coincidence," and I will not be completing the inquest today until I know how two men with no connection with Bristol came to meet the same end here,' he said.

Less than two weeks later, at Arshad's main inquest hearing, police reported there was no sinister connection, but few details emerged. Privately, the coroner was shown a statement from a man who knew Arshad which said the latter knew a woman in Bristol, although the taped message made no mention of a woman. A full statement from the owner of the guest house where Arshad had stayed, Jenny Worth, was also shown privately to the coroner. She had been questioned on her statement at the preliminary hearing, but only on certain parts. The parts of her statement which were not disclosed at the hearing would later raise uncertainties over the suicide verdict.

At the time, she considered it 'strange' that few facts

had emerged at the inquest, but she felt that it was better not to question the system. Not even Arshad's family, who had suspicions of their own, questioned the authority of the coroner's court. They formed the impression that the coroner's authority was unassailable. They therefore said nothing when his officials told them to stay away from the inquest. It was not in their best interests to attend, said the officials. So the family obeyed. And the coroner brought in an uncontested verdict of suicide.

Nobody realized at the time that the death method, described by a local paper as a 'bizarre rope trick', was probably unprecedented. Neither was anyone aware of the importance of Arshad's work. In fact both he and Vimal were employed by the same company, Marconi, a British electronics firm specializing in defence systems, although they worked at separate locations. It seemed at the time that a work connection between the two men within the diverse and seemingly amorphous Marconi group was remote. But there were connections. And their work was not the only one. Both were programmers on low incomes working on highly sensitive projects. Both were Asian. Both lived in London and both killed themselves inexplicably in Bristol, more than a hundred miles away. If that did not raise suspicions that these may have been more than isolated suicides, there were other strange deaths. They too were scientists, not just at Marconi, but at other defence establishments. And they were working on sensitive projects. Some died long before Vimal and Arshad. All were seemingly unrelated deaths which were never explained but quickly forgotten. Even in the six months after Arshad's death, a succession of scientists apparently killed themselves in strange circumstances or died in accidents at home. Again, the cases were forgotten as quickly as yesterday's news.

The fact there was no official inquiry into this series of

deaths is, perhaps, surprising. The West's technology is always in demand by the Eastern Bloc particularly to aid their command and control systems – the systems which use computers and telecommunications to partially automate the control of weapons. UK citizens who sell such computer technology directly or indirectly to the Eastern Bloc can, and have been jailed.

There is, however, something that can be more valuable to the Warsaw Pact than computer equipment. Something the West may be powerless to stop them acquiring, although Western intelligence agencies have tried.

That something is know-how, the knowledge that people have gained through practical experience or familiarity with a project. World War Three, should there be one, is likely to be a war controlled by electronics. Acquiring information about the other side's electronic strengths and weaknesses during peacetime could be a decisive factor in a war fought by push button.

The Soviet Union does its utmost to protect its electronic secrets. So does the West. But Western democracies cannot intern people for merely knowing too much. The State cannot stop former defence employees leaving their country. It cannot stop former defence employees joining Western companies which may have Eastern Bloc connections. It cannot stop defence employees leaving their companies and taking their knowledge with them. Or can it?

CHAPTER TWO

Three Asians

In the months before Vimal Dajibhai was found dead beneath the Clifton Suspension Bridge on a Monday night in the summer of 1986, he was working at Marconi Underwater Systems on the guidance electronics of a torpedo called Sting Ray. In the months before Arshad Sharif drove from his London home to Bristol, where he apparently hanged himself in his car on a Monday night in Autumn 1986, he was working for Marconi Defence Systems on an airborne electronic warfare system called Zeus. It emerged much later that the two projects had a technology in common, a technology little known outside defence circles but one which can decisively affect the outcome of every modern war: electronic warfare (EW).

At the time of his apparent suicide Vimal was happier than he had been for many years, according to his widow Nita. He was playing squash regularly, enjoyed weightlifting, was ambitious and looking forward to starting a new job at a financial systems consultancy in the City of London. He died in his final week at Marconi. Nita and Vimal had lived in a semi-detached house in a pleasant and prosperous part of Kenton, North London. A few miles away was Vimal's employer Marconi Underwater Systems at Croxley Green near Watford. Even closer was Marconi Defence Systems, the headquarters of the group, and where Arshad Sharif worked.

Nearly six months after Vimal's death, Nita gave no impression that the passing of time had relieved the sadness and burden of bereavement. She still appeared bewildered; it was as if her life had been frozen in the expectation that, one day, Vimal would again come through the front door.

He had been a powerful force in their short marriage, as diligent in his efforts to redecorate the entire house as in his attention to detail in the administration of the household accounts. At first Nita had received overwhelming support from an immense number of friends and family, but, inevitably, this had diminished and now Nita seemed alone in a large house. She sat rigidly on a plainly coloured settee, her small frame hardly making an impression on the cushions, and tried to recall, unsuccessfully, any events which could have had a bearing on Vimal's death.

'I can't think of any reason why he would want to do something like that,' she said softly but distinctly. Most of her answers were unintentionally curt. But clearly she felt that Vimal had not jumped willingly from Bristol's Clifton Suspension Bridge.

'He didn't know anyone in Bristol,' affirmed Nita.

She understood little of Vimal's work, though she knew he was heavily involved in computer simulation. Other members of the family confirmed later that simulation represented an important part of Vimal's work. One said that Vimal was working on a 'giant simulator'.

In relation to others areas of defence, simulation work might appear relatively unimportant. Most people associate simulators with computerized aircraft cockpits which are used to train pilots. But simulators at Marconi Underwater Systems have more of a direct defence application. They are used to test torpedoes. A Marconi booklet giving details of the firm's real-time simulators states: 'Basically these are extensive computer suites which embody the operational software and control hardware identical to that being used in the weapons being developed. Currently we have two simulators, one each for Sting Ray and Spearfish torpedoes.'

In fact Marconi's Croxley Green site has one of the largest computing facilities devoted to underwater technology outside the United States.

Vimal joined Marconi Underwater Systems in 1983 after graduating from Loughborough University with a Bachelor of Science degree in computer studies. Loughborough is well known in academic circles for its research work in the field of underwater warfare. For the first two years at Marconi he worked on Tigerfish, a heavyweight torpedo already in service with the Royal Navy, which was undergoing improvements to its guidance system. One of these modifications was to enable the weapon to automatically climb from depth to attack the most difficult types of surface targets. As Tigerfish is fired, a wire, which carries guidance information, is dispensed from both the torpedo and the submarine. When close to the target Tigerfish begins pinging to locate its exact position, while its internal computer performs steering calculations. At the same time sonar data on the target is fed back to the submarine to update its own computer memory. Early versions of the torpedo apparently had their weaknesses, but these are said to have been overcome. Indeed, Vimal's friends credit him with having resolved a number of difficulties with the guidance system software.

His work on Tigerfish drew to an end in early 1986 and he was transferred to Sting Ray, a 'fire-and-forget' lightweight torpedo designed to be launched by military planes and helicopters. At about the same time Marconi offered overtime work. He accepted, although many of his colleagues declined because they did not feel the money made it worthwhile.

As work progressed on Sting Ray, Vimal received

frequent requests from a Marconi employee who wanted help with his own work. There is some disagreement over whether or not Vimal was happy to oblige. The employee, who was also a member of a religious cult, said later that Vimal was the only person left at Marconi with a specialist knowledge of Tigerfish. He asserted that Vimal did not mind helping him. Others at Marconi say Vimal was irritated by the frequency of the requests, though he rarely complained. Whatever the truth, his relationship with the employee must have been at least semi-cordial because, following a number of requests, Vimal, Nita and a relative accompanied him on a casual visit to his religious group, the so-called Anoopam Mission in Buckinghamshire in April 1986. Afterwards Vimal, who had always maintained that he was an agnostic, said the group was 'friendly'. But he declined to join them, saying it wasn't his cup of tea. Light-heartedly, he reaffirmed to friends that he was committed to agnosticism.

His mood, at home and at work, remained unchanged. A busy schedule of overtime, regular squash, weight-lifting and do-it-yourself tasks continued without interruption. But he felt the need for a job change and more money. An application form he completed for a recruitment agency which specializes in placing computer programmers stated that he was seeking another £2,000 a year on his existing salary of a little over £10,000. With a chronic skills shortage in the computer industry, graduate programmers usually receive several job offers, and Vimal accepted a post with a company which specializes in providing computer consultants and programmers for companies in the financial sector, particularly those based in the City of London. At the time, the City of London employers were anxiously seeking skilled programmers like Vimal to develop the systems to cope with an expected influx of business following financial deregulation, known as

'Big Bang', due to take place in October that year.

Vimal handed in his notice at Marconi in the first few days of July 1986, by which time most of his friends at the firm had already left. Due to the cyclical nature of defence projects, it seems that the turnover of staff in his department had been high. Many of those who had completed their projects began to seek new jobs, but Vimal had stayed longer than most. By this stage he had a rare understanding of aspects of underwater warfare which no formal academic training could have given him. It was the sort of knowledge acquired only by specialist on-the-job training, practical experience and computer experimentation. In addition, he had gained a useful working knowledge of the sort of computers used not only in defence but also in the financial services sector.

It was this experience he was due to take to his new job in the City, though there was one slight snag. The City firm wanted Vimal to start at the beginning of August 1986 but Vimal anticipated having to work a month's notice at Marconi beginning 1 August. He asked his immediate superior if he could 'swing things' so that he could leave on 8 August. Marconi agreed.

In his penultimate week at Marconi, beginning Monday, 28 July 1986, Vimal took some holiday entitlement and spent a few days with his new employers. At the end of the week he told friends he was excited about the prospect of working there full time, and on the Saturday he bought a new suit for £130.00, some shoes for £31.00 in a sale and a book on the financial sector called 'Big Bang' for £11.00. He bought a durable hardback version despite the fact that it was available in paperback.

On Monday, 4 August, at the start of his final week at Marconi, Vimal went to work as usual. At lunchtime he received a telephone call from his former landlord and friend, Manu Mistry, who wanted to meet with him that evening. Manu wanted help with the computer language Fortran, which is used extensively at Marconi and at many large scientific computer sites, and he regarded Vimal as having a particularly good knowledge of the language. Vimal agreed to meet him and left work as usual at about five in the afternoon. His body was found beneath the Clifton Suspension Bridge the following morning. There were no eyewitnesses, and there was no suicide note.

What happened between the time he left work and when he died is not clear. What is certain is that he never met Manu Mistry that night. A message from Vimal found at his house said that Manu could not come that evening and added that he had taken the car and would be back late. Why had he mentioned specifically that he had taken the car? He was the only driver in the family and took the car with him everywhere.

If the note was a clue, it wasn't followed up. Vimal's red Renault 18 estate, which had been found in a car park near the bridge, was returned to the family without fingerprints being taken. When the car was eventually fingerprinted, more than a week later, 'practically everybody had touched it', said one family friend. Police confirmed that initially only cursory, non-forensic tests had been conducted on Vimal's car.

Vimal's manager at Marconi spent several weeks investigating the death, but was unable to establish what had happened. Another friend, Hitesh Shah, used Vimal's car to retrace his journey from London to Bristol. Hitesh even interviewed staff at a garage in Ruislip where Vimal bought petrol on his Access card, but, though they had a vague recollection of the car, they could not remember Vimal's face or whether he had had anyone with him. Hitesh also spoke to the tollkeeper at the Clifton bridge, but was told that there had been no confirmed sighting of Vimal. He even visited fifteen branches of the Peter Dominic off licence chain with

Vimal's photograph. It was bottles of Peter Dominic's own brand of red wine that had been found in Vimal's car. But nobody remembered him making the purchase.

At the inquest the coroner Donald Hawkins had been told that Vimal was 'happily married' and 'had everything to live for'. A report mentioned that, when found, Vimal's trousers were pulled down to below his buttocks, where there was a small puncture mark. In Vimal's car was a card belonging to the employee of Marconi who was a member of the Hindu religious cult he had visited four months earlier. Curiously, the authorities drew much attention to the Hindu cult. The police, Marconi and the coroner all mentioned the cult but only to say that it was not involved in the death.

The coroner returned an open verdict, which meant, in effect, that there was insufficient evidence on which to conclude that he had committed suicide, died accidentally or had been killed unlawfully. Vimal's family, friends and colleagues were concerned about what they saw as a shallow police investigation. Less than two weeks had elapsed between the discovery of the body and the coroner's verdict. Most of Vimal's closest friends wrote individual letters, some several pages, to the coroner and Marconi requesting a thorough investigation and expressing scepticism over the suicide theory. The mention of the cult, even to dismiss it, particularly puzzled friends.

'I never thought of him as being religious,' said a woman who had worked with Vimal. 'I do not think he committed suicide.'

Inderjit Sandhu who was Vimal's manager at Marconi Underwater Systems in Watford was also one of his closest friends. After Vimal's death he spent many nights sifting through the facts in his mind, trying, unsuccessfully, to come up with a theory.

'The police were never able to do anything,' he said. He hadn't meant to sound resentful. Time had mitigated his anger. Inderjit was particularly perplexed at the level of apparent planning which went into his friend's death.

'The whole thing is very strange. I have a friend who was very close to suicide. He said it happens straight away, or, at least, the decision is taken only a few minutes before. A decision to take your own life is unlikely to be taken so long beforehand.'

Letters written to Marconi and the coroner by other friends and colleagues displayed unanimous scepticism of the suicide theory. Rohail Bhandari, who had known Vimal for about five years, wrote a letter under the heading 'Reasons Why Not Suicide – Character Analysis'. He described Vimal as secure, stable and independent, a man who had learned to cope with stress as part of a 'childhood of neglect' spent for much of the time without his mother and father.

'He was sincere, honest and devoted to people who cared for him,' says Rohail's letter. 'At work he was clever, logical and methodical. He had an easy comprehension of problems confronting him ... He had little to say in conversation unless his opinion was required. This was more due to the fact that he always refused to impose himself on people. However, his opinions were valued by those who required them. Vimal was known as a good companion for those in need, always more than willing to help, and was not known to refuse.'

Though Vimal had a 'lack of imagination', according to Rohail, he was admired for his clear and concise thinking 'even when everything around him was heated'.

'However, Vimal was not positive in his views and thoughts and would suppress them so as not to offend. Vimal was very much involved with groups ... he would join in all the activities. We often clowned and played pranks on each other, although if the pranks were directed at him he always managed to keep calm. I remember only the once when he was provoked into losing his temper. It lasted all of five seconds, short and sharp. He never sulked or showed signs of depression.'

Rohail added that Vimal's strength was his ability to adjust to pressure. At home he relaxed by doing household and do-it-yourself chores.

'Vimal had a good family who cared and gave him support,' continues Rohail's letter. 'He was busy at home making a life for him and his wife ... All the above aspects give support to a healthy and a well-controlled mind. Vimal had everything going for him and no reason at all to commit suicide ... Vimal was a tall and strong man. His breaking point to overpowering stress was extremely high. I believe suicide can only be labelled to Vimal with extreme difficulty.'

Another letter, from a friend who knew Vimal at university where they shared a flat, stated:

'In all honesty Vimal was probably the only person I have known about whom no one had an unkind word ... He was often quiet and reserved, slightly shy of strangers. Among his friends, however, he was well-liked and well-respected. He was always enthusiastic about sports and other activities at university – and his enthusiasm was infectious. Vimal was generous to a fault with his time and money, and often people took advantage of this. He helped out some of his friends with their coursework and projects, and when things were not going too well with any of his friends he would try to motivate them and gee them up. Most people are self-centred and let their feelings and emotions get the better of them, but Vimal never allowed his emotions to cause him to react negatively. I respected him for his honesty, integrity and reliability, and he would be one of the first I would think of if I needed to talk about a problem. He was very independent in that he did not just go along with what people were saying ...'

The friend's letter continued:

'We all admired Vimal's inner strength and commitment to his friends and family, and to himself. He had the drive to achieve what he set his mind to. On many occasions he slept only three or four hours a night, waking up early in the morning to honour a commitment. He was the last person I could imagine who would let himself or his friends down, because he believed in the quality of life and friendship. In his final year at university, I am sure that one of our flatmates, who was on the same course as Vimal, would not have passed if it were not for Vimal's encouragement and support. On several occasions Vimal completed his friends' reports and courseworks. From what I gather he had an unhappy childhood but he rarely talked about it. He seemed to miss his family and tried to arrange for his brother to come over to England. Vimal talked so rarely about his problems that most people thought he didn't have any. Only after a long and deep conversation would he open up his heart and talk about them. Most of us were selfish and poured out all our sorrows onto him. I stayed with him for two days, a few days before he died. I was feeling a bit depressed at the time and so once again I talked about what was bothering me. At the time he seemed quite happy. Not at all depressed.

'Vimal never appeared to be the type of person who would commit suicide. His beliefs and convictions were such that he respected life and the lives of those around him.'

The author of a third letter said he had spent six days collating information and talking to the family. He had seen all Vimal's credit card statements and wrote: 'All his bills were paid in full, well in time.' The letter adds, 'He had mentioned to his family how things were really looking up for them.' The letter's author goes on to devote several pages to speculation on the possibility that Vimal was murdered and thrown off the bridge when the tollkeeper was not looking. The multiple injuries inflicted during the killing, says the author, would be similar to those sustained and compounded in the fall.

His suggestion, which he stresses is purely speculative, is that Vimal returned home from work on the Monday and had been at home for only a few minutes when there was a telephone call. Someone wanted Vimal's help. Whoever wanted to see him could have been desperate for a meeting, because Vimal had taken the previous week off to work at his new employers. Was it possible that the request had come from a colleague who had 'little access to him outside work'? Whoever requested the meeting, adds the letter's author, could have accompanied Vimal home from work.

'It was quite common for Vimal's friends to call on him when they were distressed,' continues the letter. 'In fact during the previous week an old college friend required such consoling and stayed over with Vimal. It is my impression that a similar person, known to Vimal, required the same type of consoling. He may have been with Vimal or phoned to arrange a meeting, the latter being the most likely. The strength of this person's demands would have been seen in Vimal's rush to go and help, the letter on the door implying he had taken the car because his contact was not local and had no means of transport himself. As Vimal was the only driver in his family there would have been little reason for him to mention the car, had not its use been important. As Vimal prepared to leave he took with him two spare pairs of shoes and two pairs of sandals ...'

The letter suggests the sandals could have been intended for decorating work as Vimal was an 'excellent DIYer'. Vimal had filled up his car with petrol near the M4 and later met his contact who had supplied the wine. The contact had placed one of the bottles of wine behind the driver's seat. It would have been a difficult manoeuvre, the author contends, for Vimal to have placed a bottle of wine behind his seat himself, but easy for someone in the passenger's seat.

'It would be important to note that Vimal hardly ever drank alcohol and never when driving. In fact Vimal was one of those people who would agree to drink only under protest. And then never wine.'

The author of the letter also finds it strange that the point at which Vimal fell from the dimly lit bridge at about midnight was close to the tollkeeper's office. He believes the body was somehow smuggled onto the bridge, disposed of at the earliest opportunity, with the person or persons unknown returning past the tollkeeper's office unnoticed.

The letter concludes: 'I understand that the speculations I have put forward may be hard to believe. What is even harder to believe is the suggestion that Vimal committed suicide at his prime and when enjoying the best years of his life.'

Vimal's friend, Hitesh Shah, also wrote a letter to the coroner, saying that, if Vimal had a black side to his character, it would have shown itself in the six years he had 'lived, studied and socialized into the late hours' with him. 'It never did,' he said.

Hitesh goes on to ask: 'Would he be able to rewire and replumb his complete house from scratch in a negative state? Would he, within a year of driving a car, be able to completely overhaul a car engine? I am completely dumbfounded ... he seemed more content than ever before.' Hitesh's letter concludes with a request for an investigation. Two other letters, one from a Marconi employee, Raj Mistry, are addressed to Marconi Underwater Systems at Blackmoor Lane, Watford. Both request an investigation.

Raj Mistry's letter states: 'Vimal was my best friend at work. In the two and a half years that I have known him, since I joined Marconi, I have found him to be a very pleasant and mild mannered person and a very dear, trusted friend. It was I who found Vimal and his wife their first flat. The news of his death was a great shock to me, but an even greater shock is the fact that he may have committed suicide. I cannot understand why he should do this. If in fact he did, he had no reason to. He was about to start a new job, higher salary, capable person, nice wife, new house ... I feel that there is something fishy somewhere although it is not clear what. I hope you keep the inquiry open until a result is obtained without doubt.'

All these letters clearly show that Vimal's death, and the suggestion that it could have been suicide, came as a surprise to his family, friends and colleagues.

In fact, it appeared that only one of Vimal's colleagues was convinced he had committed suicide, the Marconi employee who had invited him to visit the religious cult.

'Vimal was a friend of mine,' said the man. 'He visited me while he was working on Sting Ray. He was coming in early to get some extra cash ... He was the only one left who really knew about Tigerfish.' He insisted that Vimal's death was 'definitely suicide', although he could not explain why. Without prompting he added: 'I'm sure nobody got to him.' Asked about the importance of Vimal's work he said: 'It is one piece of a jigsaw.'

Of course the man's assumptions about Vimal's death may have been correct. But less than three months after Vimal died another Marconi employee apparently took his own life in even more bizarre circumstances, again in Bristol.

Arshad Sharif, a 26-year-old computer programmer at Marconi Defence Systems in Stanmore, Middlesex, died late on Monday night or early Tuesday morning on 28 October, 1986 after apparently tying together four lengths of blue nylon rope, attaching one end to a tree, tying the other end around his neck and driving off in his father's Audi 80. Although the Bristol police said they had never known someone die using such a method, the facts, at first, seemed to weigh heavily in favour of suicide. According to the police Arshad had bought a cassette recorder and a cassette tape and, before he died, recorded a suicide message. The tape, which was found in the car, was marked: 'Please hand to my father'. The authenticity of the writing on the tape and the message, which was spoken in Punjabi, was later verified by Arshad's father. According to one report, the taped message said that Arshad had done something to dishonour his family, though it did not say what. Neither did it say why, even if he had done something wrong, he was committing suicide.

Donald Hawkins, the Bristol coroner, said at Arshad's inquest that he was 'satisfied' that the message on the tape 'clearly showed the intention of the person on the tape to take his own life'. The coroner's officers spoke at length to Mr Sharif, Arshad's father, to express their belief that the case was a straightforward suicide. But despite their assurances Mr Sharif, a frail, profoundly contemplative man, was quietly sceptical.

'It was all too perfect,' said Mr Sharif, faintly.

For the first time since the funeral, Mr Sharif allowed himself to discuss Arshad, though with difficulty and in a tone, throughout, of doleful incomprehension. A loss of such magnitude was difficult enough to bear, but the fact that he did not know why his son had died and suspected that an unknown group or an individual may have been involved, made the pain of bereavement torturous. At times, he would recover thoughts from his subconscious which would evoke a momentary smile. It was such recollections that also provided an insight into his mental suffering. As soon as the smile disappeared he sank deeper into melancholic bewilderment, as if he had suddenly remembered that, of course, Arshad was dead.

It appeared from talking to Mr Sharif that the local papers had made some mistakes in reporting his son's death. Perhaps the pressure of deadlines had made scepticism impractical, but the papers conveyed an unquestioning acceptance of the suicide theory, even though the inquest had failed to give either an explanation for his death or a reason for possible depression. The papers did not consider it odd, for instance, that the evidence they were presenting asked readers to believe that Arshad had decided voluntarily upon a ghastly method of suicide and had made elaborate preparations for the event more than ten hours before his body was found.

One newspaper report said: 'Computer engineer Arshad Sharif died using a bizarre rope trick at a beauty spot ... The macabre death method broke his neck as his car crashed into a wall. Bristol coroner Donald Hawkins was told that mystery still surrounded why Sharif had driven 140 miles from his Walthamstow home to Siston Common, Warmley, Bristol, for his death ...'

The report continued: 'Sharif had left his London home two days before the death and had spent his last night at a guest house in Bristol. The day before he died he bought two lengths of blue nylon towing rope from a car spares shop near Siston Common. Retired bus driver Mr Haaji Sharif said his son was a 'helpful and obliging young man' who was due to marry a woman from his native Pakistan this month, but the wedding had been put back to January because of visa problems ... Roofer Christopher England told the Bristol hearing how he saw the Audi crash into a wall at Siston Common. He said: "I found a young lad in the car with the rope around his neck. He was in the driver's seat." '

Possibly the factual errors were minor but it was equally conceivable that reporters had been given incorrect information, making the mistakes more significant. No obvious damage resulted from the misleading reports, although the incorrect mention of the existence of a witness to an otherwise bizarre death might have put off a larger scale media investigation.

The two references to Arshad's car crashing into a wall seem curious in the light of Mr Sharif's affirmation that, when he went to Bristol to collect the car, he found it unscratched. It seemed that it could not have been going fast when the rope tightened, apparently breaking Arshad's neck. It had travelled a total distance of less than 25 yards.

'It should have hit the wall very hard,' said Mr Sharif. 'It was a very powerful car.'

The reference to roofer Christopher England having seen the car crashing into a wall was also misleading. Detective Sergeant Chamberlain, an assistant to the coroner, later confirmed that there was neither a crash nor eyewitnesses.

Other inconsistencies came to light. When Mr Sharif went to Bristol to identify the body, he inspected the car and saw a wheel hub spanner, about eighteen inches long, on the floor, between the driver's seat and the accelerator pedal. His immediate reaction was to go to the boot to see if it belonged with the car's tool kit, but the police refused to allow him to open the boot. The local paper report also mentioned that Arshad had bought two lengths of towing rope from a car spares shop the day before he died. In fact he bought only a single blue tow rope from the shop near Siston Common, which matched a blue one he already had in the car. According to the shop manager James Bickley, Arshad told him that he wanted a blue tow rope of a make called Cyclone.

'He just seemed to want to buy a tow rope which matched one he already had,' said the manager. When the body was found there were four lengths of blue nylon rope tied together. Arshad bought nothing from the car spares shop except one length of tow rope. Where did the other two lengths of rope come from?

The purchase of the tow rope took place at about

10.45 a.m. on Monday, 27 October, though Arshad did not die until late that Monday night, or possibly in the early hours of Tuesday morning. The Bristol police were unable to establish what he did, or who he may have seen, during the hours leading up to his death, following the purchase of the rope. Both the owner of the guest house, where he spent his last night, and the spares shop owner said Arshad had not acted unusually or shown any signs of depression. On the Monday morning Arshad ate breakfast at the guest house and chatted to the owner Jenny Worth who said:

'He seemed such a normal and contented sort of chap; not at all the sort you would expect to do something like that. I nearly fainted with shock when I heard he'd died. There never was a reason. He was really looking forward to getting married.'

Arshad was to have married a young woman from Pakistan. The date for her arrival in England had been set for January, two months after he died. Originally she had been due to arrive in England in November, but this was put back because of difficulties with her visa. Such a delay had happened in the past and was not entirely unexpected. On the day he died, Arshad was due to see his local Labour Member of Parliament, Eric Deakins, supposedly about the delays. Arshad had arranged the appointment with Deakins's secretary less than a week before his death. The secretary recalled later that she had allocated a particularly early date because of Arshad's anxiety to meet Deakins.

Other unexplained facts came to light after the inquest. Three cigars were found in Arshad's car, partially smoked, even though the dashboard carried a large 'no smoking' sign. Shortly before he died Arshad had complained of a sore throat. It also emerged that the guest house in Filton, Bristol, where Arshad spent his last night, takes much of its custom from British Aerospace a few yards down the road. Arshad had worked there, long before joining Marconi, on the Rapier surface-to-air guided missiles. The Filton plant is involved in civil and military contracts. It is also working on a long-term project, partially funded by government, to give computers the 'intelligence' to automatically locate targets – giving the homing head in an anti-tank missile, for instance, the ability to distinguish between a tank and a car. On this project, British Aerospace is collaborating with Marconi and other establishments.

The taped message Arshad left for his father is particularly curious. What apparently happened is that, while in Bristol, Arshad bought a tape recorder and three cassette tapes. The short message which police described as 'tantamount' to a suicide note was contained on one cassette tape, which was handed over to Mr Sharif. When he received the other two tapes they were blank. The coroner had been in possession of a transcript of the so-called suicide tape when he asked police to reopen their investigation to see if there was a possible link between the deaths of Vimal and Arshad. Furthermore, the Assistant Chief Constable of Avon and Somerset police, John Harland, during a long television interview over Arshad's death, indicated that he was not totally sure of the implications of the tape. When asked by a television reporter why police had repeatedly declined to release details of the tape, he said: 'This is a matter for the coroner. A tape recorded by a person who is, one assumes, about to take their life, is confidential.'

Certainly Mr Sharif believes the cassette tape could be irrelevant. 'The tape says nothing about his death,' he insisted. 'It doesn't say anything at all.'

Later, after the story of his son's death broke internationally, Mr Sharif became further perplexed by off the record statements made to journalists by police sources. The police were saying that Arshad had been having an affair with his former landlady in Bristol (not the landlady of the guest house where he had stayed on his last night, but the landlady of the place where he had stayed during his spell at British Aerospace).

It appeared police had found an electronics engineer, working in a petrol station in London, who said he had been a close friend of Arshad's. In the man's statement to the police, he suggested that Arshad had known an Asian woman in Bristol, his landlady, with whom he may have been having an affair. He also suggested that Arshad may have been depressed about a row with his father. The engineer told police this could therefore have been a reason for suicide.

But Mr Sharif had not heard of the suggestion before and knew there was no mention of a woman on the tape. He rang the Bristol police officer who seemed to be the source of the story to check its authenticity. The police officer told Mr Sharif he did not know the origin of the rumour of an alleged affair, even though, in fact, he had mentioned it to several reporters, including one from the BBC and, separately, a reporter from Independent Television. Furthermore, the policeman asked Mr Sharif not to talk to journalists, but by this time Mr Sharif had become slightly sceptical of what he was being told by officials. Newspaper reports continued to appear which linked his son's death to an unnamed woman in Bristol. None of the reports quoted official sources.

'Even if he knew a woman in Bristol,' said Mr Sharif, 'why is that a reason to kill himself?'

It transpired that, during his time in Bristol, Arshad had lived with an Asian family in the city. According to Arshad's family, the landlady was happily married, had several children, was fervently religious and helped teach him the Koran. The woman herself stated categorically that she had not seen Arshad since he left British Aerospace three years before. She described as 'rubbish' suggestions that they were having an affair and said: 'He was a nice man when he lived here.' It also emerged that a cherished photo of his fiancée was found in Arshad's pocket when his body was found. Apparently, he always kept it with him.

At times Mr Sharif was resolute in his desire for an investigation into the death. 'Why would he kill himself? There was no reason. He had everything,' he would say. At other times his mood was ambivalent, alternating between restrained anger at the lack of information, and placidity as he submitted to the realization that a lost life is irreplaceable.

Arshad had graduated with honours from Manchester University, had a job in which he was progressing rapidly, was looking forward to getting married and was a powerful influence on his brothers and sisters, who he constantly encouraged to work hard to better themselves.

'It hurts to think about him,' said Mr Sharif, on one of the rare occasions when he failed to keep emotion in check. 'It really hurts.'

As the head of a large family Mr Sharif had always been conscious of the need to be seen to treat all his children equally. But Arshad had proved the most difficult to regard impartially. A large picture of Arshad dominated a small sideboard in a far corner of the front room of his Walthamstow home. Arshad looked immaculate and impressive in his graduation gown and mortarboard. With so few ornaments or furniture in the room, the picture was eerily conspicuous.

'I don't know what happened,' said Mr Sharif, shaking his head morosely. 'I never interfered with his life. I never asked him about his job and he never spoke about it. I just don't know whether he killed himself or whether someone killed him. My cousin came across something similar many years ago when he was a GP. He thinks Arshad was dead before someone put him in the car and put the rope around his neck.'

Mr Sharif had spoken at great length about the death

with his cousin, a retired doctor who had performed many post mortem examinations. His cousin had recalled a case where he was called by police to examine a woman who was found hanged. He had arranged for the body to be taken to the local mortuary and conducted a post mortem the following morning. It established, said Mr Sharif, that the woman had been killed before being hung by a rope from the ceiling.

Why hadn't Mr Sharif expressed his doubts to the inquest? 'I didn't go to the inquest,' he said. 'The coroner told me not to go. He felt it was not in my best interests to go. None of my family went.'

Although Arshad's death had some of the hallmarks of suicide, many questions were left unanswered at his inquest. Indeed the absence of the Sharif family from their son's inquest was, in itself, irregular. There was nobody else to say, as was common at hearings where there was an apparent suicide, that the deceased had tried on previous occasions to commit suicide or made threats to do so. Often a witness will intimate that the balance of the deceased's mind was disturbed by a particular event or personal circumstances. There was not so much as a hint at Arshad's inquest that he had been suffering any stress. In fact, Arshad's desire to willingly kill himself was never firmly established in public. Work had its ups and downs for Arshad, as it does for most people. Mr Sharif, however, could not remember Arshad showing any deep-rooted dissatisfaction with his job at Marconi.

'A few weeks before it happened he came home with his salary slip and held it up and showed me and said: "Look, I've had an increase," ' said Mr Sharif.

'He was due to get another rise when he got promotion. He had been promised a job looking after a whole department, as a project leader in charge of about fifteen people. He would have taken over the department last month.'

Mr Sharif said his son never discussed his job and

neither he nor his other sons and daughters had expected him to discuss it. They accepted that the work was secret, that Arshad was an automatic test engineer and that he worked at Marconi Defence Systems in Stanmore, Middlesex. At the time, the fact that he never talked about work seemed due to Arshad's natural reticence and apparent introversion. Later it became clear that his taciturnity was as a direct result of the importance of his work.

'I never asked him about his job. I do not interfere with my children's lives at all,' added Mr Sharif.

He knew, however, that Arshad had been recruited by Marconi because of his particular skills as an automatic test engineer working on missile systems, and that he had been promoted on more than one occasion.

'He worked at Marconi in Portsmouth for nearly a year,' he said, without expression. 'Marconi used to send a car to pick him up at the beginning of the week and bring him back on the Friday. They booked a hotel for him. They were paying about nine or ten pounds per day extra for his work there.'

There appeared to be little detail Mr Sharif could add about Arshad's job except that he had been highly regarded by Marconi.

'He was working in Farnborough and left to join Marconi because they offered him a lot more money. Marconi had said they wanted the best automatic test engineer they could find. Marconi nearly doubled his salary.'

Mr Sharif did not express any strong feelings about the events which followed his son's death although he was a little perturbed by Marconi's attitude.

'After his death they (Marconi) never contacted me. There was not a word from anyone at work,' he said, surprised but not indignant. 'I rang to speak to one of his friends at work but he was not there so I spoke to his manager who said he would leave a message on the friend's desk. He did not return my call. I know he got my message to ring. His manager said he had got the message. When I got through to him he said he would have to call me back because his manager had just come in.'

As with Vimal's death, those close to Arshad remained unconvinced that he had committed suicide. Arshad's brother Pervez, a London Underground train driver, had been unable to raise questions at the inquest because, like the rest of the family, he had bowed to the coroner's wishes and stayed away.

Pervez spent several weeks immediately after his brother's death trying to interview Arshad's friends. On occasions he went to the Marconi factory where his brother worked, but said he was unable to find out anything. What began as a determined effort ended in submission to the family's view that the truth would never emerge.

Arshad was, perhaps, closer to his younger brother Masood than any of the others. The two had met regularly in Portsmouth for dinner when Arshad worked for Marconi there. Masood was studying at Portsmouth Polytechnic. By his own admission Masood was not as academically gifted as Arshad and had looked to his brother for help and encouragement. Without his brother Masood had become disorientated, devoid of motivation. He had failed in his studies and regularly had nightmares about Arshad's death. Masood said Arshad had shown no signs of depression. Even just before his death he noticed nothing unusual in his brother's behaviour. Arshad had rarely spoken about his work but he had mentioned the site where he had worked in Portsmouth for nearly a year, Marconi Underwater Systems.

So both Arshad and Vimal had worked for Marconi Underwater Systems, though at different sites and on apparently different projects. While in Porstmouth, the hotel that Marconi had booked Arshad into was the Holiday Inn at Cosham, just outside the town centre. The Holiday Inn is Portsmouth's only four star hotel. There is none with a higher rating.

Although coroner Hawkins returned a verdict of suicide at Arshad's inquest he made it clear by holding a special inquiry that he considered it a little strange that two Marconi programmers from the London area had come more than 100 miles to Bristol to apparently kill themselves, within three months.

It was always possible that Arshad had been depressed because he had had a row with his father. Relatives said family tiffs were not unusual. But police did not know why Arshad or Vimal had gone to Bristol and had not disclosed any reasons why either of them had apparently committed suicide. They told the coroner, after a further short investigation, that there was no link between the two cases. In a subsequent television interview about the deaths Hawkins explained: 'I adjourned the second (Sharif) inquest to enable the police to see if there was any evidence of a connection between the two people. The police carried out that investigation. A police officer attended the resumption of the inquest on Mr Sharif and assured me that there was no connection. That satisfied me completely.'

In another interview Hawkins would add nothing further about the deaths except that he recalled some controversy over the possible involvement of a religious cult. On being pressed he said that he held several hundred inquests a year in Bristol and could not remember two in particular. But Hawkins's assistant, Detective Sergeant Gerald Chamberlain, was a little more forthcoming. 'The Dajibhai death is a complete mystery,' said Chamberlain. 'We don't know why Dajibhai came to Bristol. We don't know why he killed himself.'

He spoke about Arshad Sharif's case in a more confident tone. 'The other death is more straightforward. He definitely committed suicide.'

Why?

'I'm afraid I cannot go into that. It's a personal matter. The coroner said he was absolutely satisfied that Sharif took his own life. He left a tape, you know.'

What did the tape say?

'I'm afraid I am not at liberty to divulge that.'

Was a transcript of the tape read out in court?

'I don't believe it was.'

Chamberlain confirmed that there were no eyewitnesses, and, curiously, that no exact time of death had been established.

'We estimated the time of death to be sometime on Monday night,' said Chamberlain. 'It is a spot where courting couples often stop, but there don't appear to have been any there that night. The body was found on Tuesday morning by a man walking his dog. We spent some time looking into any possible link with the other man but they were completely different.'

On 19 March 1987, with the worldwide publicity over the Marconi programmers showing no sign of diminishing, Bristol police called a press conference. Its purpose, according to one Bristol reporter, was to 'kill the speculation and innuendo'. According to police, it was to show that there had been no cover up.

The religious sect was introduced at an early stage of the proceedings. Detective Superintendent Ford explained that Vimal Dajibhai had visited the cult called the Anoopam Mission purely as a matter of interest.

'There is no suggestion that he was in any way involved with them,' said Ford.

It seemed a little curious that Ford had revealed the name of the cult, apparently for the first time in public, adding that Vimal had visited its premises and that a card from a member of the cult who worked at Marconi had been found in the car, all to make the point that he had been in no way involved with it. He also said that there was nothing suspicious about the puncture wounds found on Vimal's left buttock when his body was recovered from the footpath beneath the bridge. At the time of Vimal's death the police had referred to a single puncture mark on his left buttock. By the time of the press conference, the mark had been transformed into 'puncture wounds'.

The conference was told that the second post mortem, conducted by top Home Office pathologist Professor Bernard Knight, had shown that the 'wounds' were caused by fragmented bone being pushed through the skin because of the impact. The impact of the fall also accounted for the fact that Vimal's trousers were found down around his thighs.

With reference to the wine found in Vimal's car, Ford said he 'believed' Vimal had bought the bottle himself. There were 'traces' of alcohol in his blood which 'suggested he had drunk it himself'. No explanation was offered for the fact that another full bottle of wine had been found in Vimal's car, or the fact that Vimal did not like wine. Ford, however, admitted that the reasons for Vimal's death, and why he had chosen to apparently end it all in Bristol, remained a mystery.

'We have been unable to establish any logical reason why he should have taken his own life,' he said. 'He was a happily married man with good career prospects and no financial problems.' There were good reasons, however, for thinking that Arshad committed suicide, according to Ford. 'But they are private and confidential, and I am not prepared to go into them,' he said. Then he seemed to do just that. 'Just prior to his death he was suffering from depression, and there were domestic pressures as well.'

No explanation was forthcoming as to why Arshad may have been depressed. No clue was given to the contents of the tape recording made by Arshad just before he died. No mention was made of the half-smoked cigars found in his car, or the fact that he had spent his last night a few yards from British Aerospace where he had once worked. No mention was made of his forthcoming marriage or his promotion. No explanation was given of where Arshad acquired all the tow ropes, or why his car was undamaged, or for the spanner by the accelerator pedal.

There was no explanation of why his father had not been allowed to look into the boot. There was no explanation of what Arshad had done, or who he had seen, in his last twelve hours or so. And despite the fact that Ford himself agreed that Arshad's death was 'bizarre', and that he had never come across a similar suicide, there was no attempt to explain why he had used such a spectacular and unprecedented method. It was a grotesque way to die, especially for someone who was afraid of pain. Only a few weeks earlier Arshad had refused to mend an aerial on his father's low roof because he thought the ladder was unsafe. As an intelligent man, Arshad could surely have thought of a number of easier ways to die.

Perhaps Arshad was unhappy over the postponement of his fiancée's visa, although he was apparently told that he could have speeded up the process by paying a small sum to the Pakistani authorities. According to his brothers, Arshad rejected that because he considered it unethical. Masood added that such action would have been contrary to Arshad's deep-rooted religious beliefs. Sometimes at religious festivals, according to Masood, Arshad would persuade his father to join in all-night prayer. Moreover, Arshad's forthcoming marriage was not some loveless arrangement. His father and brothers insisted he was in love with his fiancée.

By the time of the Bristol press conference, however, the police had more to contend with than just the apparent suicides of Vimal Dajibhai and Arshad Sharif. On Thursday, 8 January 1987, 26-year-old Avtar

Singh-Gida, studying for his Ph.D. at Loughborough University, had been doing experiments with a colleague at a reservoir near his home in Loughborough, Leicestershire. Avtar's colleague went off to buy some lunch. When he eventually returned, Avtar was gone. He could not be traced anywhere.

Police insisted there were no suspicious circumstances. Avtar had had his passport with him and there had been some speculation that he had left simply to opt out and travel the world. But, instead of simply adding Avtar's name to the files containing the details of the thousands who are reported missing every year the police launched a search of such magnitude that it attracted the attention of the local papers and television stations. There were no signs of an abduction, no hint of a struggle, no suggestion of foul play. Yet the search resembled a murder hunt.

Up to thirty detectives were put on the case, frogmen dragged the reservoir and, later, Loughborough University and water authority staff were asked to use their sonar equipment to carry out echo-sounding surveys. The police carried out two systematic searches of the area around the reservoir. Scotland Yard was notified and Interpol was asked to check addresses in three countries. The authorities could not conceal their anxiety to find Avtar.

Nobody thought to question the reasons for the search at the time of Avtar's disappearance. He had been described simply as a researcher attached to Loughborough University's electronic, electrical and civil engineering departments. However, when he had been missing for three months, his lecturer at Loughborough University, Dave Goodson, revealed that Avtar had been working on a project for the Ministry of Defence. He asked, however, that this be 'played down'.

It also emerged that Avtar had been working on signal

processing, a technology with defence applications closely related to electronic warfare and encompassing aspects of Vimal Dajibhai and Arshad Sharif's work. That was not all. According to Avtar's 25-year-old wife Vali, her husband had been visibly upset when he heard about Vimal's death.

Avtar had stayed at Loughborough to do a science Ph.D., to add to his B.Sc. in electronic and electrical engineering. His disappearance was probably not in the least sinister or, at any rate, linked to his work but speculation proved impossible to suppress. It struck many people as strange that he disappeared only a few weeks away from completing his four year Ph.D. course. Vali was clearly upset by her husband's disappearance. There was a widely held view among the authorities that she had fallen out with her husband because he was a Sikh and she a Christian. The exact origins of the rumour were unknown, Vali called it absurd. Two days before he went missing, Avtar had bought Vali a £150 wedding anniversary present.

The University's attitude towards her had also caused some consternation.

'They made no effort to contact me,' she said. But one day a representative from the University turned up at her house and took away 'hundreds of floppy discs' relating to Avtar's experiments. No reason was given for the 'friendly' raid, but afterwards she placed a copy of his thesis with his solicitor. She said she understood little of her husband's work, though the emphasis was clearly on software and simulation.

Loughborough University insisted that Avtar's work was neither sensitive nor classified. According to Goodson, many of Avtar's findings were 'not entirely new to the scientific world'. The University also placed great emphasis on the fact that Avtar had been receiving a small grant from the Ministry of Defence and that was only after his allowance from the Scientific and Engineering Research Council had run out.

This was misleading. Avtar had indeed received a very small grant from the Scientific and Engineering Research Council but this was replaced with the equivalent of a respectable salary funded by the Ministry of Defence. Moreover, he was working, at the time of his disappearance, on a technical paper co-authored by a member of staff from the Ministry of Defence's Admiralty Research Establishment, which is involved in many highly classified projects, including submarine stealth technology and EW. Avtar's thesis was called 'Underwater Signal Processing'. At the same time he was working on a separate technical paper, with the title 'A High Power Flexible Sonar Transmitter'. The paper, published in March 1987, carried Avtar's name together with that of a J.C. Cook, Professor J.W.R. Griffiths and A.D. Goodson. Cook worked at the Admiralty Research Establishment, and Professor Griffiths, regarded as an authority in the field of underwater warfare, was head of Avtar's section at Loughborough. Indeed, in October 1988 Professor Griffiths was on the technical committee of a conference held in London on undersea defence technology. So sensitive, in fact, is the whole area of sonar that fishing boats containing primitive sonar sets for detecting schools of fish cannot be sold to Eastern Bloc countries without a special licence.

Avtar was eventually spotted in France in May 1987. Or rather, his whereabouts were divulged to a provincial newspaper, the *Derby Evening Telegraph*. A reporter on the paper, Tony Tweedie, went to Paris to interview Avtar who was working in a boutique in the red light district. Avtar's immediate concern, apparently, was that he 'did not want anything to bring him to the attention of the authorities'. Later, under the pressure of publicity

Avtar returned to the UK. He said: 'I just walked off to get away from things. I can't really explain why, and I had certainly not planned it. I think I did it because the pressure had been building up over the previous months.' A full explanation, however, was not forthcoming. 'It's all a bit hazy now,' said Avtar. 'I walked away from the reservoir and caught a number of buses. I can't remember exactly but it was a day or two later when I got to Paris. I just wandered around. I didn't have much money or any clothes. I was just in a state of confusion.'

His comments did not entirely solve the mystery. In particular, why had he been apparently anxious to hide from the authorities? And why had the authorities shown such anxiety over finding him?

Most peculiar of all was a remark made by a senior Bristol detective during an earlier television documentary about the deaths of Vimal and Arshad, and the disappearance of Avtar. The detective seemed to hint that, long before the local paper 'traced' Avtar, the police had already discovered his whereabouts. His exact words were: 'As I see the issues now, we here will close the files on Mr Sharif and Mr Dajibhai and I feel that my colleagues in Derbyshire may be doing that in a few months time in relation to their case as well.'

Indeed, it was about two months after the policeman's remarks on television that Avtar was traced. Furthermore it emerged that the local paper which found him was acting on a tip-off from the police and the British authorities.

The tip-off came a few days before a particularly controversial inquest into the death of another defence scientist. The scientist, a well paid family man, apparently did a U-turn on his way to work one morning and drove at high speed into a disused café. The extra cans of petrol in his boot exploded into flames, and the man and his car were burnt beyond recognition.

Again, there had been no eyewitnesses or suicide note. But any deep-rooted interest among journalists and broadcasters in this third mysterious death was killed off by Avtar's return. The general feeling was summed up by the editor of a weekly ITV documentary series. His assessment of the story: 'But that chap from Loughborough returned, didn't he?'

Avtar eventually returned to Loughborough University to complete his Ph.D. He has told his family that he does not want to talk about his disappearance, or about his former acquaintance with Marconi computer programmer Vimal Dajibhai.

CHAPTER THREE

Britannia Rules the Waves

Vimal and Arshad were working on different projects which, seen from the ground floor level, had little in common. Take an overview, however, and the picture changes. Both were working on a technology which is at the heart of modern weapons and communications. It contains many secrets, shared only by Britain and the US. The influence of the technology on a future World War is incalculable. It is a technology which is understood by few people outside the defence industry. The American authorities fully realize its sensitivity. At one military aircraft factory in the US, staff working on this technology have the highest security clearance and work in a special area of the site which visitors are not allowed to see. Even employees who assemble jet fighters are not allowed to enter. The technology is known as electronic warfare, or EW.

Unlike tangible weapons such as guns, missiles and torpedoes which have obvious roles in battle, the effect of EW cannot be known until there is a war. The technology centres on the use, and particularly the deceptive use, of radio and sound waves which make up what is known as the electromagnetic spectrum. Whichever side controls the spectrum is likely to control the outcome of a war.

The growth in the importance of EW is the result of the military's increasing dependence on electronics and communications in modern warfare. On today's battlefield, troops have computerized missile systems which use signals plucked from the air to detect an attack by an aircraft beyond visual range. Using information passing through the airwaves the missile system automatically tracks several targets simultaneously, selecting those that represent the greatest threat, and fires missiles which use in-built radar to lock onto the target. All this may happen before the troops can even see or hear the attacking aircraft.

The equivalent of airwaves in the context of underwater warfare are acoustic or sound waves. Today's torpedoes have an artificial 'brain' and 'ears' which detect the acoustic signature of a submarine. The torpedo's 'ears', or sensors, pass the information to its 'brain', an onboard computer system, which makes an assessment of the strengths of its target. The torpedo can identify the make of a submarine and attack its weakest point.

Yet, despite the sophistication of modern weapon systems, things can, and do, go wrong. The US Aegis missile system shot down a civilian Iranian airbus in 1988, with the loss of many lives. Despite their ability to track and destroy targets, today's weapons cannot be relied upon to distinguish between what is friendly and what may be an attacker. This is, perhaps, one of the most striking weaknesses of modern military electronic systems. There are many other inherent flaws but, for obvious reasons, these are kept secret. As any future war is likely to be fought by push button, the knowledge of these weaknesses could be critical. Thus Western forces and Eastern Bloc countries have embarked on a covert war to discover each other's electronic strengths and weaknesses before any future hostilities break out.

EW is at the heart of the undeclared war. In essence, EW is the practice of technical opportunism, exploiting weaknesses in the Warsaw Pact's use of electronics for its weapons and sensors, cleverly taking advantage of features of the WP's equipment design or its use of electronics.

The development of EW owes much to advances in signal processing, a technology which can be traced back to 1896 when a young inventor travelled from Italy to Britain to show the world's largest navy a device he hoped would revolutionize shipping communications. The young inventor's name was Guglielmo Marconi. The device was the wireless or radio set.

The world embraced Marconi's wireless telegraph. Within fifteen years of his arrival in Britain, the 23-year-old inventor had been awarded a Nobel Prize for physics and had established a company to exploit the growing interest in radio signals. By the time of the First World War, it was realized that ruling the ocean waves went hand in hand with ruling the airwaves. Marconi soon discovered ways of transmitting messages over vast distances, while the military began to master the art of sending false signals, to fool those who were eavesdropping. At the same time techniques were developed to convert messages into code form. But while the German Navy was encoding messages, the British were busily decoding them.

One of the first references to EW was made as early as 1914 when, according to a sub-committee of the Committee of Imperial Defence, discussions were led by Admiral Charlton, assistant director of torpedoes, on ways of blocking or 'jamming' radio signals. It was also during this period that spycatcher Peter Wright's father worked alongside Marconi, or G.M. as he was known, developing direction finding equipment for the Navy.

By the time of the Second World War, the interception, interpretation and manipulation of radio signals was an established and highly secret technology. This was the secret war referred to by Winston Churchill in his famous 'Their Finest Hour' speech: '... the secret war whose battles were lost and won unknown to the public.' Churchill continued: 'No such warfare had ever been waged by mortal men. The terms in which it could be recorded or talked about were unintelligible to ordinary folk. Yet if we had not mastered its profound meaning and used its mysteries even though we saw them in the glimpse, all the efforts, all the prowess of the fighting airmen, all the bravery and the sacrifices of the people, would have been in vain.' In his war memoirs, Churchill called EW 'the wizard war'. He referred to the bombing of Britain by the *Luftwaffe* and the so-called Battle of the Beams, in which the Allies prevented German aircraft getting their navigational bearings by radio in 1940. Some of the German aircraft became so confused that they landed at British air bases.

During the late 1930s, British scientists had also developed the area of radio technology now known as radar. This, too, played a central role in the 'secret war'. In 1942, for example, RAF Coastal Command was using a radar which operated in a frequency range, known as L-band, as an aid to locating German submarines which had to surface to recharge their batteries. The radar was successful, until the German submarines began using receivers which could detect L-band radar signals. This gave the submarines enough time to crash-dive before being sighted by searching aircraft, and in general the effectiveness of the RAF anti-submarine effort decreased. The Allies realized what had happened and installed new 'S-band' search radars aboard their aircraft in the early part of 1943. As a result the rate of interceptions rose sharply. German submarines sitting on the surface listening for L-band signals became vulnerable targets for British aircraft now using S-band. As the submarine sinkings increased the Germans tried frantically to determine what method of detection the Allies were using. Since reports from surviving submarines stated that no signals had been heard in L-band prior to the attack, it was thought that perhaps an infra-red detection device was being employed. Considerable effort was spent in an attempt to combat a non-existing infra-red threat, and submarine activity was greatly reduced by the time the German High Command realized that, in fact, a new high frequency radar was in use.

If the Germans had been doing electronic reconnaissance on flights over England and intercepted the new S-band signals during the development and testing stages, they could have countered the new threat by replacing their L-band receivers with S-band versions. The Allies gained an enormous military advantage achieved by suppressing what was, in effect, a simple secret, demonstrating that a basic requirement of EW was, and still is, information. Today, those very same security considerations have since led to EW equipment being developed and tested in laboratories and on large-scale simulators, rather than in the open air, where electronic emissions may be hoovered up by reconnaissance satellites and other surveillance equipment. The Marconi group from its origins has spearheaded the intelligence gathering effort, from its early construction of signals stations to its manufacture today of intelligence gathering EW equipment.

For example, a technical paper published in 1986 by EW scientists at Marconi Defence Systems in Stanmore, where Arshad Sharif had worked, emphasizes the need to protect one's own secrets and to acquire information on potential enemies. Entitled 'The Role of Advanced Technologies in Future EW Systems', the paper states: 'Specification of the environment must use knowledge of friendly and hostile radar fits, and the probable deployment of these radars. Since it would be extremely difficult (not to say unwise) to generate such environments as parts of an exercise, processor proving must rely increasingly on digital simulation.'

A separate Marconi document makes it clear that in

any weapon system compromises are inevitable. Simulation, however, pinpoints weaknesses which might, for example, make a torpedo vulnerable to acoustic jamming. 'Performance of the weapon can be assessed against a wide range of different targets,' continues the Marconi document. 'Our Sting Ray Real Time Simulator has been approved by the Ministry of Defence as evaluating performance ... The most difficult and complex task that had to be faced was that of modelling the underwater environment. Many hundreds of hours of data have been gathered by in-water equipment, enough to show that traditional textbook models of the environment are not adequate.'

Simulations, in fact, are at the centre of America's Star Wars project which was launched in 1983 by the then president Ronald Reagan. He had announced that the US was about to embark on a programme to develop a system for the defence of the United States against attack by intercontinental ballistic missiles. The plan became known as the Strategic Defence Initiative (SDI) or Star Wars. The Initiative envisaged deploying a variety of exotic weapons, such as space-based lasers and 'rail guns', to provide a technological canopy over America, shielding it from conventionally armed or nuclear tipped missiles. The plan, which cost an average of about $4 billion a year, has caused much debate over its technical feasibility. What has been almost forgotten in that debate, however, is that the technology being applied to SDI is being researched in other projects and for other purposes. SDI has given these other programmes an added impetus and direction. It has also added to their secrecy.

The *Observer* newspaper reported in 1987: 'The Americans emphasize the importance of "extraordinary security" for computer programmers – the heart of the SDI project – to prevent sabotage and the leaking of information.' And according to the magazine *Jane's*

Defence Weekly, those technologies which share a common military application with SDI will be 'classified top secret' to prevent such technologies 'falling into the hands of the Soviets'.

The Americans have given countless warnings to Europe that the Soviets are carrying out a 'massive global effort' to improve their weapons by acquiring Western technology. The former US Secretary of Defence, Caspar Weinberger, said in a Pentagon statement that the problem was 'far more serious than we had previously realized'. He spoke of the thousands of Warsaw Pact intelligence officers and scientists, diplomats and espionage agents that 'make use of unscrupulous Western collaborators'. He said there was a need to stop the 'dangerous' flow of the West's superior technology to potential adversaries and added: 'Technology security is a very vital component of our defence. Without the Western technological lead that we have, our ability to maintain an effective deterrence would be very seriously jeopardized.' This attitude is unlikely to soften because of the dismantling of the Berlin Wall.

Some would go so far as to say that the Americans are paranoid over the need for secrecy. Others would argue that its concern is understandable given that an expensively researched technological breakthrough in the defence industry is of little value if a potential enemy can find out enough about it to design and build countermeasures.

Companies can lose their cherished security clearance if employees cannot be trusted to maintain discretion over classified information. In the UK, defence industry employees are inculcated with the need for secrecy, in the interests of national security and also to show the Americans that the British are capable of keeping secrets.

The Americans would refuse to share their intelligence information with British defence contractors and Ministry of Defence establishments if they suspected that UK employees were not trustworthy and, indeed, there is no evidence that British employees cannot be trusted. But codes of confidentiality cannot take into account every eventuality. What if an employee has discovered the methods which will give a company, or even its country, a technological edge? That employee is always free to leave one company to join a competitor. Naturally such an employee would be expected to respect the confidentiality of information acquired in previous jobs, but it is questionable whether such an obligation is legally enforceable. Some of the electronic secrets contained within weapons systems may be worth, potentially, hundreds of millions of pounds. Sometimes, it may be a single programming procedure, capable of being memorized by a bright individual, which can hold the key to a technological breakthrough.

It is against this background of secrecy that British companies and establishments embark on a variety of SDI and technologically related projects. Many seem, at first glance, to have disparate interests in the programme. However, like so many computer-related defence projects, the areas of technology overlap. A number of British companies, for example, are working on contracts relating to battle management C3 which is perhaps the most technically challenging part of SDI. It has been described as the glue which will hold any future SDI system together and includes the development of computer systems which will automate elements of decision making, reducing the time taken to react to an attack. Due to the speed of modern warfare, the systems must make a split second assessment of the threats and automatically activate firing sequences. Companies awarded SDI contracts relating to battle management C3 include British Aerospace, Plessey, Marconi and its sister company Easams.

Of course, SDI can never be tested. So a large part of research is based on computer simulation. Hopes for the entire development of SDI depend heavily on highly complex computer systems which mimic large scale threats. Proponents of SDI argue that a combination of small scale testing and the use of computer simulators could substitute for actual systemwide testing. One particularly advanced simulation project, called Cosmos, came to light during the investigation by journalists into the deaths of Vimal Dajibhai and Arshad Sharif.

A project leader at Marconi Underwater Systems at Croxley Green, where Vimal worked, described Cosmos as 'a bit like video war games'. Television screens display three dimensional graphics which enable weapons designers to read almost every conceivable underwater situation. The technology, said the manager, was three years more advanced than anything in the US and ten years ahead of the Russians. The simulator had 'immense potential' for Star Wars. 'Our software is unique,' he said. 'It allows us to home in directly on multiple targets, either from sea, air or space.' One critical area of the SDI programme is the development of weapons systems which can distinguish real Soviet warheads from perhaps thousands of decoys. The Marconi manager said that such a system could be developed. 'You program into the missile's computer all possibilities so that it recognizes a missile fired from a particular launcher,' he said. 'But this is in the realms of highly sensitive information.'

Some of the computerized war games used by the military and those that people buy for their home computers in the shops may not appear, at first, significantly different. Both types may, for example, show a Western torpedo attacking a Soviet submarine. The real difference is that the shop version makes only assumptions, some of them well informed, about the enemy's capabilities and weaknesses. It may only guess at the ability of a torpedo to find its target, its potential speed, and its immunity to enemy countermeasures.

The military 'game', on the other hand, can call upon

highly classified intelligence information with which to make the simulations rather more accurate. Data derived from the covert surveillance of Soviet submarines, for example, can be programmed into military computer simulations. It is therefore likely that a large-scale SDI simulator, which would be designed to show many types of military engagement, would contain much highly classified information.

Whereas, in the past, classified data was locked away in filing cabinets and handed out on a 'need to know' basis, with few people gaining an overall picture of a project, simulators can display an entire underwater, air or space battle. They can not only show the strengths and weaknesses of a missile under development, they can also simulate the environment in which it is programmed to operate. In short, simulators can calculate the odds on a successful outcome, while at the same time accurately estimating how long it would take to respond to a particular threat.

Clearly, 'war games' are no longer as frivolous as the name implies. These days the most realistic simulations are those which contain within their computer programs accurate and highly sensitive intelligence information such as communications and infra-red frequencies, or, perhaps, the electronic order of battle and signals details of hostile radar. This sort of information is acquired by covert surveillance which can take many forms. There is now little, in fact, to differentiate some simulations from actual weapons performance. With the use of supercomputers, which can perform many millions of calculations per second, simulations can provide test operators with a far more comprehensive picture of a weapon system's performance, and its role in a battle, than they would gain by witnessing a live test firing.

As one graduate employee at Marconi Underwater Systems put it: 'A real "engagement", from seeing the target to launching a torpedo, may take two hours or so.

My program has to run a hundred times faster than that. On our computer one engagement takes a maximum of five minutes, so that we can do a large number of runs and analyse the results statistically, to obtain probabilities for hits and misses.'

Britain, then, holds technological secrets which are applicable to the most sensitive aspects of modern warfare. Marconi, especially Marconi Underwater Systems and Marconi Defence Systems where Vimal and Arshad worked, is at the hub of those secrets.

It was not surprising, therefore, that Marconi attempted to play down the importance of the dead men's work. Marconi's official comment at the time when the story of the deaths originally surfaced in 1987 came from its public relations advisers. A press officer said he knew of no reason why the two deaths should be connected and added: 'The two dead men were junior employees who worked on different projects at different sites for different Marconi companies. As far as we are aware they did not know one another. They were very junior members of staff.' However, he could not remember the particular sites where they had worked, although he said he knew there was no link between the two.

Referring to the press investigation into the deaths, he continued: 'Marconi was most concerned about what has been said (by its employees). There were internal checks to establish who had said what, and we realized we had a lot of problems.

'There were loads of telexes and faxes going between different buildings with details of who had said what. Some of the things you were told has given slight cause for alarm ... You might have been given information that would be useful to an enemy.

'Some people have given you bits and pieces that, put together, would be of use to someone ... People have said too much, and it has caused mild panic.'

Was the company absolutely certain that there was no link between the deaths?

'There was no link,' he said. 'They both worked at different parts of Marconi. The only link is that they both were part of some sect or particular temple. That's the only link we are aware of. Apparently they were both members of the same sect.'

Whether this final comment was deliberately meant to be misleading is unlikely. Even the police acknowledged that, while Vimal, a Hindu, had indeed visited a sect once, Arshad, a devout Muslim, probably did not even know of its existence.

The claim that both men were 'junior programmers' was also bewildering. Both men were graduates and had probably already had considerable work experience by the time they obtained their degrees. The application of those skills to specialist defence projects, together with their innate ability, acknowledged by their colleagues, to grasp an understanding of more complex areas of their work made them more than just 'junior programmers'. In fact Arshad had been promoted and was to have taken over a department of fifteen people. He had his own office, unlike many others who worked on a large factory floor. Moreover, unlike those on the factory floor, he had an understanding of the equipment itself. It also emerged later that he had been familiar with large scale test equipment which enables the operator to test a single circuit board by simulating its role in an entire system. One of Arshad's tasks had been to test the circuit boards in a particular EW system.

In fact, the £100m Zeus project with which Arshad was involved is said to be a multi-purpose EW countermeasures system designed by Marconi Defence Systems and American defence contractor Northrop. According to defence specialists, it can intercept and measure the electronic emissions from 'all radar controlled systems likely to be a threat to an aircraft'.

Zeus's digital processor then displays details of the enemy radar threat on a computer monitor in the aircraft.

Detailed information on Zeus is not easy to come by, although Marconi Defence Systems, in a three page booklet for graduates, mentions EW work and the Zeus project before any other. In the brief reference it states: 'During the Second World War, British bombers dropped chaff to interfere with enemy radar surveillance. The modern equivalent is our Zeus system.'

When the Ministry of Defence commissioned Marconi Defence Systems to develop and manufacture Zeus in 1984, Air Commodore G.S. Cooper, writing in the *Daily Telegraph*, reported that, with Zeus's advanced technology and compact size, enhanced sales prospects for installation in a number of foreign aircraft would be good. There were particular plans to sell Zeus to the US. The Ministry of Defence was quoted as saying that Zeus would provide the Harrier jump jet with the 'most advanced EW technology in the world'. The RAF was to get sixty Harrier GR 5s, the new Anglo-American version jointly developed by McDonnell Douglas and British Aerospace, all equipped with Zeus.

Both Vimal and Arshad had worked on test equipment and simulators. According to one of Vimal's colleagues, he was more experienced in his particular field than any other member of the Marconi group. Vimal was a member of Marconi's Advanced Software Group which was investigating aspects of the application of artificial intelligence to computers, with more than a passing reference to EW. Moreover, the Sting Ray torpedo, which Vimal was working on when he died, is a weapon of considerable versatility. Designed to be launched from aircraft and ships, it was said to be the only torpedo capable of penetrating the titanium hulls of the deep diving Soviet submarines and is designed to ignore decoy targets and other attempts to seduce it away from its real target. The accuracy of its guidance systems, assessed during water trials and detailed computer simulations, is said to be up to 95 percent. In April 1987, it was reported in the technical press that Marconi had developed an advanced algorithm, or set of mathematical rules, which 'radically improves the kill capabilities of Sting Ray'. The algorithm was said to form a critical part of Sting Ray's guidance system and was used for target location and tracking.

According to a highly regarded *Jane's* defence reference book: 'It seems certain that in place of blast type torpedo warheads, some form of directed energy payload is required to counter modern submarines. Such devices require highly accurate guidance to ensure that the torpedo strikes its target in the most vulnerabale place at the right angle. This suggests that Sting Ray incorporates both very precise guidance and an enhanced warhead, but this cannot be categorically confirmed as yet.' No wonder, then, that the Ministry of Defence, in what Marconi described as the 'largest order ever for a single weapon system', ordered more than 2,500 Sting Rays at a cost of £200,000 each.

To recognize an enemy submarine, Sting Ray's on-board computers need to know in advance the target's acoustic characteristics or signature. The torpedo therefore needs to be programmed with highly classified information.

There is considerable secrecy surrounding submarine intelligence gathering missions, although Royal Navy personnel are aware that they are frequent and sometimes highly risky. Occasionally such missions are joined by perhaps one or two plain clothed staff, about whom there are few, if any, questions asked. According to Royal Navy officers the plain clothed passengers will generally be communications or EW personnel.

Once at sea, sophisticated and highly sensitive listening equipment is used to secretly record the signatures of Eastern Bloc submarines. Despite Soviet advances during the 1980s in techniques aimed at suppressing the amount of underwater noise made by their submarines, some of them can still be heard more than 100 miles away by Western boats. At the 1987 Royal Navy Equipment Exhibition on Whale Island in Portsmouth, a company which installs command and control systems aboard British submarines demonstrated a simulation of how its computer system was designed to discern a potential enemy submarine from the mass of underwater noise. On each of a row of screens were different pictures which changed rapidly. Although the pictures lasted for only a few seconds, one showed the number of blades on the approaching submarine's propellers, the number of shafts and the type of engine. A company spokesman said: 'This demonstration has been sanitized, of course. We can actually tell rather more than the type of enemy submarine.' He added, in a lowered voice, 'We can tell what fridge he's using.'

Each side is continually trying to come up with new ways of disguising the inevitable noise of its submarine propulsion systems. Both Nato and the Warsaw Pact countries frequently change their propellers to thwart the other side's attempts to pigeon-hole their acoustic charateristics. Military experts are currently experimenting with a quiet propulsion technique called a propulsor, where the blades rotate inside a duct or shroud, not unlike those on a paddle steamer. Some of the techniques of the propulsor programme are applied to Sting Ray's propulsion system to make it less prone to detection.

So, clearly, Vimal and Arshad were working in areas which are not taught at university. Interviews with a number of graduate employees in the area of defence electronics have established that an understanding of underwater or electronic warfare can be gained only by practical experience and experimentation, working either for a defence contractor or for the Ministry of Defence. In fact Vimal and Arshad were possibly more familiar with the technical intricacies of their projects than some of their superiors.

Although Marconi is a primary British contractor to Star Wars neither Vimal nor Arshad were working directly on the project. But the technologies in which they specialized have direct implications for Star Wars. In particular Vimal and Arshad were at the leading edge of computer simulation technology, a field in which Britain leads the world, according to senior Marconi employees.

The most advanced military simulations can contain intelligence information derived from covert reconnaissance missions or from 'spy' satellites. In the West military authorities spend tens of billions of pounds on computer simulations. They are used to test the key electronic parts of weapons. They are used in the design, development, final testing and later enhancement of EW systems. They are at the centre of the Star Wars project. In short, military simulations can contain some of the most sensitive defence secrets in the West.

The Marconi company, from its inception, has worked closely with successive governments on the most sensitive developments in defence technology, even where intelligence information is involved. It has even manufactured intelligence-gathering equipment. Therefore it was not surprising that Marconi turned down several requests to discuss the details of Vimal and Arshad's work. It is also not surprising that they would not give the names of other scientists who had apparently killed themselves or died accidentally. But others there were.

One particularly mysterious case involved 43-year-old employee Robert Wilson. In 1972 Robert, who until a year earlier had worked at Marconi's Chelmsford plant, was clearing out his attic when he apparently came across a pile of Marconi documents marked 'secret and confidential'. He duly presented the documents to Marconi's security officers, saying he wanted to return them, and after a lengthy interview went home. The following day he was cleaning his .45 revolver when he accidentally shot himself in the chest. The incident was clearly out of character. As a marksman at the local gun club, he might have been expected to know better than to clean a loaded gun with the barrel pointed towards him.

The *Sunday Telegraph* carried a report at the time under the headline 'Mystery of the Shot Marconi Expert'. It described Robert as an electronics engineer and described Marconi in Chelmsford as being 'concerned with radar, sonar and guided missiles schemes'.

In fact Robert, who survived the incident, had been employed by Marconi as a technical author in the company's information department where he would have had access to a wide range of material on Marconi research projects. A year before his accident he had resigned to join a rival electronics firm. He offered no public explanation of how he came to have secret papers at his home, but Marconi insisted at the time that national security was not involved.

Robert, speaking from his hospital bed, told a reporter:

'There has been a certain amount of tightening up of security at Marconi over the last two years. Quite fortuitously, in the course of a clear out of the attic, I came across some obsolete stuff which was too bulky to burn. I returned it instead of destroying it because of the sheer volume of it. It was classified when it was printed. About twenty-four hours thereafter I had a shooting accident. I was cleaning and checking the action of the pistol.

'The nature of the blunder lay in the fact that I was

handling the pistol while the muzzle was pointing towards me. It was an error so grotesque that I have shivers.'

The following year a story appeared in a local paper about a colour television engineer who had died shortly after being admitted into hospital. The story continued:

'He was Robert McClean Wilson of Spalding Way who was taken to Chelmsford and Essex Hospital from the fume filled garage at his home whilst servicing his car. A post mortem was carried out yesterday.'

So Robert had survived the accidental shooting incident only to die, apparently accidentally, in his garage.

At his inquest the coroner was preoccupied only with the dangers of servicing cars inside locked garages. He recorded a verdict of accidental death by carbon monoxide poisoning and said: 'It is part of the purpose of an inquest to warn others. I hope this will serve to warn other people about the dangers of running car engines with the garage door closed.'

Dr Kenneth Turk, a consultant pathologist, told the inquest that people did not seem to realize just how dangerous carbon monoxide can be.

Barbara Wilson said her husband always serviced the car himself. On the day he died he was servicing it prior to going to the West Country. When their daughter came home from school, she heard the engine running and went in to see her father. She found him lying unconscious against a wall. Mrs Wilson said: 'My husband was an extremely sensible and sane man. We had no worries.' She added, 'He was earning a good salary.'

PC Anthony Barker said he was called to the house by Mrs Wilson and said he found a note beside the car containing a list of jobs to be done on the car. He added: 'I can only imagine that Mr Wilson was overcome by fumes while he was working on the car.'

At around the same time as Robert's death, the local paper carried a story which took up a large portion on a front page in May 1973 under the headline 'Knife Death – Body in Flat.' The story read: 'Last night police still had not named the dead man who is believed to have been a student.'

The article added that the man had been found in his flat with a knife wound in his chest. His landlord had found the door to the man's flat ajar.

By the time of the following week's brief article police had ruled out foul play. 'Detectives investigating the death of a 22-year-old man found with a knife in his chest in a Chelmsford flat have ruled out crime. The body of Gerard Jack Darlow, a Marconi worker, was discovered lying on a bed in his second floor flat above County Car Sales' showrooms in the cul-de-sac part of Baddow Road soon after midday last Thursday.

'A team of detectives, including the head of Essex CID, Detective Chief Superintendent Len White, was called to the flat close to the town's inner ring road. On Friday an inquest in Chelmsford was opened and adjourned for six weeks. PC Dick Lucas told Essex coroner Dr Charles Clark that forensic evidence was being analysed. He added that crime had been ruled out.

'The body was discovered by landlord Mr Gerald Ager who lives in the first floor flat. He called police after finding Mr Darlow's body on a bed.'

Mr Ager said he went into the flat shortly before 1 p.m. after he saw the previous day's milk and letters outside the door. Head of Chelmsford CID, Detective Chief Inspector George Raven, and a team of police began investigations. They were later joined by other senior detectives.

A Home Office pathologist was called in from London and later the body was taken to Harlow for a post mortem. During the afternoon Mr Darlow's parents visited the flat from their RAF Wattisham home near Ipswich. Apparently Mr Darlow had lived in the flat for about three years.

About four months later, in September 1973, the incident which had prompted a front page story was concluded with a brief report on page twenty. It did not name Gerard Darlow's employers, and described him only as a 22-year-old 'apprentice'. It said that he had 'stabbed himself to death'.

Mr Eric Darlow, an RAF training instructor from Lincolnshire, said his son had tried to kill himself in July the previous year by stepping in front of a lorry. Mr Darlow said his son had shown signs of a slight manifestation of schizophrenia and was receiving drug treatment. He said of his son: 'He started work in November. He appeared to be making very good progress from Christmas.' He last saw his son alive on the previous Monday before his body was found in a top floor flat. His son had been to see a doctor on the Monday. Afterwards Mr Darlow was 'completely relieved'. And he added: 'The doctor felt there was no immediate danger. He said he could start back at work.' Essex coroner Dr Charles Clark recorded a verdict that Gerard Darlow took his own life while suffering from schizophrenia.

Gerard Darlow and Robert Wilson died in 1973. Vimal Dajibhai and Arshad Sharif died in 1986. On Friday, 25 March 1988, 52-year-old Marconi engineer Trevor Knight was found dead in his fume filled Ford Capri car at his Harpenden home. A hosepipe led from the exhaust into the car. On the day before he died, Trevor telephoned his mother Rachael. He telephoned her nearly every day and visited her regularly. 'On the day before he died he phoned me twice,' said Rachael. 'He sounded quite happy and said he would see me over the weekend. He never talked about his work but he was always happy and a wonderful son to me. I don't think we shall know why Trevor died.'

Trevor, a former grammar school pupil who was separated from his wife, although they remained good friends, had worked for several companies before he joined Marconi. In his spare time he was keen on jogging and took part in several mini-marathons, raising money for cancer and leukaemia research. The police did not treat his death as suspicious, although a Labour Member of Parliament, Doug Hoyle, who also represents the interests of the Manufacturing, Science and Finance Union, which counts many research scientists among its members, raised the matter in the House of Commons.

At the inquest it was made fairly clear that Trevor had intended to take his own life. The coroner, Dr Arnold Mendoza, said that Trevor's friend, Narmada Thanki, who also worked at Marconi, had found three notes on the kitchen table which, said Dr Mendoza, gave 'a clear indication of his intention'. Narmada told the inquest that she had known Trevor for nearly eight years, but that they had kept their relationship quiet in order not to upset his wife and family. She said he had disliked the work he was doing but had not shown signs of depression. Trevor's estranged wife, however, told the inquest he had appeared depressed, but that he had not talked about harming himself. It was further reported that Trevor had suffered continual problems for a five year period as a result of 'road accidents he had been involved in', and that he had also suffered from migraine. Consultant pathologist Dr Sarah Hill confirmed that death was due to carbon monoxide poisoning and that there was no evidence of excess alcohol in his blood or urine. Recording a verdict of suicide Dr Mendoza said: 'He didn't like his work and was a bit depressed, and he left notes which gave a clear indication of his intention.'

It seemed like a tragically conventional suicide although one or two further facts are worth noting. A close friend and confidant said later that, contrary to newspaper reports, which quoted the authorities as saying that Trevor did not have 'direct access to classified information', Trevor had been, in fact, handling 'very sensitive' data. He was not, as the authorities insisted, an 'engineer', but rather a computer services manager. Less than two years before his death he had worked at Marconi Underwater systems at Croxley Green, where Vimal Dajibhai worked. He had later moved to Marconi Defence Systems at Stanmore, where Arshad Sharif had worked, which was deeply involved in a number of highly sensitive EW contracts. Trevor had also, according to the source, been involved in 'very sophisticated' real-time simulations.

Furthermore, no clear indication was given at the inquest of the contents of the notes on the kitchen table. Even Trevor's close friend, who had seen the notes, refused to talk about them. The friend, who had spoken in a relaxed manner for about half an hour, suddenly went quiet when asked if the messages were suicide notes or straightforward letters. After a long silence the friend said: 'No comment.'

Marconi had, according to the Bristol police, been 'very cooperative' during the investigations into Vimal Dajibhai and Arshad Sharif's death. When asked, however, whether the security services had been consulted, the police would only say that they could not 'discuss matters of national security'. It seems likely from this evasive reply that the security services had been alerted, and at least one national newspaper reported as much.

What is, however, virtually certain is that Vimal Dajibhai, Arshad Sharif, Robert Wilson, Gerard Darlow, and Trevor Knight were all working in areas important to national security. They were working for a company which is at the leading edge of some of today's defence technologies.

Britain still leads the world in some aspects of

underwater warfare technology. Its anti-submarine sonar and weapons are regarded as some of the most advanced, and the Marconi group specializes in those areas. Britain also excels in other defence technologies. The very fact that it is an island and therefore relies on its navy to prevent invasion has led to a concentration of skills in electronics-led naval and anti-submarine warfare. But a modern navy needs back-up from the air, and Britain has also forged a lead in air defence with its use of computerized command and control systems. Vast amounts of information on an unfolding underwater, sea or land battle can be sieved by computers and displayed in an easy-to-read form on computer screens. In the Falklands War, information about air defence, naval and underwater warfare was brought together by electronic means. Military authorities, watching computer screens at a base in England, were able to monitor the progress of the war in the South Atlantic 8,000 miles away.

In the summer of 1988, two defence company employees, Brigadier Peter Ferry and Alistair Beckham, apparently took their own lives. Both men worked for separate companies, Marconi and Plessey, so it was widely assumed that there were no connections between their fields of work. In fact, with the media adding their names to a list of seemingly disparate cases, the distinctive and not wholly dissimilar circumstances surrounding the deaths of Peter Ferry and Alistair Beckham became blurred. Peter had apparently wired his teeth to a mains supply. Alistair, also, had apparently wired himself to the mains.

The deaths brought a mixed reaction from journalists. The coincidence theorists became more convinced that all the deaths were unrelated. They said that the two new deaths had straightforward explanations. The conspiracy theorists became hardened in their conviction that one or two deaths may have been coincidental but that more than that smacked of something strange.

On balance, there were more facts to support the coincidence theorists. Why would anyone want to murder them? How could it have been done? The door of Peter Ferry's flat had been wedged almost shut from the inside. The door of Alistair Beckham's shed was locked from the inside. Peter's death could be explained by the depression brought on by a road accident three weeks before his apparent suicide. Although no reasons emerged at Alistair's inquest to explain his death, the trade press subsequently received an anonymous telephone call from a man saying he was a colleague of Alistair's and that Alistair had been under considerable stress. Certainly Mary, Alistair's wife, knew he had been working hard. He had once mentioned that he was doing the job of three people. But he had never shown signs of stress, and he was usually home by 6.30 p.m.

The events leading up to Alistair's death on a sunny, Sunday morning in August 1988 suggested nothing untoward. Mary got up at 6.15 a.m., allowing plenty of time before leaving for her job as a part-time nurse at a nearby residential home. She tried to persuade Alistair to stay in bed, to enjoy a Sunday morning lie in, but he insisted on getting up. He wanted to get on with painting the front windows. As a do-it-yourself enthusiast, he had already redecorated many of the rooms and built several cupboards. The Beckhams lived in a double-fronted detached house and there was always something that needed doing. Alistair got up at about 6.30 a.m. and joined Mary for breakfast. At 6.50 a.m. they set off for the residential home in his Vauxhall Cavalier, chatting casually about going on a long weekend to the Isle of Wight in a few weeks time. They planned to get the children out of school early on a Friday afternoon.

Alistair dropped Mary off at about 7 a.m. and he agreed to pick her up at 2 p.m. when her shift finished. 'Oh no I won't forget,' he had told her. It was the last time she saw him alive.

Sometime in the morning, while their three daughters, on whom he doted, slept in their rooms, Alistair had apparently electrocuted himself in a shed adjacent to the house. When Mary arrived home on her own she found the shed door locked and a neighbour helped her break in. He was sitting on a tea chest, his back against the wall. 'He felt cold,' she said. Inside the shed were the tins of paint and brushes he would have used.

Mary later reconstructed her husband's movements on the Sunday morning and became confused. Until going into the shed to apparently electrocute himself, everything had seemed normal. After dropping off Mary he had returned to the house, fed their small dog and checked his football pools. He had also taken the dog for a walk and bought their usual Sunday newspapers. The police, however, treated the case as a straightforward suicide. Although they could not establish a motive they said that Alistair's death had been a well-planned, deliberate act. Mary believes that a third party was involved, though she has no idea who or why. She and her husband had no particular financial worries, having paid cash for their house on a small site close to Woking town centre in Surrey. Although they lived on a tight budget, his job at Plessey Naval Systems was well paid and she supplemented her income as a nurse by letting out some spare rooms in the house.

'We had a very good relationship. There weren't any other women involved and there weren't any other men involved. There was nothing. I don't know why he did it, if he did it. I don't believe that he did do it. He wouldn't go out into the shed to kill himself. There had to be something.' Mary suspects that threats may have been made to harm their children and that Alistair was coerced into turning the key locking himself in the shed.

Alistair's death, and that of Brigadier Peter Ferry a month later, had something in common: their work.

Before the road accident on Tuesday, 2 August 1988, which changed his life, ex-army officer Brigadier Peter Ferry was a reliable, respected member of the military community. He was soon to retire from full-time work as business development manager at Marconi and was to settle down in a new house, to pursue his personal passion, restoring veteran motorcycles. He had planned to do a few hours of work a month for Marconi, keeping up his contacts. After all, as his wife Ann put it, 'he knew an enormous number of people'. 'We lived in America for three years,' she said. 'We were with the British Embassy on the defence staff. Peter was research and development attaché from 1975 to 1978.' Although no bones were broken in the car accident, it turned a robust 6 foot 2 inch, self-confident individual into a shell-shocked soldier, shaking, shivering and even crying at times.

A policeman who had investigated Peter's death said: 'What basically happened was that he had an accident on 2 August and had been depressed since then, a totally changed man. The accident blew his mind and he just committed suicide.'

Just because of an accident?

'It would appear so.'

Was it that serious?

'He was trapped in the car for a while. Although he was not seriously injured there was petrol pouring everywhere, I'm told, and he was obviously thinking he was going to be burned alive. If someone had lit a match it would have gone up.'

Peter's car was apparently hit by a truck travelling on the wrong side of the road. Ann said: 'The car was driven over by a ten ton truck going at 65 m.p.h. in a lane just outside our house. My husband had to be released from the car before it exploded. There is nothing he could have done. It is a very narrow lane. You could just get two cars past but a lorry and a car is almost impossible.'

Three weeks after the accident, Peter was found dead in a cottage in the grounds of the Marconi factory at Frimley near Camberley, Surrey. He had been staying there during the week, travelling home to Wiltshire at weekends. 'He took a wire off a lamp, stuck one side of the wire to the right molar tooth and the other side to the left molar tooth and plugged himself in,' said a detective who investigated the death. Police ruled out foul play. The cottage was out of bounds to all unauthorized personnel and the factory has twenty-four hour security measures.

Ann is convinced that her husband's death is not connected with those of the other scientists. 'To me he died in that car crash. It was most terrifying watching him disintegrate,' she said. 'It is such a waste of such a super person. He had never had anything in the least like a mental breakdown or stress. He handled anything. He was tremendously outgoing and popular with people.'

At the inquest Ann said that after the accident her husband had 'started to panic about everything and was frightened he would lose his job'. On 19 August he had admitted he had tried to drown himself in a nearby river but the water was only 18 inches deep. Two days later he drove to Frimley to talk to his employers about his future. Afterwards he telephoned Ann to say he wasn't going to be fired. He was going to Brussels in September to 'sort out Nato'. He added that he would be back the following evening. Ann said that her husband had spent a lot of time in Brussels and had found work no more stressful than anyone else in the job.

David Halsall, Marconi's personnel director, said that he had spoken to Peter previously. He had found him a 'robust individual, a typical ex-army officer, full of confidence, a professional'. But when he later saw him at Marconi on 22 August he was a totally changed man who had aged considerably. 'I said I had heard about the accident and how he was lucky to be with us. He said something along the lines of: "I doubt it." ' Peter had been concerned that the company might not wish to keep him on but Halsall said: 'I told him he was quite wrong. As far as we were concerned we were more than happy to continue employing him but could see him changing to part-time work around Christmas when he was due to retire.' Peter was assured that he had valuable work left to do and was asked for his help in finding a suitable successor. However, because he was concerned about his health it was arranged for him to see the company doctor the following day.

The next day a cleaner reported that she could not open the door to Peter's room in the cottage and that she had seen sparks coming from the room. Halsall went to the cottage and found the door was slightly ajar but wedged. He could see a plug half inserted in the socket and heard an electrical discharge. He reached through and switched off the electricity and removed the plug. Peter was found lying behind the door. The police discovered two notes in his handwriting in a dustbin but the contents of the notes were never disclosed.

It seemed obvious that depression had led to the Brigadier taking his own life. No evidence emerged which suggested foul play, although certain questions went unanswered. Ann Ferry described as 'extraordinary' the fact that some of the scientists who had died had also previously been in inexplicable car accidents and went on to say that her husband had had 'one or two accidents' even though he was a 'very skilled driver'. She described an accident in April 1987, when his car had been stationary for a few seconds at a pedestrian crossing in London and a lorry had crashed into the rear of his car. He had suffered whiplash neck injuries. It must have been coincidence that the inquest on Marconi computer services manager Trevor Knight was told that, before he was found dead in his garage, a few months before Peter's death, he had also been in car accidents which had left him with whiplash injuries. Questions also remain over Peter's depression. Individuals who have access to highly sensitive information are regarded as potential security risks. Brigadier Ferry had, after all, turned overnight from being a military character of exemplary reliability to a mental wreck, worried about the security of his job and his financial future. It was highly unlikely that a potential enemy might have wanted to exploit these vulnerabilities. But was it inconceivable? And was it unthinkable that the security services might have been concerned about Peter's depression?

His knowledge of some of Nato's military strengths and weaknesses was extensive. Ann said: 'He had had a busy summer. He did a lot of work for Nato. I know his title was assistant marketing director but in fact he was more in the actual nuts and bolts of the various bits of equipment and so on.' And she added: 'He was chairman of something called NIAG, the Nato Industrial Advisory Group.'

The coroner said it appeared that Peter's problems had started from the time of the accident. 'I have to be satisfied that if a person takes his own life he is intent on doing it. I am not convinced that that was the direct intention of Brigadier Ferry. He tried once before, but in the circumstances, because of the doubt, the only verdict I can return is an open verdict.'

On the face of it, there were no similarities between the work of Brigadier Peter Ferry and Alistair Beckham. Peter was based at Marconi Command and Control in Frimley, Surrey, and Alistair at Plessey Naval Systems at Addlestone, a few miles away.

Plessey's 1988 handbook for potential recruits summarizes the work of the company's subsidiaries. The handbook refers to the work of more than twenty separate divisions, including Plessey Network and Office Systems, Plessey Wound Products which deals with transformers, Plessey Semiconductors, involved in the manufacture of circuits and even a plastics subsidiary. The entry under Alistair's division, Plessey Naval Systems, begins: 'The Command System Unit within Plessey Naval Systems is responsible for the design, development and manufacture of command and control systems for military and civil applications.'

Both men, therefore, were working for large defence contractors, at the divisions which dealt specifically with C3. If there were any doubts that Alistair was involved personally in C3, they were dispelled by a report he wrote on 23 May 1988, less than three months before his death. It was entitled:

Command Systems – Addlestone
Analysis of Manufacturing Faults 1987/8

Alistair's job was described by the company as quality control engineer and, certainly, he had a profound understanding of the type of recurring faults found in wiring assemblies, test units and at the final inspection department.

But documents at his home suggest that his military interests were more extensive and apparently diverse than his job title implied. One of his folders contained more than thirty separate, numbered hand-prepared documents, containing meticulously presented military drawings, some of detailed specifications of equipment ranging from tanks to aircraft carriers. Tiny imperfections have been covered with typing correction fluid.

The first page is entitled:

The Navy
The Grand Home Fleet
1st (main) NORTH PACIFIC FLEET

Below that are listed the specifications of, for example, armoured battle divisions, cruiser and frigate flotillas, and an aircraft carrier division showing the number of aircraft carried. Subsequent pages show details of the minelaying squadron of the 2nd South Pacific Fleet, including destroyer and attack submarine flotillas.

Page seven lists the knots, tonnage and numbers of 'enemy ships'. Glued on the page are photocopied pictures and specifications of aircraft.

On another page are columns showing the locations of 'HQ army bases' and 'HQ navy harbours' in, for example, the US, Canada, Mexico, Guatemala, El Salvador, Nicaragua and Chile. The bases are ports defined as first, second or third class.

Elsewhere in the folder a curious mixture of subjects seems to be covered. For example, the mineral resources of various countries are depicted. On a black and white map of the US, Alistair has drawn a small green circle showing a location in the USA where the metal titanium can be found.

There are also details of the composition of a 'Rapid Deployment Force', an intricate design of a 'basic shelter model Nato type 11', a Plessey Radar document and a set of rules for radiological safety officers which contains the paragraph:

'It must be impressed on every individual working with ionizing radiations or radioactive substances that he has a duty to protect himself and others from any hazard arising from his work and that he must not expose himself or others to ionizing radiations to a greater extent than is reasonably necessary for the purposes of his work.'

Why Alistair was taking an interest in all these subjects is not clear. Perhaps he regarded defence as a hobby as well as his profession. Curiously, he had drawn the various stages in the feasibility and development processes of what appeared to be an intelligence command system. Also, there is a tree diagram of various committees, painstakingly hand-drawn in several colours. At the top of the tree are small boxes labelled 'House of Representatives' and 'House of Peoples Assembly'. Under this is a box showing the composition of the 'Full Main Board Senate', which, it says, has one meeting a year. Below this are six boxes marked federal, industry, government and international councils. These are marked in black. A further box, labelled 'Defence Cabinet', is singled out in red. Below it are further branches indicating the 'HQ War Office', an intelligence sub-committee and a 'Local Defence Ministry'. A detailed breakdown of the defence cabinet is given on the next page showing sub-sections which included intelligence, counter intelligence, camouflage, decoys, security, war games and simulation.

Today, Nato and Eastern Bloc countries are putting an unprecedented effort into the development of computerized command and control. As with EW both sides are also continually trying to find loopholes in their potential opponent's systems, fuelling a war of information, known as the Infowar. Britain is uniquely positioned in this peacetime conflict. She employs thousands of people to gather intelligence and has intelligence gathering bases throughout the world. Furthermore Britain has an accord with the USA which allows the mutual exchange of intelligence data. Marconi, through its association with military authorities and with governments for nearly a century, is a unique recipient of intelligence information. EW equipment manufactured by Marconi contains some of these secrets. Command and control systems also share these secrets. It is clear that the field of EW has suffered a number of mysterious peacetime casualties. So, too, has the field of command and control.

CHAPTER FOUR

The Defence Network

Before the bizarre death of David Sands in March 1987, few people outside the world of defence electronics had heard of Marconi's sister company Easams. Despite employing 900 people and announcing Star Wars contracts in early 1987, Easams appeared to enjoy its status as a little known specialist electronics company and computer consultancy. 'It is probably the most secretive company within GEC,' said one defence specialist. For example, the company refused to divulge its turnover on the grounds that this information might be useful to a potential enemy. The argument goes that such a figure would enable an assessment to be made of how long it would take the company to complete a particular, highly sensitive, defence contract. The same contract that David Sands was working on before his premature death.

Founded in 1962 as Elliot Automation Space and Advanced Military Systems Ltd, Easams specializes in the field of testing by 'simulation modelling' of large computer-based defence projects. As we have seen, for security reasons, it is considered better to simulate an EW system on computers than test it in open air military exercises, where potential enemies may use electronic eavesdropping devices such as satellites to scoop up its electronic details and develop countermeasures which would render the system useless.

Easams also specializes in underwater and airborne EW defence systems. The company's special

Underwater Group carries out studies into future underwater systems, including sensors, torpedoes and acoustic countermeasures. Another division, the Land/Air Group, focuses on the development of computer-based command, control and communications (C3) systems and the assessment of Soviet threats. In a leaflet intended for prospective clients, the company states: 'Easams has a wide experience in the performance assessment of radars, missiles, decoys and jammers ... The effective communications and use of data in a hostile electronic warfare environment is all important. Easams's simulation and modelling of data links in this type of scenario has been extended.' And the leaflet also states that 'electronic warfare is possibly the fastest growing defence technology today'.

The cause of 37-year-old David Sands's road crash was never established. When the police found his burning car embedded in the wall of a solitary, disused building at the side of a long, straight road, they were baffled.

On the morning of Monday, 30 March 1987 he got into his well maintained Austin Maestro car and set off at about seven o'clock on his usual journey from his home in Itchen Abbas, near Winchester, to Easams in Camberley, Surrey. His wife Anna had not noticed anything unusual in his demeanour or behaviour. The driving conditions were good. When David reached Popham, near Basingstoke, about thirty minutes after leaving home, he apparently did a U-turn on the A33 dual carriageway and drove at high speed into a slip road. The reason for the U-turn has never been established. In the slip road he crashed into a boarded up Little Chef café at a speed estimated to have been about eighty miles per hour. The car exploded into flames and police later found two cans which had each contained five gallons of petrol, in the boot of the wrecked car. In the fireball that followed the impact David was burned beyond recognition. A formal identification was possible only with the help of dental records.

The spot where the incident occurred was, according to a policeman, 'as straight as an arrow'. There were no skid marks, no apparent attempt to steer away from the building and, as with the other deaths, no eyewitnesses were present. Even stranger was the fact that David had been wearing his seat belt. It was another horrific, spectacular death which could have been an accident, suicide or perhaps even murder. Almost immediately the police were at pains to point out that the death was being treated as just another traffic incident. It looked like an accident, they said, but they were keeping an open mind on the possibility of suicide.

Nobody realized at the time that David, a graduate of Bath University, was a knowledgeable scientist working in a highly sensitive area of defence, who had been considering a change in lifestyle and the possibility of getting a job outside the world of defence. This uncertainty over his future could have been a contributory factor to suicide. His father's chronic heart condition could also have been a factor. But for the most part David was a dedicated father of two young children, a son aged six and a three-year-old daughter, with a happy marriage. According to relatives, he and his wife had just returned from an enjoyable holiday in Venice to celebrate the successful completion of a three year project. It was particularly puzzling that the police were able, within two days of the car crash, to state that David's death was 'most positively' not linked to the deaths of the other scientists. It was even more puzzling when, at David's inquest six weeks later, although the police had still not ascertained the cause of the crash, they were still unambiguous in their assertions that there was no connection between it and any of the other deaths.

Details of David's work were never officially

divulged. Easams would say only that he was a senior engineer working on 'communications'. A spokesman for David's company Easams said at the time: 'He was highly regarded and extremely good at his job. It is a terrible shock for everyone. It is too early for us to comment about the connection with other scientists who have died. We cannot say what project he was working on. It is confidential.' Its importance can be gauged, however, by the guarded comments of his colleagues. Peter Peacock, a marketing executive with Easams, described David as a 'highly respected and senior member of the staff'. But he refused to give any details of the project David was working on, saying that all work carried out by Easams was 'extremely sensitive'.

On a separate occasion an Easams spokesman said David had been engaged in a range of studies for the Ministry of Defence 'of a conventional nature'. According to the spokesman, the work related to 'information management systems', some of which were classified. He added: 'There is no connection, as far as I know, between Mr Sands and projects worked on by any other scientists who have died or disappeared recently.'

Evidently, much secrecy surrounded David's work, though some months after the inquest a former senior Marconi employee made a point of mentioning that David had been an authority on military communications and command, control, communications and intelligence (C3i) systems. Shortly before his death he had been working on a Ministry of Defence C3i contract, one of the most important of its kind for several years. The former Marconi employee named the project as the Air Defence Command Information System, (ADCIS), which is due to come into service with the British Army in Germany in the early 1990s.

The former Marconi employee said little about David's death or his work, but made clear his belief that both warranted further investigation. 'David knew a great deal,' he said without further elaboration.

As part of the run up to bidding for the ADCIS contract, David had evaluated various C3i systems overseas. Little has been published about ADCIS itself. At one point a spokesman for the project at Easams would say only that the objective of the system was to 'speed up procedural control'.

Why was that important?

'If only you knew how important that is,' said the spokesman enigmatically. 'But I cannot go into it further. It is getting into dangerous ground.'

Just how dangerous that ground is can be judged from an article on European air defence by Juergen Hoeche who, at the time, was Chief of Air Planning Team in the Operations Division at the Supreme Headquarters Allied Powers in Europe.

In his article published in the magazine *Nato's Sixteen Nations* Hoeche says: 'Should deterrence fail and should the Soviet Union and the WP (Warsaw Pact) consequently decide to go to war against Nato, their initial action on the ground would most likely be accompanied by a deep air attack campaign against vital Nato assets in the rear of Nato territory. The primary targets would probably be the tactical nuclear as well as the defensive and offensive counter air capability, of Nato, complemented by attacks against the command and control installations.'

Work on the £90 million ADCIS project appears to have started with a feasibility study in July 1984. In February 1985 Easams's rival, Software Sciences, a subsidiary of the Thorn EMI group, issued a press release declaring that, along with Easams, it had won a Ministry of Defence contract for a competitive engineering study charged with the design of ADCIS. It added that the two parallel design studies would last about fifteen months.

The system was due to be installed in a 'very short timescale', and would facilitate more effective use of air defence weapons such as the Rapier missile system. 'In today's highly sophisticated theatres of war,' continued the press release, 'there is a problem identifying friend or foe when troops with ground to air weapons are confronted by low flying, high speed aircraft. Rapid dissemination of information using fast and accurate communications is needed to avoid destroying friendly aircraft.'

The nature of the problem of identifying friend from foe was further explained in graphic terms by Bill Ellis, marketing director of Thorn EMI Software, who said: 'At the moment our troops will only recognize an enemy plane when it starts firing missiles at them.'

It transpired that, not only had David been involved in the design of ADCIS, but he had also written a paper based on Easams's work on the project, published seven months before he died. The paper, written with unusual clarity and authority and without any of the literary pomposity which afflicts many such technical papers, is headed 'Short Range Air Defence Command and Control' and refers to other command and control systems as well as ADCIS. It describes how Easams had completed studies with the Ministry of Defence on ways of linking up different systems and refers in particular to the idea of linking up British systems in Germany and those of other Nato nations on the Central Front.

Referring to ADCIS, David writes: 'A critical assessment of user requirements was completed. This was followed by the production of a generic system design and then the preparation of a detailed software design ...'

He continues: 'The objective of the Army's air defence is to prevent enemy air forces interfering with operations by our own ground forces. It is therefore essential that air defence weapons are given as much freedom as possible to engage enemy aircraft.' He mentions Rapier and other unnamed weapons which simply he called 'the new high velocity missiles' and adds: 'Currently ... notification of friendly air movements, warnings of enemy air movements and the subsequent procedural control to weapons are distributed manually through the command hierarchy using congested voice communications and employing manual encryption ... This is a slow and potentially error prone process which results in weapons being unnecessarily restricted for long periods. Real-time command and control of so many weapons is very difficult to achieve ... For these reasons the Ministry has decided to develop and field a command information system ... The pace of the air battle will demand that, for the first time, a land tactical command and control system capable of true real-time operation must be developed and deployed.'

To reduce cost, risk and implementation timescale of ADCIS, tried and tested technology would be used 'wherever possible'. Digital communications would be provided by Ptarmigan, a military communications system developed mainly by British electronics group Plessey. One of ADCIS's strengths would be that it would cover a battery with any mix of weapons and 'substantially more weapons platforms than are currently deployed'. Easams even put forward detailed plans for the size and type of armoured vehicle needed to accommodate the ADCIS equipment. There could, however, be shortcomings, what David referred to as the 'compromise always inherent in the tactical area where the demands of the computer system ... must be balanced against operational realities'. The potential weaknesses are not detailed, but it is most probable that David was aware of them. In his paper he also speaks of the importance of simulation and modelling in showing the effectiveness of ADCIS.

Furthermore, he reveals that Easams built a large scale 'user demonstration' as part of the project. Simulation software was supplied for the demonstration by the Ministry of Defence. This software 'simulated battlefield activity and provided a representative communications environment'. In other words, it would appear that the software provided by the Ministry simulated, among other things, how ADCIS would stand up to EW attacks.

ADCIS's job, then, will be to better defend some of the most valuable British military assets in Germany, such as airfields, missile sites and command posts. Its importance as a deterrent can be measured by the fact that it will be employed at what defence experts predict will be a likely flashpoint for a possible East/West conflict.

The ADCIS technology is also related directly to Easams's Star Wars work on battle management and C3i systems. It is unlikely that David was working specifically on Star Wars but, like most other companies, there is considerable integration of skills within Easams. In fact the company is quite open about its SDI involvement. At its Camberley offices, where David worked, a number of staff working on Star Wars have their names on an office door clearly marked 'Strategic Defence Initiative' displayed only a few doors away from a typing pool.

None of the facts presented at David's inquest proved foul play. Police Superintendent David Pearcey even gave evidence to the effect that there had been 'no grounds to link the death of Mr Sands with any other incident'. Evidence was brought that there were no skid marks and that the vehicle could have been steered into the building or 'deviated into it for some other reason'. However, the coroner John Clarke said: 'Why he should choose to do a U-turn, one can't explain. He was happily married and he had been successful in a difficult and demanding job working for Easams of Camberley, Surrey, who held him in high regard.'

The inquest heard from Graham Leach, personnel manager at Easams, that the company was engaged in 'technical work'. He said that David was a senior project manager in an engineering post, engaged on a communications project. He agreed that the work involved satellites but declined to give any further details. He said David was highly thought of and dedicated. He had never expressed reservations about what he was doing, and could have switched to other projects if he had wanted. Superintendent Pearcey, of the Basingstoke police, told the inquest he had carried out inquiries following the speculation that David's death might be linked to those of other scientists working for GEC companies. He said he had liaised with all other police forces involved, but there was no evidence of a link. Pathologist Dr Roger Ainsworth told the inquest that David was badly burned in the crash and died from multiple injuries. David had not been drinking.

What the inquest did not hear was that, according to a *Daily Telegraph* report, Easams was 'visited by Special Branch' the week before David's death, while he was on holiday in Venice. The Special Branch officers allegedly spoke to the firm's security officer and its personnel manager. Easams, however, has since categorically denied Special Branch visited the company.

What is not in dispute is that David went missing for six hours on Saturday, 28 March 1987, shortly after he returned from holiday. He had told his wife he was going to buy some petrol, but when he failed to return she telephoned the police. Why Anna Sands called the police after David had been missing a relatively short time is not clear. One suggestion is that she was worried for his safety, although, according to defence specialists, the disappearance, even for a few hours, of a scientist with a top level security clearance, must be reported to the police. Whatever the reason, PC John Hiscock went to the Sands's large detached house to wait for David's return. Hiscock told the inquest that David reappeared at 10.20 p.m. and told his wife that he had been 'driving and thinking'. He wanted to go inside and talk with her. Hiscock said he did not get the impression that there were any domestic problems. Anna also confirmed at the inquest that David had explained his absence by saying that he had been driving about and 'having a long think'.

'It was very out of character for him to be away for so long,' said Anna. 'He was a considerate and kind man. We were very happy together.' She added that she did not think that David had realized how long he had been out. He returned confused but otherwise happy. 'He was upset about his father who was, at the time, on his death bed. David knew that he was dying and had got to that state through overwork and smoking.'

'He was wondering if there was a need for a change in his life. He thought that maybe he could do with a complete change of lifestyle. He felt that he was in a rat race and did not want to end up like his father.' The following day, Sunday, David had complained of headaches and tiredness.

The coroner, however, said that David's evident concern about his father was not a sufficient reason to conclude that he had committed suicide. He also said that there was no significance in the two petrol cans which were found in the boot of David's burnt out car. They were, apparently, carried in the car as a matter of normal practice. Coroner Clarke therefore concluded that, from the evidence before him, David had died of multiple injuries caused by the crash, and that severe burns, probably caused by a fire started after the car's petrol tank ruptured, were a secondary factor.

'I would be unsafe in arriving at any suicide verdict without positive evidence that Mr Sands intended to take his life,' added the coroner. 'The evidence is quite to the contrary. He left no notes, he didn't explain that he was depressed, and, indeed, seemed to be going to work in the normal way.' But he said the available evidence 'clearly excludes any foul play', and recorded an open verdict.

'The evidence does not specifically reveal the facts on which any other verdict could be brought.' It meant, in effect, that he could not determine whether the crash had been an accident, suicide, or, somehow, an unlawful killing.

As a military C3 specialist David would certainly have known, through simulation, the probabilities of success, or otherwise, of a major enemy air attack over Germany. He was alive at a time when the Ministry of Defence had taken delivery of software which, in effect, recommended the best positions to site sensors in Germany to detect an invasion, and which also revealed gaps in Nato's air defences. It showed, for instance, that Eastern Bloc aircraft which knew Nato's 'safe corridors' in Germany could pass overhead undetected. If they knew certain compass headings and altitude settings, they could avoid Allied radar and EW sensors which can only operate within finite height ceilings and distances.

The sensitivity of this sort of information is summed up in an article published by the Royal Military College of Science which clearly states that the basic defence against EW is to 'ensure that the communication and Infra Red frequencies are kept secure. An attacker will put much effort into gaining such information in peace and war.'

David Sands's spectacular death was not the only bizarre incident to involve a specialist in the field of C3. What happened to family man, David Greenhalgh, aged 46, on 10 April 1987, was never explained. At soon after eight o'clock on that Friday morning, David Greenhalgh left his detached home in Maidenhead, Surrey, and set off as usual for the drive to work at Winnersh. The following day he was due to fly to Brussels and, according to his friends, the bags were already packed.

At about twelve noon, several hours after leaving home, David was found only a few miles away, barely alive, after apparently falling 40 feet from a railway bridge onto an embankment, close to lines which carry high speed Intercity trains between London and Bristol. He was found by train driver Mick Hughes, who said David's wallet, containing travellers cheques, lay nearby. He was also reported to be carrying an unusual red identity card and wearing an expensive business suit. And, according to British Transport Police, one of his wrists had been neatly slashed. It transpired later that this was not true.

David was taken to the Royal Berkshire Hospital at Reading with multiple injuries. He was not expected to live. Considerable secrecy surrounded the incident, and it proved difficult and sometimes impossible to obtain information from the hospital on his condition. Over a period of several weeks, however, it emerged that David's condition, although grave, was stabilising. His company later revealed that he was moved to different hospitals and eventually recovered sufficiently to return to work, although not in his original job.

Paradoxically, in view of the circumstances of the fall, which had all the hallmarks of a suicide attempt, hospital staff attributed David's survival to what they described as an 'amazing will to live'. His company confirmed that, even a year after the fall, his injuries left him able to walk only with considerable effort. Like David Sands, David Greenhalgh had shown no signs of being suicidal, in fact he was apparently in good spirits. He had a happy marriage and was a devoted father to his children. Furthermore, no explanation has ever been forthcoming regarding what happened in the hours between David's leaving home and when he was found under the bridge.

David's friends say he cannot remember exactly what happened or why.

There is no doubt, however, that the authorities wanted the news of David's fall suppressed, perhaps because it was an embarrassment coming so soon after the unexplained deaths of other defence scientists. It is conceivable, however, that their anxiety sprung from a concern that evidence might emerge indicating that the incidents were, in some way, related. Attempts to keep the news quiet indefinitely would probably have succeeded but for the tenacity of John Askill, a journalist in the Maidenhead area. A few days after David's fall, John, who has some good police contacts, heard that a defence company employee involved in secret work was unconscious and critically ill after being found under a bridge.

After the *Sun* carried John's exclusive story on the fall, several days later, the authorities became more open. Berkshire police said they knew about the incident, but that it was purely a matter for the British Transport Police, as the incident had taken place on British Rail property. A British Transport Police spokesman said: 'We're treating it as an ordinary incident.' But he added, a touch ingenuously: 'It's an unusual one, this. I've got a telex here saying I can't give his name, address or occupation. That's never happened since I've been here.' On being given David's name, address and occupation from a newspaper cutting he said he could not comment, but remarked: 'It's not far out.'

Another British Transport policeman described David as a 'defence contracts manager' who worked at the defence division of International Computers Limited (ICL). The policeman, who seemed to be reading from notes, also said that David's fall occurred only 130 yards or so from Woodley police station. 'A bit strange isn't it?' he added. 'He'd just finished a major contract.'

On a third occasion yet another British Transport

Police spokesman said he was reluctant to comment on the case because a Detective Constable Ryan was 'dealing with it' at the Royal Berkshire Hospital, where David was being treated. But the spokesman went on to confirm that David 'sort of had connections' with the Ministry of Defence, and also said casually: 'We had a visit from officers telling us that under no circumstances was this story to be released to the press ... But a freelance journalist rang up and said he knew everything about it. We could not deny it.' The policeman claimed the visiting officers were from Special Branch.

A spokesman for ICL, Britain's largest indigenous computer company, described David as a 'salesman', a description which was used in many of the newspaper reports of his fall. When, however, it was put to ICL that he was a defence contracts manager, the spokesman asked some questions to authenticate the source of the information and said eventually: 'We regard all our managers as salesmen.' The spokesman added: 'We have looked into it (David's background) and he was not working on any sensitive project. Any suggestion that he was is clearly wide of the mark.'

Asked what David was working on if it was not sensitive, the ICL spokesman answered curtly: 'He works at ICL. He does not work for Marconi.' He did not elaborate.

In fact it is indeed possible that David was working on unclassified projects just before he fell from the bridge. But a short time before that he had been working on one that involved the processing of classified information. It was of such sensitivity that security considerations had prevented a number of UK defence contractors from being granted authority to bid for the contract.

Furthermore, David's friends said that he was responsible for a group of people and had one of the highest security clearances within the company. He had had access to Nato secrets.

ICL Defence Systems in Winnersh near Reading, where David worked, specializes in command and control systems. An example of one of these systems is the Air Staff Management Aid (ASMA), a version of which was used extensively and successfully in the Falklands War. It was also installed in the headquarters of RAF Germany in Rheindahlen, in early 1987. With more than 400 computer screens at 70 different locations, the system provides the RAF with information on the state of readiness. Details typed in at one terminal can instantly update the data shown on remote screens at other locations. A typical screen will show a table of rows and columns with headings at the top which include Base, Role, Squadron Aircraft, Combat Ready and Total. At the side are details of the available aircraft and crews. The number of crews available for combat within twelve hours is shown, along with the number of those available in more than twelve hours.

Also shown are the numbers, types and roles of aircraft available before and after twelve hours. A typical line might detail the availability or otherwise of a Harrier, its identification number and EW role, its location and the squadron to which it is attached. The total column shows, on a regularly updated basis, the state of readiness of British air forces in Germany. This typifies the sort of sensitive information handled by command and control systems. Anyone with access to ASMA on a regular basis would be able to calculate the RAF's average operational strength and the approximate number of crews ready to go into combat within twelve hours.

Three weeks after David's fall, ICL announced that it had won a contract for another command and control system which would manage information similar to that on ASMA, but on a much larger and wider scale. The new system was to be called UKAIR. The contract had actually been awarded three weeks before the announcement. According to his friends, David had been involved in the project.

UKAIR is a command and control system for the strategic air defence of Britain, designed to last well into the twenty-first century. Speaking about UKAIR in August 1987, Lord Trefgarne, the Minister of State for defence procurement, called it an 'automated command and control information system for the UK air forces'.

He went on: 'This technically challenging system is based on the most up-to-date data processing equipment. When it enters service early in the next decade, it will provide the Nato Commander-in-Chief UK Air Forces with the means for effective, secure and survivable command and control of air operations during exercise, tension and war. The system will be installed at RAF Strike Command headquarters at High Wycombe and other sites throughout the UK. It will provide comprehensive facilities for the operator, with multi-level security features to ensure that each user has access to the information he needs but not to other sensitive information.'

Lord Trefgarne predicted that UKAIR would be operational in 1991 and would be 'one of the most advanced systems in the world'. It would form one of the first links in the Air Command and Control System to be established throughout Nato and would be a key element in the overall Nato 'shield'. Lord Trefgarne added that UKAIR would link up with other command and control systems, including a vast £7 billion UK air defence project called the Improved United Kingdom Air Defence Ground Environment (IUKADGE) which will cover Britain's sea defences and which will link up with command and control systems in Nato's central region in West Germany. Work on IUKADGE started at the beginning of the 1980s, with the completed system due to be handed over at the end of the decade, although technical difficulties have meant that IUKADGE was still nowhere near completion by 1989. So, through IUKADGE, the UKAIR project, which had involved David Greenhalgh, may link up with David Sands's ADCIS system. Moreover, according to Air Commodore David Cowley, director of command and control within the management information systems group of the RAF, UKAIR will carry air attack and 'intelligence' data. The reason for the high security was becoming clear.

It would appear that the UKAIR project and David Sands's ADCIS are not totally dissimilar. Both are air defence information systems designed to operate well into the twenty-first century. Both are a new generation of computerized military information systems. And both are command and control systems, systems which can influence the balance of power.

It further transpired that UKAIR data would be carried by particularly sophisticated communications links to be developed and built under a contract code-named Uniter, a project which involves a number of UK companies including Marconi. Uniter is one of the first communications systems of its type, built to resist EW attacks and hardened against the effects of nuclear explosions.

One of the other companies working on Uniter is British electronics group and communications specialists Plessey. GEC, Marconi's parent company, took over Plessey in 1989 in collaboration with the West German firm Siemens following a previous unsuccessful takeover attempt by GEC alone in 1985. The 1985 bid was blocked by the Monopolies and Mergers Commission, following complaints by the Ministry of Defence that a merger would reduce competition in its equipment buying. GEC's reasoning behind the 1989 takeover was the need to create a company big enough to compete in the deregulated, single European market, due to be introduced in 1992. Apart then, from working on joint contracts there had been a considerable overlap between the activities of GEC and Plessey, particularly in the areas of radar and communications. Nearly every major Royal Navy surface ship, for example, has radar manufactured by either Plessey or Marconi. Following the failure of the 1985 bid, GEC and Plessey agreed to merge some of their telecommunications interests to form a new joint company GPT (GEC Plessey Telecommunications).

In 1987, a Plessey scientist who had been working on a project which involved GEC, died in an unusual car accident.

If Michael Baker had followed his instincts on Sunday, 3 May and refused to join two men on a fishing trip, he would probably be alive today. His epitaph was a few paragraphs in his local paper, the *Echo* in Southampton. The story read:

'Angler Michael Baker died in an accident on Upton by-pass on Sunday morning. Mr Baker, 22, of Knights Road, Bear Wood, was taking two friends to the Kingsbridge lakes near Lychett Minster to teach them to fly fish when his BMW crashed through the central reservation and overturned on the opposite carriageway.

'Two years ago he was the first person to catch a salmon in the river at Lychett Minster and he had booked a fishing holiday in Ireland in August. An electronics engineer for Plessey at Poole, he was in their sports team. He played darts and golf.

'Educated at Hardye's school Dorchester, he lived at home with his parents and sister and was in the SAS Signals Squadron of the Territorial Army.'

His father was quoted as saying: 'He was one of the happiest boys going. He was rarely miserable. All we can be thankful for really is that he was driving the car he loved.'

As with David Sands's and David Greenhalgh's

incidents, there were no eyewitnesses, even though Michael Baker's accident happened in clear weather on a dual carriageway at around mid-morning on a bank holiday weekend. Michael was found slumped over the wheel and death was declared to be the result of brain damage. His two passengers, one of whom was sitting in the passenger's seat, were uninjured. Several weeks later it proved possible to contact one of the passengers in Michael Baker's car at the time of the crash. Politely he made it clear he did not want to discuss the accident. Several months later, Michael's inquest failed to establish the cause of the accident. It was said that he must have momentarily lost concentration. The coroner recorded a verdict of accidental death.

Sergeant Leonard Wayman, one of the accident investigators, who had given evidence at the inquest, stressed that there had been witnesses to the car crossing the carriageway and overturning, but that nobody had seen the start of the accident or knew why it had happened, even though, he said, the road 'carried a fair bit of traffic'.

Had Michael had an accident before?

'Dunno.'

Were there skid marks?

'There were scuff marks, scrape marks, gouge marks and roll marks.'

No skid marks?

'Everything but skid marks.' Sergeant Wayman added that the car was not travelling at an excessive speed and was 'well maintained' for its year. Commenting on the death, a Plessey spokesman was emphatic that Michael's work was not related to defence. 'He was working at Plessey Major Systems in Poole on System X and not at Plessey Defence Systems at Christchurch,' said the spokesman.

Later a very senior member of the Plessey board of directors denied that Plessey Major Systems's main product, the System X digital telecommunications exchange, developed jointly with GEC and currently being installed as part of British Telecom's modernization of the public telephone network, had any defence applications. It emerged, however, that System X was, in fact a key component of IUKADGE. Furthermore, the SAS squadron, of which Michael was a part-time member, is heavily involved with EW.

Finally, there was something a little unusual about the circumstances leading up to Michael's fatal journey. 'He did not want to go,' said his mother Mrs Isobel Baker. 'But someone came to the door for him and he went.'

As with the other scientists, it is impossible to know exactly how much Michael knew about any sensitive defence projects. But it is certain that he would have learnt much through his part-time work with the SAS. Much of the work of the SAS signals squadron is enveloped in secrecy. An article about the SAS in the magazine *Defence, Communications and Security Review*, distributed to UK and US Government and armed forces security personnel, GCHQ security officials and security staff in industry, mentioned the signals squadron only once. Sandwiched between advertisements for grenades, sniper rifles and storage equipment for tanks, the article mentioned that the SAS was formed in 1941 with the motto: 'Who Dares Wins'. The unit was used to getting behind enemy lines by land, sea or air. Today its members are volunteers from all regiments and corps and are 'very carefully selected'. They are trained in all forms of raiding and sabotage, according to the article. It went on to say that the names of SAS members are never intentionally released, they are never allowed to be photographed and their activities always remain secret. The Ministry of Defence never divulges where they are, what they are doing or what they have done unless it is absolutely vital to do so.

The article continued: 'It is known that there are three

SAS Regiments (battalions) in the British Army, the 22nd is a fully regular regiment, the 21st and 23rd are Territorials. There is also an SAS signals squadron.' No further details of the signals squadron were given, although the article mentioned that volunteers are trained to use and fire 'every' weapon likely to be used by the British and other armies, including prospective enemy weapons. In the signals squadron, 'enemy weapons' also means Eastern Bloc EW equipment.

Michael's death could have been an accident, his work on System X and military part-time job coincidences. Perhaps it was also a coincidence that his accident was one of five mysterious incidents involving computer company employees to take place within five weeks in spring 1987. Michael's death, however, was not the first involving a System X and digital communications expert. Jonathan Wash, a 29-year-old System X engineer, fell from a hotel balcony in the early hours of Tuesday, 19 November 1985, shortly after expressing a fear for his life.

His fatal fall could have been recorded as suicide if it had not been for the fact that Jonathan's father refused to ignore the unanswered questions. John Wash has lost count of the number of letters he has written to try to find out why his only son died. As the months and years have gone by, his doubts have hardened into a conviction that the truth has been covered up, that his inquiry has been ensnared in what the BBC documentary programme *Out of Court* described as a web of official contradiction, unhelpfulness or deceit.

The implications are enormous. Although the authorities had initially interpreted the facts of Jonathan's death as suggesting suicide there is evidence that points to the fact that he was killed because of a personal problem, or because of something he knew.

Jonathan, who held an honours degree in electronics, had been employed on research and development by the

British Telecom Technology Executive at Martlesham. Martlesham is an establishment which undertakes secret Government defence work as well as commercial research. Strong ties exist between the Martlesham research centre and GCHQ.

At the time of his death, Jonathan was working on a temporary basis for a British Telecom subsidiary called Telconsult, which advises foreign governments on telecommunications systems. He was said by his parents to be outgoing and friendly, with a bright future. His mother Lenore said: 'He was very practical. He enjoyed doing things. He was very good with his hands and he was always ready to help anybody. His friends, when they wrote to us on the occasion of his death, said that he had helped them so much with different things.'

Jonathan had been working in Abidjan, capital of the Ivory Coast in West Africa and one of the most prosperous and sophisticated cities in French speaking Africa. He was using his expertise and knowledge of telecommunications exchange systems to help provide an independent assessment for the Ivory Coast government of the rival tenders in a bid for a multi-million pound digital exchange contract. As an engineer who had been involved in the design of the System X digital exchange, Jonathan was ideally qualified for the role. It was his second visit to Abidjan. On the first occasion in 1984 he had helped draw up the project specifications and again in September 1985 he had returned to assist in the adjudication of the contract tenders. On Tuesday 19 November, six weeks after he had arrived, he was found dead on the flat concrete roof beneath his bedroom balcony. British Telecom officials told his mother and father that Jonathan had recently been under strain and that he had problems with a local black girl who was pregnant. Officials said that his work had gone to pieces. The inference was that he had committed suicide.

However, his father John Wash said: 'He was not the sort of person who would contemplate suicide. He had never been depressed in his life. He went out there full of beans. He was enjoying life. He was saving up to buy a new car when he returned. In fact, looking through his diary, you can see the entries where he has actually put the figures showing how much he had saved toward his car, right up to the week before he died. He had written back saying "hoping to see you soon". Nothing would give us any indication that he was particularly concerned about any problems.'

A letter which Jonathan wrote to his parents six weeks before his death made no mention of any problems. The tone was hardly that of someone who was suicidal. 'I've been here for two weeks now – but the time has really passed so quickly that it seems more like a couple of days,' Jonathan wrote. 'The hotel is marvellous – the normal rate is £51 a day!! but we've got it for a mere £23 because it's for a long stay. The swimming pool is absolutely enormous, the food is acceptable and there's a ten pin bowling alley and an ice-skating rink here too! Now that Mike (a colleague) has gone back to England to resume his university course I've been appointed driver (which is quite exciting because of the 'standard' of driving, or lack of it, and the fact that it's a left hand drive car, a Renault 12 estate).'

The letter continues: 'We've had a fairly easy start to the work for the first week – but now it's hit us! We had five bids, from Thompson (France), FATME (an Italian subsidiary of Ericsson), FACE (an Italian subsidiary of ITT), GTE (yet another Italian company offering an American designed system) and Interbras, which is a Brazilian subsidiary of Siemens ... The total documentation for the five bids (six copies of each had to be supplied) weighed more than one ton! We are at present working 8 a.m. to 6 p.m. (with about one and a half hours for a very pleasant leisurely lunch at an excellent French restaurant nearby!). Of course, we are also working Saturday mornings, but the two weekends so far have mainly been spent around hotel swimming pools. I'm about to go to bed now. I hope the shock of getting a letter from me is not too great! See you in December – I hope the early part. Love from Jonathan.'

The last person to see Jonathan alive was Telconsult's team manager Lionel Haynes. Hours before his death, Jonathan had a discussion with Haynes about his girlfriend during which he confessed she was pregnant. He had asked to go back to the UK as soon as possible. Together they discussed Jonathan's problems at the hotel until the early hours of the morning of his death. In a report to his superiors, Haynes states that Jonathan was under stress because of his girlfriend's pregnancy. But two months after his son's death John Wash was told by his solicitor that Haynes had been detained by the Abidjan authorities who were now investigating Jonathan's death.

John said: 'When my solicitor here in Bedford told me he had had words with the coroner, and the coroner had said that there was a possible prosecution pending, that put an entirely different complexion on the whole affair. We wondered exactly what was going on, whether we had got the right information. From that point onwards I was extremely sceptical of what I was being told by British Telecom.'

Haynes was subsequently released and has proven impossible to trace, although it appears that he is still employed by British Telecom. But during his detention by the Abidjan authorities, Haynes wrote a strange letter to John Wash. It seemed to contradict his earlier statements that Jonathan was worried about his girlfriend 'There is evidence suggesting that he had another problem which he kept to himself,' wrote Haynes. 'It is, I believe, possible that this terrible thing has occurred as a result of this unfortunate problem. I hope that the inquiries concerning this matter can proceed in a clear atmosphere and that the person responsible is brought to justice.' Unfortunately Haynes's letter fails to clarify what he meant by this. But Haynes adds: 'Neither the girl concerned, nor any of Jonathan's colleagues who were in Abidjan had any knowledge of his other secret or the circumstances which resulted in his death.'

Further evidence emerged which contradicted earlier suggestions of suicide. Many of Jonathan's possessions, such as his shoes, diary and watch were found in a room two floors above his bedroom, where mysterious messages were found scratched on the wall:

> British Télécom Kill?
>
> Mum and dad, I love you,
> sell the shares
>
> BT Kill by 3rd party
>
> If there is a god, He knows the truth
> Haynes, British teleconsult wants Wash
> dead or mad
>
> Abidjan, asylum or death, no chance of
> reaching England

British Telecom knew of the messages, yet the family only found out exactly what was in them some eight months after Jonathan's death. There was yet a further puzzle. A post mortem conducted by a doctor in Abidjan listed injuries to the face and body which may have been consistent with a struggle. In fact, the doctor said that this was '*beaucoup plus plausible*' (much more plausible) than a simple fall as the explanation for the circumstances surrounding Jonathan's death. There was even a mention of injuries which had probably been caused by blows with a sharp instrument.

However, when the body came back to England a

second post mortem was conducted by UK authorities. That report concluded that the suggestion of a fight was 'difficult to accept'. Dissatisfied with the UK report, the Wash family sought to have their own post mortem carried out.

The coroner was unwilling at first, and spoke of the problems of multiple post mortems. But after critical press coverage, including headlines such as 'Officials Clam Up On Strange Death of BT's Man in Africa', the coroner allowed the authorities to hold a third post mortem, although he only told the family about it afterwards. This third post mortem concluded with the remark: 'I could not confirm the presence of any defensive injuries.'

The family were still unconvinced, especially as they had been unable to send a representative to the third post mortem. So they had their own fourth post mortem done. This time the injuries found were closer to those described originally by the Abidjan doctor. The conclusion: 'It is impossible to exclude the hypothesis that he might have been involved in a minor struggle before he fell or that he might have been pushed.'

More than four years after Jonathan's death his father is still no nearer to solving the mystery. Each new piece of information that has come to light has strengthened John Wash's belief that his son was murdered. But despite the fact that he has managed to unlock many doors that would have remained closed to the unperservering enquirer, official secrecy still blocks the way to the truth.

Particularly curious is the role of the authorities in the whole affair. Because of incompetence or perhaps something more sinister, the Foreign Office's translation of the Abidjan post mortem report left out some references to injuries which suggested that there could have been a struggle.

Other facts have come to light which make the sugges-

JONATHAN WASH CASE HISTORY

September 1985. Jonathan arrives in Abidjan to evaluate bids for digital exchange.
15 November. Takes the day off work and moves belongings to another hotel. Books early flight to the UK for 20 November.
17 November. Persuaded to return to his original hotel by Telconsult. Expresses concern to his girlfriend about his life.
18 November. Has five hours of discussions at the hotel with Haynes and members of Telconsult team which finished at 1.20 in the morning of Tuesday 19 November. During the discussions it is stated that Jonathan's girlfriend in Abidjan is pregnant.
19 November. Jonathan's body found on flat hotel roof at about 6.34 a.m.
December. Most of Telconsult team returns to UK. John Wash begins attempts to find out how and why his only son died.
February 1986. UK authorities hold post mortem which contradicts that held in Abidjan which called the theory that there had been a struggle 'much more plausible'. UK post mortem finds that injuries are consistent with a fall.
July 1986. UK authorities refuse to allow John to have his own post mortem. A letter from the coroner states: 'You will appreciate the difficulty of there being multiple post mortems ...'
August 1986. Nationwide publicity alleging a cover-up.
26 August 1986. UK authorities hold another post mortem, without informing the Wash family, during which it is alleged evidence on the body was destroyed. More injuries are noted, however, but no suggestion of foul play.
27 August 1986. UK authorities write to Wash family allowing, for the first time, an independent post mortem. Subsequently, similar injuries are found to the original Abidjan post mortem.
October 1986. Home Office minister Douglas Hogg, in answer to questions in the House of Commons, states that, as the investigation into Jonathan's death is incomplete, the case remains 'sub judice'. This suggests that the case was under judicial consideration and therefore any comment was prohibited.
November 1988. UK coroner returns open verdict after hearing conflicting evidence. UK authorities continued to insist that Jonathan's fall was not suspicious. John's family and Abidjan coroner pointed out that there were signs of a struggle.

tion that Jonathan committed suicide less plausible. It transpired, for example, that Jonathan had secretly booked a seat on a British Caledonian flight back to the UK scheduled for Wednesday 20 November, a few days before his work in Abidjan was due to be completed. It also emerged that Jonathan moved from the Hotel Ivoire, where the British Telecom project team was staying, complaining about the security there. He was later persuaded to return. Nobody can explain why he might have wanted to break his contract and return home early or why he was worried about hotel security although Jonathan's girlfriend, Mary Donkor, said: 'Jonathan expressed a fear for his life, especially a couple of days preceding his fateful end. Jonathan told me that the relationship between him and Mr Haynes was not cordial, and since the circle of dislike had widened to include his working mates, he had decided to break the contract and leave for England to see his most senior superior.'

Like Michael Baker, Jonathan was involved in work on System X. In fact he had a special knowledge of UK digital exchanges, System X in particular. Like Michael and many of the other scientists who had died mysteriously, he was working in a field related directly to command and control, and in an environment where he may have had access, wittingly or not, to secrets beyond the scope of his project or his level of authorization.

He had worked for a branch of BT which was working on defence and government contracts. While at British Telecom he had spent some time at GEC, a prime contractor in the Uniter project.

The suspicion was that Jonathan had fallen not from his own room, but from the room two floors above, where the mysterious messages were found. Yet after four post mortems the exact circumstances of the death are still unclear. There seems little doubt that, for reasons which are not clear, details of injuries on his body which suggested a struggle were omitted. The procrastination of the authorities over John's attempts to commission an independent post mortem on his son's body would probably have deterred most parents in similar circumstances. Indeed it was only the family's sedulous investigation, especially its insistence on double checking the veracity of official versions of Jonathan's death, that transformed an apparent case of suicide into one which had the hallmarks of murder. One cannot avoid wondering what new evidence, in the cases of the other apparent suicides and accidents, may be lying beneath the surface, hidden from those families who do not have the means and motivation to investigate the deaths further.

CHAPTER FIVE

The Establishments

It is not only the big electronics companies that undertake the research of EW and military communications. Some of the institutions funded by the Ministry of Defence also undertake highly sensitive work in this field. The Ministry of Defence research establishments employ about 14,000 scientists and researchers who are categorized as civil servants. At the time of writing the government was considering reorganizing four establishments – the Admiralty Research Establishment, the Royal Signals and Radar Establishment, the Royal Armament Research and Development Establishment, and the Royal Aerospace Establishment – into a semi-autonomous Defence Research Agency. Concern over security, however, had been expressed in defence circles. There were suggestions, for instance, that the Ministry of Defence should retain control over certain projects.

The research establishments maintain close ties with defence contractors. In 1988, in a move aimed at further commercializing defence research, the government allowed private companies to use the establishments' facilities for a fee.

Detailed information about some of the establishments is not easy to come by and it proved particularly difficult to discern which of them are deeply involved in EW. One which certainly is concerned with the various aspects of EW is the Royal Armament Research and Development Establishment (RARDE). RARDE has thousands of employees and is scattered across several sites in the UK. A booklet written for RARDE recruits clearly states that RARDE has a special interest in C3i. And it adds: 'The intelligence gathering area shows the greatest growth. Here the objective is to produce efficient, easily read intelligence which will give a picture of what enemy forces are doing and compare it with our own situation.'

According to the booklet RARDE is responsible for the operational analysis of future weapon systems which are either under development or which are being considered for purchase by the British Army. To perform this work, RARDE uses a great deal of simulation, and has an American Cray supercomputer, one of the most powerful computers in the world.

'Increasingly, battlefield intelligence is an essential defence ingredient and we provide the scientific background necessary to make the right assessments,' continues the RARDE booklet. 'Separate war games for the direct and indirect fire weapons are used to investigate future tactical concepts, procedures and performance in a battlefield environment, where the effects of enemy countermeasures can be introduced ... The indirect fire battle is studied in the Divisional War Game set up to permit explicit representation of the military command relationship, and also the simulation of the future battlefield in an EW environment.'

The Divisional War Game is described as a 'unique facility within Nato' in which game positions are played by military officers 'with appropriate specialist knowledge'. The US 'regularly supplies players'. In fact ties between RARDE and US research establishments are cemented by a formal technical co-operation programme. Furthermore, RARDE is at the forefront of Star Wars research in the UK. In 1986, the Ministry of

Defence announced that RARDE, along with the Atomic Weapons Research Establishment and the Royal Signals and Radar Establishment would lead British SDI research, with a number of electronics firms as subcontractors. Easams, where David Sands worked, was named as the leading C3 subcontractor.

Shortly before Christmas 1986, 52-year-old Dr John Brittan, one of the most senior scientists at RARDE, lost control of his car and drove into a ditch. He told his colleagues he could not understand how it happened. No other vehicle was involved. A few weeks later, on the morning of Monday, 12 January, he was found dead in the garage at his home in Camberley, Surrey. The cause was carbon monoxide poisoning, a common suicide method. Yet there was no reason for suicide. Moreover, such precipitate action would have been out of character. At his inquest, Dr Brittan was depicted as a logical and sensible scientist who had left the car engine running without opening the garage or side door, probably with the intention of warming up the car on a particularly cold January morning. A verdict of accidental death was returned. The local paper published a few paragraphs and the incident was quickly forgotten. Nobody realized at that time that John was one of several scientists who had died in their cars of carbon monoxide poisoning. Each time the inquest had been told that the deaths were probably an accident.

The events preceding Dr Brittan's death are puzzling. He had been on a long working trip to the US and on his return had been unable to sleep. In addition he had developed a virus that his doctor could not explain. The doctor said the problem would go away, but it persisted and kept John off work for several weeks. On the day before his death, John and his wife Rosemary took one of their sons back to university. Rosemary said her husband had appeared absolutely normal. They had been happily married for 25 years. On the day he died, he was returning to work for the first time since being off sick with his throat infection. He had got up a little later than usual, at eight o'clock, and had taken her a cup of tea. 'Everything was normal,' she said, adding that her son Christopher had heard on the radio that it would be a good idea to warm up the engine of the car. He had told his father this. Rosemary said she had tried to persuade John to stay at home. His throat had apparently not yet cleared up.

At about 8.30 a.m. Dr Brittan left the house to go to work. He had checked the road conditions and they were not too bad. He was not seen alive again. Christopher found his father when he went into the garage at about 9.30 a.m. to put some washing into a spin dryer. 'He was slumped over the steering wheel with his hat and glasses on,' said Christopher at the inquest. 'The window was down about half way and the car engine was running. The garage doors and side doors were shut.'

The coroner asked: 'Did he ever suggest that he might take his own life?'

Christopher replied: 'No.'

Dr David Brittan told the coroner of a telephone conversation he had had with his brother thirty six hours before his death. 'He said he had this throat trouble and was worried because it had not cleared up, but he said it was slightly better and he was contemplating going back to work.'

The coroner asked him, 'Would not a scientist have recognized that to start a car with the garage doors closed might be dangerous?'

He replied, 'I am sure he may have been aware of that but I would imagine he was thinking of warming up the car while he went back to open the garage door.' David described his brother as a 'logical and sensible scientist'.

The coroner, returning a verdict of accidental death, said there was no evidence that John had taken his own life. Surrey police said later they were satisfied with their inquiries and the coroner's verdict. Nevertheless, important questions remain unanswered. If John was thinking of warming up the car while going back to open the garage doors why was he found slumped over the steering wheel? It seemed that no attempt had been made to open the car door, let alone the garage door. A pathologist at the inquest testified that John would have had at least one or two minutes before he became unconscious.

Dr John Brittan had worked at the Military Vehicles and Engineering Establishment division of the Ministry of Defence's RARDE. The Chertsey site where he was based, is responsible for formulating military concepts up to 25 years ahead. His secretary there said: 'He was a lovely man. He is badly missed. He was in charge of testing and he loved computers.'

And an assistant officer to the head of RARDE who had known John 'very well' said:

'Although he originally came to this establishment on the computer side, he didn't actually continue with that once the new computer and everything had been installed in here some years ago. Really, for the last five or so years he had been engaged on other things, latterly heading up the trials and evaluation group.'

John had apparently enjoyed experimenting with computer simulations, but did so more as an 'outside interest' than as part of his direct employment. The RARDE officer said it was difficult to explain the exact nature of John's work in the period before he died, and insisted: 'I'm not hedging.' He went on, however, to talk in general terms about the importance of the work:

'He was manager of all the trials facilities and so on in the establishment. He was in charge of all the testing laboratories and all the equipment that we have here but it was a managerial post rather than actually operating it all and carrying out the scientific analysis himself ... He was responsible for the deployment of the equipment, for deciding who should use it and what should be done with it, that sort of thing.' This would involve assessing the effectiveness of the equipment in the light of its success or otherwise in trials, he added. 'A lot of our work involves computer simulation and therefore he was particularly interested in that.'

It emerged later that, at the time of John's death, RARDE was supervising work on ADCIS, the C3i contract which David Sands had worked on before his death.

John was not the only scientist working for a Ministry of Defence scientific establishment who had died in odd circumstances.

Three months later, on Friday, 24 April 1987, 24-year-old Mark Wisner, a quiet and hard working computer software engineer at the Aeroplane and Armament Experimental Establishment (A&AEE), died with nine feet of cling film wrapped around his face. Mark's death resembled a tragic accident. The local newspaper, under the headline, 'Computer Ace's Fatal Fetish', reported that:

'A young computer expert at the Boscome Down air base led an amazing double life as a transvestite, an inquest heard. Bachelor Mark Wisner who worked on computer software for the Tornado warplane, had a secret fetish for photographing himself wearing women's clothing. But his quest for sexual stimulation ended in tragedy two weeks ago, when he suffocated after a sexual experiment went disastrously wrong. He was found dead at his Durrington home wearing high heeled women's boots, suspenders and a PVC top.'

Sexual experiments of this nature are not unknown. However Mark had a sensitive job at an establishment which is involved in some of the most secret defence work in the UK and which has close working associations with test establishments in the US, Canada, France, Germany and Italy. The fact that for years he kept his transvestism secret, even until shortly before his death, from people at work, could not have been much comfort to those responsible for the protection of information at his workplace. Such a secret could have made him a potential candidate for blackmail. Furthermore, the circumstances surrounding Mark's death are not quite as simple as the local paper report implied. A full report was made for the coroner. It stated that Mark Wisner of 14 Downland Way, Durrington, was a single Professional Technical Officer, and was certified dead on 24th April. He rented a semi-detached house with three bedrooms. Two other men shared the house with him, Nigel Arthur and Nicholas Thompson.

The report continued: 'At about 19.30 hours on Thursday April 23rd Mark Wisner arrived home from his work. Nigel Arthur telephoned him from his girlfriend's house in Salisbury and he appeared all right. Mr Arthur did not return home that night. Nicholas Thompson was away practising Kung Fu when Mark Wisner arrived home. Thompson arrived home at 23.30 that night and heard the television on in Mr Wisner's bedroom and assumed he had been watching television. At about 7.30 a.m. on the morning of the 24th, Mr Thompson got up and heard the television in Mr Wisner's room still on. He knocked on the door to ask if he was going to work but got no reply. He then went onto work. Through the morning Mr Arthur telephoned the house on a number of occasions without receiving an answer. At 12 o'clock Mr Arthur returned home with a workmate and found a parcel had been delivered for Mr Wisner. He took this upstairs and knocked at Mr Wisner's bedroom door and said that there was a parcel. He heard the television still on but heard no reply. Mr Arthur then returned to work. Mr Arthur telephoned the house on a number of occasions and then spoke to a supervisor. At 14.30 hours on the 24th Mr Arthur returned home and found the deceased lying on the bedroom floor with a plastic bag tied around his neck ... Subsequent examination of the body found that there were three layers of cling film wrapped around the head of the deceased with a hole for the mouth. Inside the plastic bag was a tube of Evostik and some glue had been squeezed out.'

The inquest, held only five days later, heard that death was due to asphyxia. A Home Office pathologist, Dr William Kennard, told the inquest that a lack of oxygen can heighten sexual arousal. Summing up, the coroner said: 'At first sight this could be seen as a case where a young man had decided to take his own life – but that is definitely not so. Dr Kennard, a most experienced Home Office pathologist, has told me that in his opinion the deceased was perhaps experimenting ...' As with the other cases no exact time of death was given.

After spending two days considering a question about Mark's work a Ministry of Defence spokesman said: 'I don't think he had direct access to classified information.' The A&AEE at Boscombe Down was even less helpful. An official at the establishment who had worked with Mark would only confirm that he had been an employee there. The official would not even comment on the newspaper report that Mark had worked on Tornado software. 'I'm not going to say that over the telephone,' said the official. 'I am not going to comment to anybody on what we work on up here at all.'

The term 'Tornado software' means little without knowing the exact area of specialization. David Sands's company Easams, for example, built its reputation in the field of electronics and software for the Tornado fighter but the technology, and its military sensitivity, varies greatly. Low classification work might involve working on a computer program for a pilot landing display. Higher classification work could include the development of identification equipment which could link in to IUKADGE, or top secret EW equipment. It subsequently emerged that the A&AEE specializes in EW testing equipment. Ministry of Defence publications show that the A&AEE has been working on Tornado software since the early 1980s. One publication has a photograph showing an entire wall of a large room fitted with computer equipment to check and test Tornado electronics. Another describes the A&AEE as responsible for 'testing all military aircraft and airborne systems to assess their suitability for operational use by the armed services' and that the establishment has a 'unique electromagnetic radiation generator for exploring the compatibility of electrical and electronic equipment'. It goes on to say that the work covers the whole field of aeronautics and avionics, and includes liaison with defence contractors, universities and the armed services.

The establishment also specializes in what has become known as stealth technology as well as sonar projects. This demonstrates the considerable overlap in the work of the various fields of work of the Government establishments. Although not implied in its name, for example, RARDE is nevertheless involved in torpedo projects. Moreover, it is known that many computer systems, even those in use at defence establishments, are not as secure as their manual equivalents. According to a technical paper by Dr D.H. Barnes, a computer security specialist at another Ministry of Defence research establishment, the Royal Signals and Radar Establishment, computer suppliers provide glossy brochures giving the impression that, if you buy their equipment 'all your problems are solved'. But Dr Barnes goes on to say: 'If this were the case, why do we not have truly secure systems in widespread defence use in the UK today? The fact is that the only 100 percent secure computer based system is one that contains no information, and does no work, i.e., a useless system. Our research and development programmes are aimed at getting us technology which lets us get progressively closer and closer to the 100 percent secure goal, but we never reach it. The closer we get the harder and more expensive the job becomes.'

Dr Barnes adds: 'In particular we want our automated systems to be at least as good (in security terms) as the manual systems which they will replace.'

The number of times that secure systems have been breached in recent years by hackers, enthusiasts who use home computers and telecommunications networks to electronically break into secure data bases, mostly for the sheer challenge involved, bears testimony to the fallibility of defence systems.

Wau Holland, spokesman for a team of young West German hackers who broke into a computer network linking the US space agency Nasa with research centres in Europe and Asia, said: 'Computer systems often have a security loophole. The designers and users are aware of that, and that's why a lot of material isn't marked confidential or secret.'

As with the other scientists it is impossible to measure the exact extent of Mark Wisner's knowledge. Even if he were working on the least classified A&AEE project he could have overheard information or gleaned it from a data base which was intended for someone of a higher authorization. Moreover, many staff from apparently separate Ministry of Defence establishments tend to mix socially and professionally. In Dr John Brittan's case he had joined RARDE after working at the UK's foremost academy for defence technologists, the Royal Military College of Science at Shrivenham, on the border of Wiltshire and Oxfordshire. The college takes its students from the RAF, Royal Navy and the British Army, although its main area of expertise is regarded as battlefield technology. According to the Ministry of

Defence publication *Defence Science* the college has 'excellent library facilities, including a unique collection of research reports'. Its nuclear physics and nuclear chemistry laboratories contain equipment 'not commonly available in university laboratories' and courses run by the college relate to specialized technology and are not available elsewhere in the country. The publication adds: 'A course lasting nearly a year is also conducted for the Royal Navy to prepare officers for specialist staff appointments in technical fields.' Other courses include ballistics, nuclear and chemical defence, and microprocessors. A substantial amount of research by the college is done on the basis of a research agreement entered into with the Ministry of Defence research establishments and other organizations.

What *Defence Science* does not make explicit is the fact that, like RARDE, the Royal Military College has a particular interest in C3i systems and the effect of EW on them. In fact it has a world-wide reputation of excellence in this field.

The College's work in the field of EW is rarely discussed openly, but a clue to its expertise is given in a series of technical books, written by Royal Military College of Science lecturers, which are designed to instruct army officers who are 'studying for promotion examinations, furthering their knowledge at specialist arms schools or attending command and staff schools'. The books say the College has a unique blend of academic and military experts. It goes on: 'They are not only leaders in the technology of their subjects but are aware of what the military practitioner needs to know. It is difficult to imagine any group of persons more fitted to write about the application of technology to the battlefield.'

In fact one of the College's lecturers, Professor A.J. Sammes, is the editor of a publication called

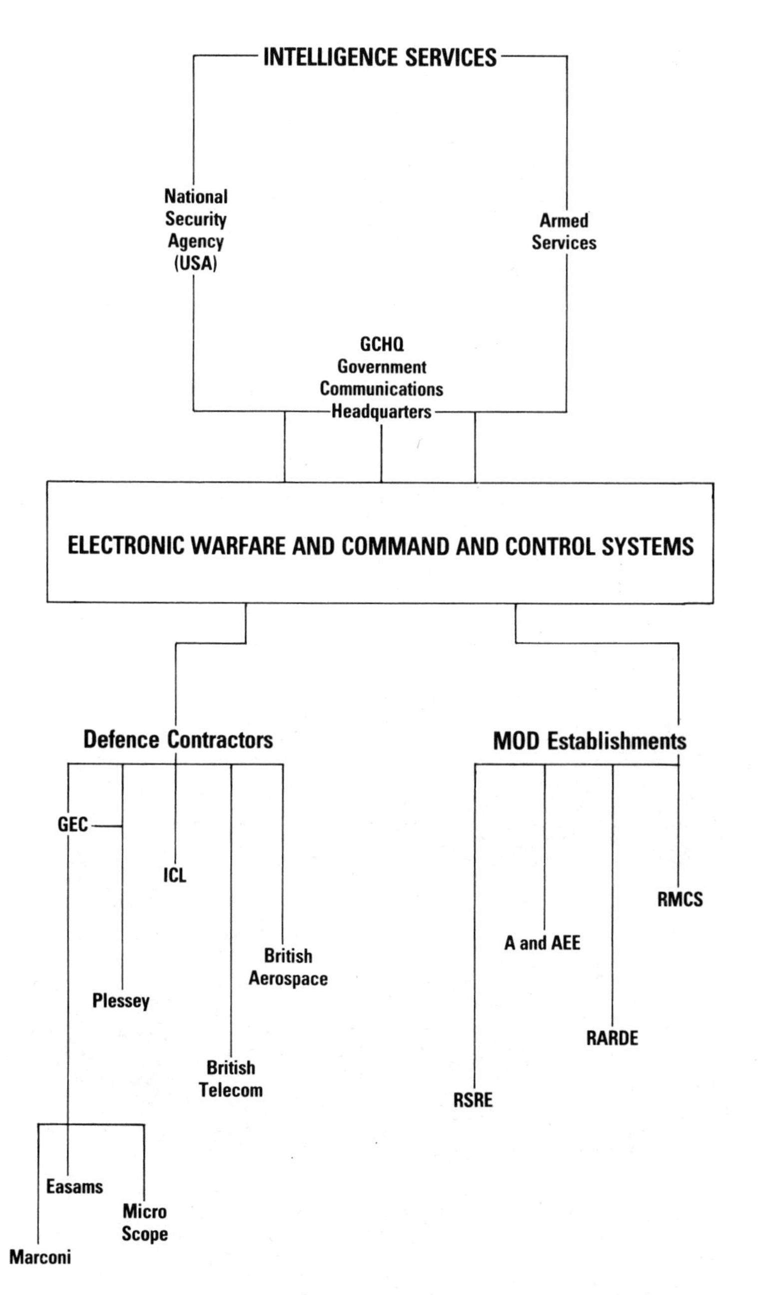

Diagram shows relationship between intelligence services, electronic warfare related equipment and some defence organizations.

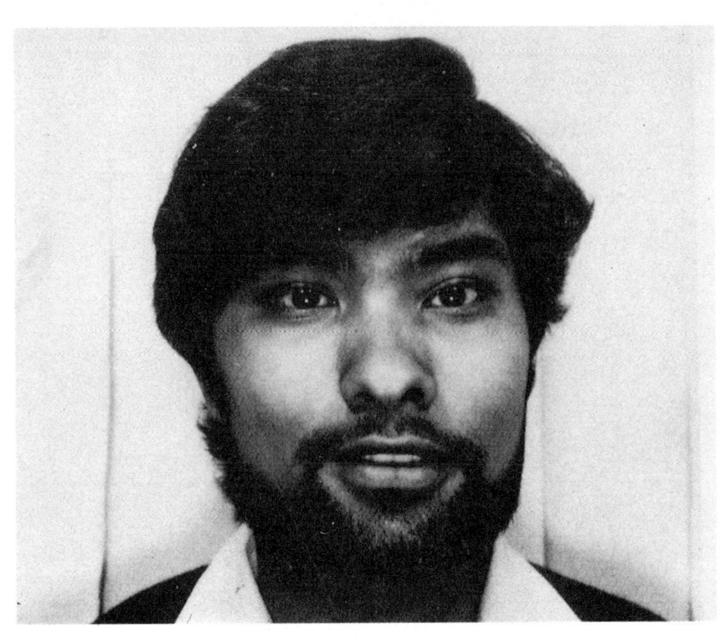

Arshad Sharif

Trevor Knight

Alistair Beckham with his wife and family

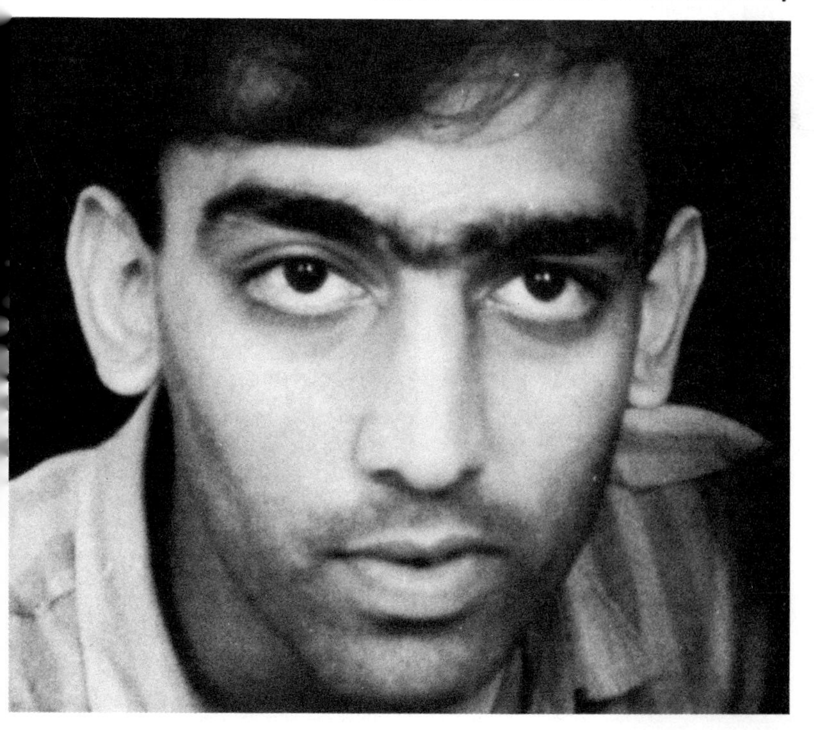

Vimal Dajibhai

Peter Peapell

The wreckage of David Sands' car

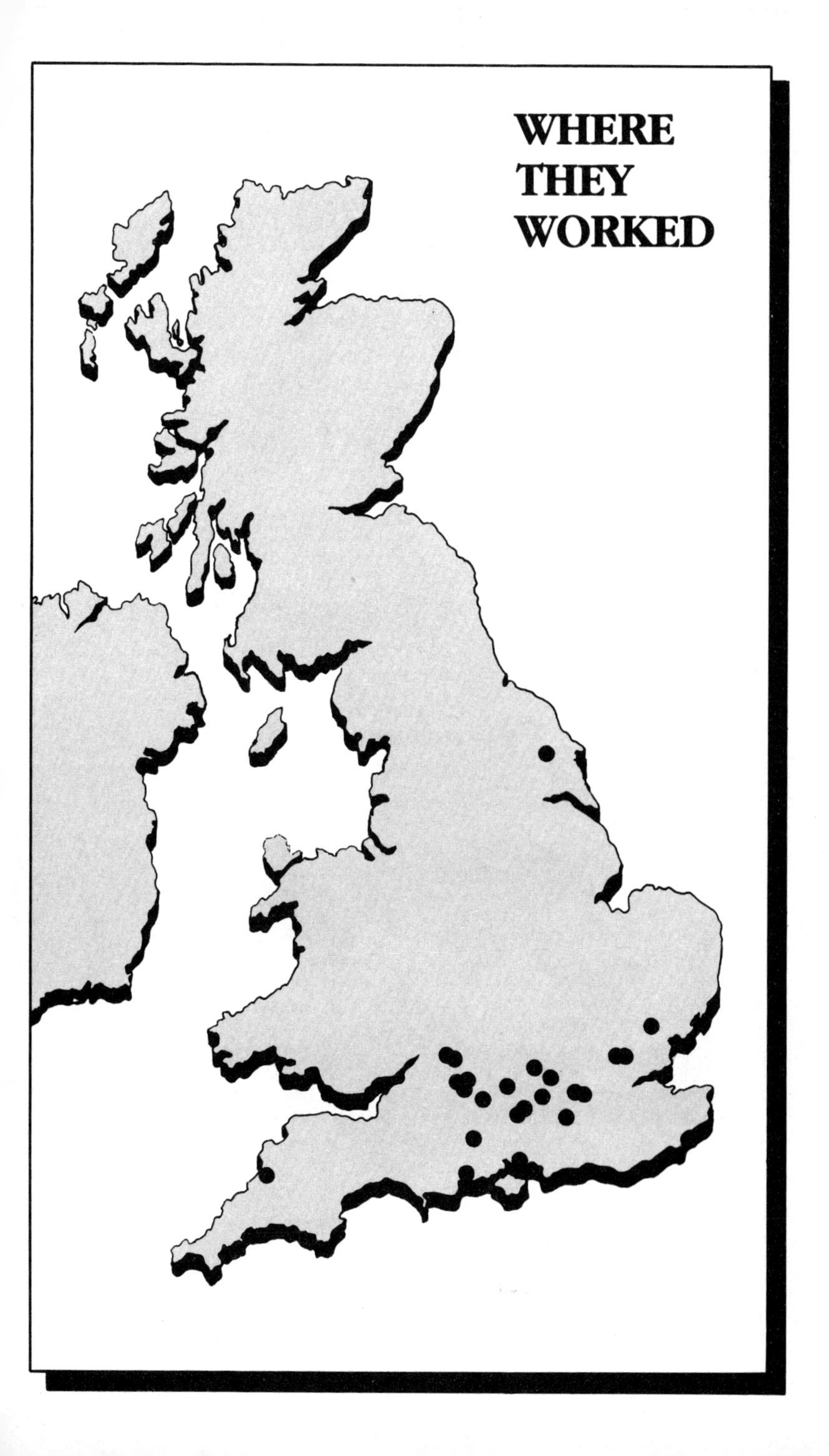
WHERE
THEY
WORKED

Cover of Easams brochure about ADCIS

Command and control bunker at RAF Northwood

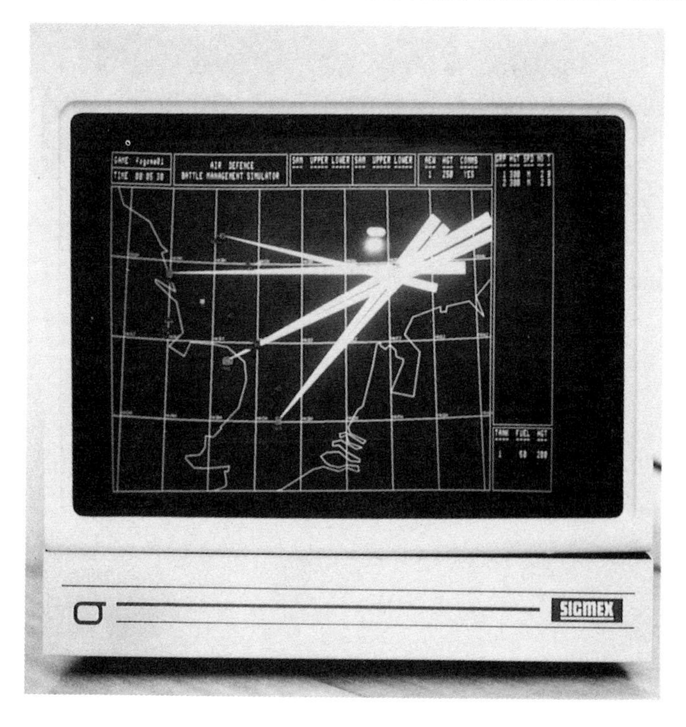

Example of a battle management simulator

Automatic test equipment in use at GEC

International Command and Control Communications and Information Systems, which boasts an editorial board comprising the commander of the UK field army, representatives from American military and academic institutions, and an assistant chief of the defence staff at the Ministry of Defence. Professor Sammes was also the key prosecution witness in a case which was heard at Bristol Crown Court in October 1986 concerning the illegal sale of Western technology to the Eastern Bloc. Alan Simmons, a computer engineer, was jailed for nine months for breaching export regulations by selling certain American computers and ancillary equipment to the USSR. British customs officials had been watching Simmons closely after they were tipped off by US intelligence staff. Sammes testified that Nato was able to counteract the superior resources of the Eastern Bloc by keeping a 'four to five year lead in the field of command and control'. Sammes added that the Soviet Union's own computers had proved unreliable in this respect and that the acquisition of the American computers would have been a real asset to the Russians.

Sammes was in a position to know about the strengths and weaknesses of Soviet technology. The College makes a point of studying Eastern Bloc military developments. In fact this had been one of the responsibilities of Peter Peapell until his mysterious death in 1987.

On the night of Saturday, 21 February, Peter, a 46-year-old senior scientist in the College's metallurgy department, and his wife Maureen, left their home in Shrivenham to join some friends for a dinner party. A thoroughly enjoyable evening ended with Peter winning a game of Trivial Pursuit. He was apparently in good spirits as they drove home in the early hours of Sunday morning. He was over the limit for driving but not drunk. During the drive he heard a slight knocking noise coming from underneath the car but was not unduly concerned. The couple arrived home at about three o'clock in the morning. Maureen got out of the car to go straight to bed. She was very tired and was asleep within minutes. Peter went to put the car away in the garage behind the house.

When Maureen woke up at about 9.30 a.m., Peter was not beside her. She assumed he had gone downstairs to make a cup of tea. She got up and went to look for him. Outside she found the garage door closed and heard the car engine running. When she opened the garage's up and over door, she saw her husband's head sticking out from underneath the car, his face upwards, almost parallel with the rear bumper and his mouth virtually aligned with the end of the exhaust pipe. She pulled him out but he was dead. Her first thought was that it was an accident, that he had gone underneath the car to check the knocking noise. But the light in the garage was broken and he had no torch.

Was it suicide? Maureen, aged 45, a part-time office worker, said that there had been no marital or money worries. Peter had been at the Royal Military College of Science for twenty-five years and had loved his job. In fact he had just received a sizeable pay rise. Furthermore, Professor John Belk, Peter's departmental head, said that he had shown no signs of strain and that his death was a mystery to his colleagues. Professor Belk added: 'None of us have got any indicators that we can think of that would have suggested anything other than a normal state of affairs.'

Peter's family and friends remain unconvinced that he killed himself. Even the police found the circumstances strange. There was no suicide note and detectives thought it 'totally improbable that he would have chosen that moment for suicide, when his wife might easily have come looking for him'.

PC William Fuller, the Oxfordshire coroner's officer, said: 'Most people killing themselves this way use a hose pipe connected to the exhaust, and then sit in the car. This case just does not fit.'

PC Fuller had experimented to see if Peter could have died accidentally. The problem with this theory was working out how his body could have ended up in the position in which it was found. PC Fuller tried to crawl under the car, and then shut the garage doors, and also to close the garage doors and then squeeze under the car. Neither was possible. It seemed that Peter's Ford Escort car had been a very tight fit inside the garage. It left no room for a man to fall beneath it.

If Peter's death was neither suicide nor an accident, was it murder? It seemed highly improbable. The killer or killers would have needed to wait until the couple returned and then ambushed Peter as he was putting the car into the garage. There would also have been the risk of Maureen coming out of the house.

There was, however, one clue. If the car engine had been running all night, there would have been black carbon deposits from the exhaust on the garage door. There were none.

The post mortem revealed that the cause of death was carbon monoxide poisoning but added that the heat of the engine made it impossible to determine the time of death. In the end, the inquest proved inconclusive. The coroner recorded an open verdict: in other words he could not establish if the death was an accident, suicide or an unlawful killing.

If it had not been for Peter's job the details of his death would have gone unnoticed except by the local paper, which had printed only a few paragraphs. Professor Belk confirmed that Peter had been responsible for checking the resistance of metals to explosions, though he said he could not be more specific. He did, however, agree that Peter worked with titanium, a very light and exceptionally strong metal which is expensive to produce in the West but which is found in relatively large quantities in the Soviet Union. It is used extensively by the military in aircraft and submarines. In fact the latest Soviet submarines are thought to have double hulls made of titanium which cannot be penetrated by conventional torpedoes. It also emerged that Peter had a high security classification. Maureen mentioned that her husband had written a book on computers and that he had been involved in military simulations. He had also written a paper on signal processing. The paper, written with a colleague called K. Topp, discusses, among other things, frequency analysis. Peter writes: 'A reasonably comprehensive computer program enables all or any part of the captured signal to be plotted out and analysed for frequency content in an attempt to characterize the signal source mechanism.' Finally, like Dr John Brittan, Peter had recently returned from a trip to the US.

Calmly and articulately, Maureen said she was as puzzled as the police. She did not believe that her husband's death had been suicide and could not see how an accident was possible. In fact she said she was planning to ask the police to explain why they were not treating his death as murder. 'I won't have a cover up,' she said a few weeks after Peter's death. She said that she had telephoned the police and that they were sending an officer the following day, Monday. A few days later, when Maureen was asked what had happened during her meeting with the police, she said she was unable to say anything. Previously, her voice had been expressive, almost animated. Now it was tremulous. It was difficult to avoid the conclusion that she sounded worried.

Peter Peapell was not the only scientist at the Royal Military College to die in unexplained circumstances. Stuart Gooding, 23, was killed on Friday, 10 April 1987 in a tragic road accident while on a diving expedition in Cyprus. His hired car was involved in a head-on collision with a lorry on what was described by a coroner's assistant as a mountain road. The lorry driver was apparently unhurt. There were, apparently, no independent eyewitnesses. In the report the lorry driver at one point is referred to as 'the accused' although later in the same report his actions are completely exonerated by a British police inspector. The report says the accident happened 'when the deceased left his lane and drove toward another vehicle which was driven by the accused on the left hand side of the road. The accused had no chance to stop and avoid the accident. The cause which made the deceased leave his lane and collide with the accused was not ascertained.'

The report goes on to say: 'From the facts mentioned, I come to the conclusion that the accused and his vehicle bear no responsibility and the accident is therefore unfortunately due to the responsibility of the deceased. It would seem from the evidence here that the deceased's vehicle was the one which veered across the road.'

At the inquest the coroner made no summing up, noting only that the deceased had 'died from the injuries sustained during a traffic accident'. There was no reference in the paperwork to where Stuart had worked. Apparently, the only personal details given were that he was aged 23, a single man and a 'scientific officer'. There is mention of the fact that he had left England on a diving expedition organized by his sports and social club, although it is not clear whether the club was associated with his employment. Stuart's father made a statement to the inquest but this also makes no reference to Stuart's work or place of employment, although he says on several occasions that his son had considerable professional driving experience. At Birmingham University, Stuart had been a member of the climbing club, and on 'many occasions' since the age of 21 had driven the university mini bus with groups of students to various climbing locations. 'Additionally, during the summer, he had been responsible for transporting club members to European locations including Chamonix and Innsbruck. Vacation employment included four weeks with a company as a van driver.'

The Royal Military College of Science described Stuart first as a student and later as a research undergraduate. It would not confirm or deny the statement in the coroner's report that he was a scientific officer. In fact it proved particularly difficult to find out any information about his job. The college seemed far more interested in finding out why questions were being asked about Stuart's death and who was asking them than in providing information. Even the exact date of Stuart's death proved difficult to obtain.

Still fewer details were available on 49-year-old Lieutenant Colonel Anthony Godley, the head of the works study group at the college who disappeared in April 1983 and has never been seen since. He and his wife had been living in the College's married quarters when one Saturday he went missing without trace. Local newspaper news editor Alan Johnson, who made inquiries, said he tried to talk to his family, his wife for instance, but 'she had packed up and left. In fact she was gone from the Royal Military College's married quarters within twenty-four hours of her husband's disappearance.'

After Anthony's disappearance it transpired that he had spent a night at a Dover hotel but left without paying the bill. His yacht went missing from Folkestone harbour and was apparently never found. His damaged MG sports saloon, however, was later discovered at Folkestone, and a pistol was found in the boot. After the disappearance Anthony's father John, a retired magistrates clerk, died leaving his son an estate worth £79,509. The money had to be claimed within three years, by the end of 1987. But Anthony did not reappear.

Death notices have been placed in national newspapers but with no response from the missing colonel. It is assumed that he is dead.

CHAPTER SIX

The Listening Post

'In the last resort there is no procedure of personnel or physical security which will offer complete protection against the ill disposed public servant who has access to secret information' – Report of the Committee on Security Procedures in the Public Service, April 1962.

To accurately represent a full-scale war scene, computer simulators need access to information about the enemy's EW and C3i capabilities. Such information is acquired by Britain's government communications centre GCHQ at Cheltenham, aided by the armed forces, surveillance satellites, covert reconnaissance missions and other methods. GCHQ supplies the electronic intelligence which can influence the design of some EW equipment. One of its least known functions is collecting intelligence on enemy radar emissions. Such intelligence is used in 'threat libraries', databases containing the electronic characteristics of different radar systems, which are built into EW equipment such as Zeus, on which Arshad Sharif was working. When deployed on the Harrier jump jet, Zeus can detect enemy radar transmissions, determine the degree of threat they represent, using its in-built threat library, and initiate the appropriate response, which might be to either jam, confuse or deceive the radar. Indeed Zeus's effectiveness is largely governed by the degree of prior knowledge of enemy electronic emissions.

Electronic intelligence is therefore one of the prime functions of organizations such as GCHQ and its American equivalent, the National Security Agency or NSA. The work of GCHQ was virtually unknown to the general public until 1982 when one of its employees, Geoffrey Prime, was jailed for 35 years for espionage. His conviction, and the unwanted publicity associated with the trial, made the government determined to take action to prevent a repetition of such an embarrassment and new security measures were introduced.

The publicity associated with the Prime trial also concentrated attention on a pact between the UK and the USA to share intelligence booty. The pact is known as the UKUSA Security Agreement. The collaboration involves, among other things, an exchange of intelligence staff. So, for example, it came as no surprise to learn in spring 1988 that a spy ring, based in the UK, had been broken after a reported two year surveillance operation by the American Central Intelligence Agency in conjunction with the British security services.

The Americans have more than a passing interest in the protection of British secrets. This is perhaps understandable, given that the Soviets are at least as predatory as the West when it comes to EW information. An essay by two Soviet defence experts, Rear Admiral Peroumov and Captain First Rank Engineer A. Partala, entitled 'A Look at the Development of Means of Electronic Warfare', states:

'The military effectiveness of electronic countermeasures, even with emph asis on real life experimentation, must be regarded as confirmed only under the condition that basic characteristics of the electronic weapons of the opponent have been revealed with sufficient accuracy.

'But the possibility of dependably uncovering and obtaining this information is an extremely difficult task

... even the most modern reconnaissance (intelligence) is not able to secure timely disclosure of all nomenclatured radio-electronic means, their tactical-technical characteristics, and special military employment.'

After the jailing of Geoffrey Prime, the government set up an inquiry into security at GCHQ which showed that Prime had suffered acute depression and had even received psychiatric treatment, but that he had not reported this to GCHQ as staff regulations required. It also emerged that Prime had built up detailed files on other staff members at GCHQ who could either be blackmailed into working for the Russians, or induced to do so with bribes. As a result, those people named in Prime's files were interviewed by both GCHQ security officers and MI5. Five members of staff were disciplined and lost their security clearances because they were not entirely frank when questioned. But GCHQ faced a problem with those who were in receipt of the most sensitive information. Disillusionment with the job can be, in itself, a security risk. Moreover legal action against someone who is only suspected of being a security risk is impossible.

Despite the additional security measures enforced at GCHQ following Prime's arrest, there is no evidence of a connection with the mysterious deaths which followed. Nevertheless, the fact that senior GCHQ radio operator Jack Wolfenden died in an unexplained glider accident within a few days of Prime appearing in court, inevitably led to speculation of a link between the two events. Prime had been charged on 15 July 1982, prompting what MP Rupert Allason called 'one of the most intensive espionage investigations ever known in England'. On 27 July 1982, the local newspaper in Cheltenham reported under the headline 'Pilot Killed in Mystery Crash', that 56-year-old Jack Wolfenden had died instantly when his powered glider suddenly went into a shallow dive and crashed into a Cotswold hillside in perfect flying weather. He was an experienced pilot and there was no sign of illness or mechanical failure to explain the crash. According to a contemporary report in *The Sunday Times*, Jack's girlfriend Judith Pither said he had acted oddly after returning from abroad and complained of feeling lethargic and indecisive.

At the inquest, Jack was said to have been suffering from severe stress. He apparently had tensions in his domestic life and was upset at his divorce settlement. But he left no suicide note. Judith, who had been living with him at his home in Harp Hill, Cheltenham, told the inquest: 'I feel that Jack would not have crashed his plane deliberately. There was so much unfinished business.' The inquest returned a verdict of accidental death.

A few months after Jack's death his colleague 43-year-old Ernest Brockway, who had worked for ten years at Irton Moor, one of GCHQ's largest ground stations in Britain, was found dead at his home. The station's work for GCHQ includes what is known as long range technical search which entails scanning the airwaves for high frequency radio signals emanating from ships and aircraft in a sector bounded by Archangel in the north of Russia and the Baltic ports in the south. Although Ernest, who had been promoted a few weeks before, left no suicide note, all the signs were that he had hanged himself. Ernest's widow Janet told reporters: 'My husband was a sick man and that's all there is to it. I have been told by the police and GCHQ to say nothing.'

After the inquest Mrs Brockway's solicitor issued a statement declaring that there had been no MI5 or other special inquiry into Ernest's death. Prime Minister Margaret Thatcher, in a reply to a question in the House of Commons, cleared Ernest Brockway and Jack Wolfenden of any suspicions of spying. In addition, GCHQ issued an internal memorandum to its 7,000 staff stating that there was no connection between the spying activities of Geoffrey Prime and the two deaths. Sir Brian Tovey, the director of GCHQ, said that the implication behind the speculation in the press and elsewhere had been that the dead men were connected with the Prime affair. He continued:

'I want all staff to be aware of the Prime Minister's statement on December 1 – that there was no reason to suspect that they were anything other than loyal, trustworthy citizens and that neither had any reason to think they were under suspicion.' He added: 'GCHQ deplored the distress and suffering caused to the families of both men by various statements, no doubt made in good faith.'

At the inquest which recorded a verdict of suicide, it was suggested that Ernest had been receiving drugs for depression but had refused to take them. The coroner was told that Ernest had been reluctant to admit he was depressed. It was not considered particularly significant at the time but depression is regarded by the authorities as one of the grounds for suspecting that an employee working in a highly sensitive field of defence is a possible security risk.

On 2 April 1984 GCHQ confirmed that lie detectors had come into force on that day as part of vetting procedures to 'weed out staff who posed a possible security risk'. Hundreds of staff were to undergo tests. Only four days after lie detector tests were introduced at GCHQ, a short report appeared in the *Guardian* newspaper which said: 'GCHQ confirmed that one of its employees had been found dead in unusual circumstances.' The employee was not named, but the report mentioned that an MP was asking for an official statement.

That statement again came from Margaret Thatcher who said: 'Any suicide, and I am aware of the one to which you refer, accompanied by a suicide note will be a matter for the coroner. The note would be in possession of the coroner, I would expect.' In reply to supplementary questions she repeated that it was a matter for the coroner. Still the dead man was not named.

It was only after several days that the *Daily Mail* revealed that the dead man was 58-year-old George Franks, and reported that he had been a radio specialist engaged in highly classified defence work. According to the *Daily Mail* he was found 'hanged at home and is believed to have left a suicide note'.

The report added that his electronic espionage work had involved operating sophisticated equipment in extreme conditions ranging from helicopters and submarines to garret rooms. 'It is understood that for this purpose he had a very high level security clearance,' it said.

Almost as curious as George Franks's death was the news blackout which followed it. Whitehall sources explained to journalists that the blackout was necessary out of concern for George's family. But if George had a family they were not in evidence after his death. The body had to be identified at the police station by one of George's elderly neighbours. The only family member to give evidence at the inquest was his sister Mrs Eva McNulty who had not seen him for four months. Moreover, according to his neighbour, George received only about two telephone calls a week, and these were usually from a man who identified himself only in the form of a code.

At the same time, the Tory MP for Cheltenham, Charles Irving, said it was 'unfortunate' that George's death had not been disclosed to the press. He added: 'It certainly is understandable that, with immense pressure upon GCHQ in recent months, sadly, something like this might occur.'

George Franks, however, did not commit suicide because of stress. In fact, according to the inquest, he did not commit suicide. He died of natural causes.

Shortly before the inquest, the *Daily Telegraph* reported: 'Police in Sussex investigating the death have ruled out hanging as the cause of death, with the evidence now pointing to a heart attack.' It appeared that George had felt a heart attack coming on and had put into effect a series of actions which, it seems, were pre-planned. He compiled a bundle of documents, including his will and testament and letters, the contents of which were never disclosed, left clear instructions for his neighbour to give the bundle to his sister, placed it in a cubbyhole in the hall outside his flat, went back in, locked the door, and died.

Dr Walter Killpack, a pathologist at the Royal Sussex County Hospital who conducted the post mortem, told the inquest: 'He must have decided not to seek medical attention for reasons not known. It appears that this behaviour is most unusual.' No mention was made at George's inquest of the nature of his work. Clumsy statements were constructed to avoid even mentioning the name of his employer. When an official representing GCHQ gave evidence at the inquest, he was described as 'an officer in charge of the place of employment where Mr Franks worked'.

On a potentially more serious note, claims that evidence was actually being suppressed arose after a letter from GCHQ, which George had included in the bundle intended to be read only by his sister, was withheld from the hearing. The message on the bundle of documents addressed to George's neighbour Charles Harvey, said: 'Charles, please give this to my sister only.' The word 'only' was underlined. Charles, however, had handed the bundle containing the documents unopened to the police.

Asked after the inquest whether the entire contents of the bundle had been given to George's sister, the coroner, Edward Grace, replied that she had received the parts intended for her. Grace said that he had read a copy of the GCHQ letter and that it had been purely to do with work and was in no way connected with George's impending death. George's sister refused to comment on the contents of the parts of those documents which she had received. The police would say only that the envelope had contained two further envelopes. On one was written 'Will and Testament'. Inside there was a sheet of paper with writing on. The second envelope was a used one, addressed to George at his place of work. Inside was another envelope containing four sheets of scrap paper with writing on them, and the letter addressed to George at GCHQ.

Other questions about the circumstances surrounding George's death remain unanswered. Why, for example, was a partially concealed, half-empty bottle of twelve-year-old malt whisky and a plastic cylinder containing 100 tablets found near the body? According to the pathologist, they bore no relevance to his death, but then why had the Prime Minister herself referred to suicide and a suicide note, when the coroner said that there was no indication at all that George had killed himself?

What had sparked off the original speculation that he had been found hanged? Why, as in the other cases, could a time of death not be established? The pathologist had told the inquest he could not establish the exact time of death because of the conditions in which he examined the body. He did not elaborate.

On the face of it, George's death could not have involved foul play. His front door was locked from the inside. But some years later a close friend voiced his reservations about the death. He was perhaps the last man to speak to George and said that he had been convivial and looking forward to the future. The friend also revealed that George had been involved in a dispute with his employers. All he would say was that it was about a matter that GCHQ had taken very seriously.

Little real evidence emerged about the deaths of two other GCHQ workers. In the case of 25-year-old Stephen Drinkwater, who was found asphyxiated, with a plastic bag over his head in 1983, there was every likelihood that his death was the result of a sexual experiment which went wrong. A short report of the inquest which appeared on an inside page of a Cheltenham newspaper referred to him only as a 'civil servant' and made no reference to GCHQ. It said that Stephen's parents had returned home and found that his bedroom door was shut. They had thought nothing more about it until they had discovered the door was locked. Stephen's father Donald had climbed a ladder up to the bedroom window and found Stephen on the bed. He immediately went inside, broke down the door and attempted to revive his son. But it was too late. The coroner recorded a verdict of misadventure.

Stephen had been a clerk in the one department of GCHQ which is permitted to make copies of highly classified documents. Although there was speculation at the time that his death may have been linked to the Prime affair, there was no evidence of a connection.

The death in 1985 of 35-year-old Stephen Oke, who worked at GCHQ's most advanced listening post at Morwenstow in Cornwall, seemed far more suspicious. The precise circumstances which led to Stephen being found hanging from a beam in the loft of his home were never established.

The North and East Cornwall coroner George Northey was puzzled by the fact that a piece of string was found twisted around Stephen's hands and tied in a reef knot but he was told by the police that Stephen could have done this himself. The police, however, admitted they could find no reason why Stephen should have taken his own life. It happened while his wife Helen and their two children were away for a few days in the Midlands. In their absence Stephen was going to redecorate the kitchen. 'What happened is entirely beyond me,' said Helen.

The Devon and Cornwall police, who investigated Stephen's death, found GCHQ responsive to their requests for assistance. 'They said that it was nothing to do with work so there was no problem about our people talking to staff,' said one of the investigating officers after the inquest. George Roberts, officer in charge at GCHQ, said that Stephen had worked there for about eleven years doing a job that involved handling communications and assisting in clerical duties. He was a traffic handler.

Roberts said: 'It is a routine job. Whether one feels it is exciting depends on the individual, but there is no mystery or security aspect to Mr Oke's death whatsoever.'

In his summing up the coroner said he was bound to wonder whether, for some reason, Stephen had decided to see what it felt like to be hanged and, maybe, his feet had slipped. He returned an open verdict.

Again, there were many unanswered questions. Cigarettes were found at the scene although Stephen apparently did not smoke. An empty brandy bottle was found in the dustbin despite the fact that Stephen was said to have disliked spirits. A meal had been put together from items in the fridge, but it was left uneaten.

Some years later a policeman on the Devon and Cornwall force remembered the case well. 'It was a strange business,' he said. And a man who had known Stephen since their school days, and knew of his work at Morwenstow GCHQ, said that an experiment would have been 'totally out of character'. But he added that he had no reason to believe that Stephen's death was connected with the others, even though Stephen had had access to the inner sanctum of one of the most sensitive departments at GCHQ.

One cannot easily ignore the fact that the authorities

are extremely sensitive to matters relating to the intelligence services, particularly where they impinge on signals intelligence. This was made clear during an Official Secrets Act trial in the late 1970s when a man, who was referred to in court only as Colonel B, told the hearing: 'Because of my knowledge of the subject, I am better aware than most of the critical need to ensure that some secrets that are more secret than others are kept as secret as possible. Sigint (signals intelligence) is one. This matter should remain as secret as possible. An individual having information concerning Sigint in his possession may only communicate it to someone else having the same type of indoctrination, or if he has been previously authorized in writing by an officer not below the rank of Major General.' He referred to leaks of certain information as 'potentially causing grave damage' to national security.

The importance of signals intelligence was further underlined in July 1988, when a 22-year-old, homosexual data processor at GCHQ, one of the lowest grade technical jobs at the estabalishment, lost his High Court battle against the withdrawal of his security clearance. Andrew Hodges's positive vetting clearance had been removed and he had been suspended after he gave a full account of his homosexual relationships to a line manager. GCHQ said that his clearance had been withdrawn because he was 'vulnerable to pressure or blackmail by a hostile intelligence service'. This was despite the fact that his homosexuality was no secret. In his twenty-first year he had come to the conclusion that he was homosexual and had told his family, friends and immediate superior. But GCHQ decided that doubt still remained about his discretion and reliability.

Such an attitude casts a shadow over cases where someone who had been in receipt of particularly sensitive information was discovered to be a security risk of some sort. George Franks, for example, had a secret taste for pornographic magazines. This was discovered by GCHQ and it was felt to be a problem. George had been a wireless operator at GCHQ during the Second World War and had remained at the establishment up until his death. He had been privy to highly sensitive signals intelligence. He told a close friend that GCHQ officers had interviewed him extensively, had mentioned the pornography and had made some unspecified accusations. How the magazines were discovered and exactly why the matter was taken so seriously is not clear. However, the withdrawal of George's security clearance, demotion or the cancelling of his pension, a matter which, incidentally, was said to have been the subject of a dispute between George and GCHQ, might have caused disenchantment. And disenchantment might have been regarded as a security risk, especially in the light of a supposed onslaught by what former Civil Lord of the Admiralty Sir Charles Orr-Ewing once described as 'thousands of Russians ... all trained to detect weakness in character, weakness for drink, blondes, drugs and homosexuality'.

One former GCHQ employee said that when he left he had to sign several forms which in effect declared his knowledge null and void. As he had several separate clearances which gave him access to information on different security levels, he had to sign a form for every clearance, declaring that he was no longer entitled to know the things he knew. But what if he was not prepared to erase from his mind what he knew? What if he wanted to leave Britain for a country which was beyond the scope of the Official Secrets Act? And what if the security services suspected him of being disaffected or even subversive, a potential security risk? 'I would rather not think of the consequences,' he said.

CHAPTER SEVEN

The Peacetime War

The proliferation of modern, electronically controlled weapons has caused a rapid expansion in the field of EW to the extent that it can be a decisive factor in a war. Missiles can be made to miss their targets by being subjected to EW. Attacking aircraft can be made to disappear from enemy radar screens through the deceptive use of EW. Submarine commanders can use EW technology to seduce an attacking torpedo into chasing the wrong target, or into 'seeing' and 'hearing' a target that does not exist. The West's C3i could be neutralized by the Warsaw Pact's use of EW coupled with the physical destruction of the key components of the systems.

Much of the technology used in EW is not top secret and can be read about in Soviet and Western technical papers. It is the ways in which EW is applied that forms the basis of some of the most highly classified secrets that either side possess. This is one reason the intelligence services play a key role in the EW effort.

According to American EW specialist Dr Curtis Schleher, 'victory will go to the side that can best control the electromagnetic spectrum', that is the whole range of radio, radar, sound and other waves that make up the tool kit of modern defence technology. The stated aims of EW are simple enough, and fall into three categories: firstly to exploit the enemy's electromagnetic emissions to provide intelligence on their order of battle, intentions and capabilities; secondly to prevent a hostile force making effective use of the electromagnetic spectrum for its communications and weapon systems; and to protect one's own use of the electromagnetic spectrum.

The Second World War saw rapid growth in the sophistication of radar systems, which in turn spawned EW measures to defeat them. An aircraft flying over enemy territory would carry electronic equipment to confuse the enemy's radar. The equipment would consist primarily of a jammer, a powerful transmitter which would overload the radar receiver, rendering it ineffective. The crew could also dump bales of aluminium chaff from the airplane which would fool the radar into seeing false targets.

Similar principles still apply today, although modern EW equipment is usually designed for a specific purpose or incorporates in its design the details of the enemy radar to be jammed or deceived.

In the 1950s and early 1960s, the West gathered such intelligence information by overflying Warsaw Pact territory, challenging radar and early command and control systems. Sometimes, the crews of these spy planes were killed as the Soviets managed to detect and identify their aircraft, assess their distance and height, and launch missiles against them. The crashes and lost lives were explained in the West as accidents involving routine navigational flights or training missions. No mention was made of the fact that the aircraft were specially adapted to assemble signals intelligence. In 1958, for example, when a United States Hercules was brought down in Armenia with the loss of all seventeen crew, the Americans announced the crash of an unarmed plane researching 'radio wave propagation'. And in 1960 a flimsy plane known as a U-2 came down over Russia. The pilot, Francis Powers, survived to face a public trial. It transpired that his plane was not engaged in meteorological research as claimed by the US, but espionage. The electronic recording devices which survived the U-2 crash were put on public display and a Soviet specialist in signals intelligence testified that:

'The radio apparatus examined is a system of airborne radio reconnaissance equipment, intended for the collection of information on the structure of the radio technical service of the anti-aircraft defence system of the Soviet Union ... A ferromagnetic tape was found to contain signals of ground radar stations of the Soviet Union.'

Dozens died as Western aircraft were brought down near Vladivostok, Latvia and Siberia.

The first real showcases for modern EW techniques were the Israeli-Arab wars. In 1973, thirteen Israeli boats armed with a total of 63 Gabriel missiles succeeded in defeating 27 Syrian and Egyptian craft carrying 85 Soviet SS-N-2 Styx missiles with about twice the range of the Gabriels. Two battles took place, one on 6 October 1973, the other two days later. In the first, five Israeli missile boats ran into a group of Syrian patrol craft. While engaging them, the Israelis detected six incoming Styx missiles on their radar. The Israeli boats dodged the missiles but eight minutes later a second salvo of six missiles was detected. One of these was destroyed by fire from Israeli guns, the other five passed overhead without doing any harm. During the second battle, a group of five Israeli boats sighted four enemy boats and at the same time detected a salvo of three missiles, followed by three more. Each time the Israelis dodged them, making a total of twelve missiles which failed to lock on to their targets. Once again the Israelis closed in, with disastrous results for the enemy. Two Syrian craft were seen to blow up and a third ran aground, to be destroyed by gunfire.

What Israeli reports did not make clear is exactly how the Styx missiles missed their targets. It was reported in some circles that the Styx's radar seekers had been decoyed by Israeli EW techniques and had been made to 'see' targets which did not exist.

Furthermore, in 1981, Israeli jets, according to the US magazine Air Force, destroyed one of their own downed aircraft in Lebanon to prevent its EW equipment falling into enemy hands. The article said that Richard Perle, US Assistant Secretary of Defence, had 'recently disclosed that the Israeli Air Force lost an aircraft carrying highly secret Israeli developed electronic countermeasures equipment' and that the Israelis had been 'determined not to let the equipment fall into enemy hands', and had therefore mounted a strike 'to destroy totally the downed aircraft on the ground'. There were reports that Russian military personnel had been trying to retrieve the equipment from the jet at the time of the Israeli attack. Some were said to have been killed.

A year later, also in Lebanon, the Israelis proved the value of their EW equipment. According to information published by the Royal Military College of Science, the Israelis found out the frequencies used by the Syrian surface to air guided weapon systems and then jammed them before attacking and destroying them with devastating success.

EW also plays a critical role in underwater warfare. If a defending submarine knows the homing characteristics of an attacking torpedo, the guidance system can be fooled into 'hearing' a false target. If the submarine's countermeasures are successful the torpedo will destroy a decoy or sink harmlessly to the ocean floor. In the Falklands war, reports suggest that one Argentinian submarine got near the British ships, only to have its attack frustrated by faulty torpedoes. According to one report, torpedoes were fired at the British yet they 'failed to explode'. Other reports suggest that the torpedoes may have been decoyed by British EW countermeasures.

In the air, EW can be used to make hostile planes appear on a radar screen as friendly, and 'smart' missiles can be programmed to try and avoid seduction by decoys and other EW techniques. In the Falklands the Argentinians lost many Skyhawk aircraft in battle against the British air to air and ship to air missiles. According to defence specialists, the British had prior knowledge of the EW equipment in use by the Argentinians and were aware of its low level of sophistication.

However, in one incident, a British Gazelle helicopter was said to have crashed in bad weather, killing four crew. Later, at the inquest, the army said the Gazelle had been shot down by Argentinians. Only after a prolonged legal campaign by the family of one of the dead crew members did it eventually emerge that the Gazelle had been mistakenly shot down by a missile fired by the British following problems with its identification system.

The most recently publicized use of EW was in the Gulf War when Iran accused the US fleet of jamming Iranian radar during what was described in newspaper reports as a 'devastating' Iraqi air strike. A senior Iranian air force officer was quoted on Tehran Radio as saying: 'The US fleet began carrying out electronic warfare against our planes. When our tankers were being bombed at Larak by Iraq, the US fleet jammed the radars and radios of Iranian planes for nine minutes.' In a separate incident a few weeks earlier, the US Navy destroyed two Iranian oil platforms in the southern Gulf, which the Pentagon said were being used as 'command and control radar stations for the Iranian military'.

These days Nato deploys specially equipped vehicles in West Germany as close to the forward areas, near the border with East Germany, as possible. Their purpose is to scan the electromagnetic spectrum and to categorize any transmissions. Similarly, in an attempt to detect and record the West's electronic emissions, the Soviet Union invests heavily in EW listening equipment. This is usually installed on trawlers and even larger vessels, which accompany Nato ships on exercises and lurk offshore whenever weapons trials are being conducted at test sites such as Benbecula in the Hebrides and the Atlantic Underwater Test and Evaluation Centre off the Bahamas. In addition, hundreds of uninvited guests are recorded as penetrating British airspace every year, many of them Warsaw pact aircraft such as the Tu-16 'Badger' and Tu-95 'Bear'. And on land there are extensive Warsaw Pact EW facilities all along the borders with West Germany and other Western countries. All this is backed up by satellites.

The pace of modern warfare, itself a product of the increasing mobility, range and deadliness of weapons systems, dictates the need for electronic communications systems. In any battle, commanders must be able to make the most effective use of their fighting forces. In any modern battle, the movement of weapons systems is fast and reactions must be equally fast. Such speed is achieved by linking together elements such as sensors and satellites which detect targets, to computers which can instantaneously process the data and display it in a format that can be easily and quickly understood. This is the essence of C3i systems. In some cases, the computer can be programmed to decide automatically what action should be taken and passed to the weapons systems. Such decisions will be based on a combination of understanding the current situation and prior knowledge in the form of a database of typical scenarios, weapons and target characteristics. Such C3i systems are often referred to in military circles as force multipliers, because of their ability to enhance a fighting force's effectiveness, making any notions of numerical superiority virtually irrelevant.

In theory, a ground based weapon system such as the Rapier missile should interrogate an aircraft with an electronic signal to see if it is friendly or hostile before an attack is launched. If the signal triggers a coded response from an aircraft that Rapier recognizes, it is allowed to pass unharmed. If the aircraft does not respond, Rapier is activated. Such a system is technically known as Identification Friend or Foe. In reality, IFF does not work very successfully.

Lecturers at the Royal Military College of Science write: 'There are still some weaknesses in current electronic IFF methods. The codes are easily broken and could be used by hostile aircraft. Jamming is also a possibility.' In other words, it is conceivable that, in the early stages of an air attack over, say, West Germany, many enemy aircraft may be regarded as friendly while, in the confusion, Nato planes could be shot down by their own missiles.

Staff involved with ADCIS say that aircraft could be identified with more accuracy by correlating information from many sources of different types. Instead of missiles and their target locating radar being operated as single, isolated systems, they could be fused together in a large scale command, control, communications and intelligence system in West Germany. This would provide a total air picture, including even the scenario behind enemy lines, and allow targets to be allocated to weapons systems even before they approach. Mobile ground troops responsible for Rapier, for example, would carry portable computer equipment which, in the event of an invasion, would carry a complete set of instructions for the missiles. Nato air movements would be notified to the ADCIS system on a minute by minute basis so that, in the event of a full-scale invasion, anything not already notified to the system could be deemed hostile.

A senior defence systems employee at one British defence systems company explained: 'The object is to know what you are shooting at so that you don't shoot down your own aircraft. ADCIS enables weapons systems to know exactly what they are shooting at and for their targets to be designated to them. At the moment, the first thing you know about an invasion is when you have just been bombed or when you have just been shot down.'

He continued: 'In any future war over Europe the air picture will be very cluttered, there will be many things flying around. If World War Three broke out tomorrow there would be a lot of Warsaw Pact aircraft, there would be a lot of us, a lot of French, a lot of Germans and a lot of you name it. Nobody would know who the others were. Consequently, we are making things fully automated.

'The decision to fire at a target or not is more in the hands of the computer than it used to be. There is obviously human input to that. The human will provide all the rules, but the computer will do all the eventual deciding and firing. So we need to work out a specific set of rules that a computer can use. Making it totally automated makes it a lot faster. If a target is identified as hostile and doesn't get shot down by the front line systems then details of its direction and velocity will be passed back along the battlefield so that the weapons further back get warning and get geared up to shoot it down. In the final result there will be less penetration by hostile aircraft because the ones that get through will be known about.'

Another ADCIS project member said: 'If we make systems that can shoot targets down automatically we need to make sure they do not shoot our own people down. The question is, how do we tell the differences between a hostile invasion and a group of our own aircraft returning from dropping bombs on Moscow? They could look both the same to an automated system which just selects targets and tries to blow them out of the sky.'

Clearly, with the greater reliance on ADCIS and similar command and control systems to reinforce the West's ability to deter, the capability of communications systems to survive conventional and EW attack, as well as the effects of nuclear explosions, are critical. Indeed some of the most sensitive information on C3i systems relates to their resistance to the effects of nuclear attack. Certain systems such as ADCIS, UKAIR and Uniter are designed to survive the effects of nuclear explosions which would usually wreak havoc with electronic circuitry. And the durability in war of communications and C3i systems may well depend on how soundly their secrets are kept during peace. Other highly classified but non-technical information, such as the location of critical data processing or command centres, must also be kept secret to avoid being destroyed by the enemy 'special forces' actions prior to an invasion. Many secrets are contained within David Sands's project ADCIS, which itself is based on Ptarmigan, a communications system used by the British Army in West Germany. Ptarmigan is described in a Marconi report as a 'military version of System X', System X being one type of modern digital telecommunications exchange currently being installed by British Telecom as part of the modernization of its network. System X is manufactured by GEC and Plessey, and also forms the foundation of Uniter.

There are extension telephone numbers at the Ministry of Defence's Fleetbank House in London which are answered by army officers who say simply 'ADCIS'. But this is the only information they are prepared to impart to any caller who does not possess the proper accreditation. An army officer with the rank of 'major' who worked in the ADCIS office suggested that he was prepared to answer questions only after the caller had fully identified himself and had given the name of his contact who had divulged the major's extension number. In this short conversation the major asked more questions than he answered. His objective, he said, was to establish the bona fides of the caller, whose name was requested, and given, on three occasions. He continued: 'There will be no announcement before contracts have been awarded, and that will be in due course. I won't say any more than that. What is your name? ... I'm sorry I can't say anything. I would be delighted to but I can't ... I'm sorry, your name again?' He repeated the name to ensure he had recorded it accurately and said goodbye.

An employee at the RSRE was a little more forthcoming: 'You are talking about Stage One of the project and I am not directly concerned with that. My job is looking at what we might do in a few years time. I am not sure what the position is from the press point of view. The project is all rather sensitive. I know some things but it is not my area and I am not working on it directly.' He added: 'There is wheeling and dealing going on so that everyone can agree on exactly what the project is going to do ... this has been going on for some time.

'From the project point of view I am looking at the way ahead for ADCIS in, let us say, about 10 years time. We are thinking about what we would like to do given that we have got the technology. What you are talking about on the present ADCIS is a system that is being implemented now because it is doable (sic). There are things we can't do at the moment which we are looking at for the future, but the release of any information on that is subject to security considerations.'

He added that the crux of the problem was the rapid identification of low flying aircraft. 'There you are into requiring faster communications and faster processing. You cannot take large crates of computer equipment into the field. The key issues are questions of affordability, and whether it is small enough, and reliable enough to do what you want to do.'

As the British defence contractors STC put it, in an advertisement in the publication *Defence, Communications and Security Review*: 'Tomorrow's battlefield will be dominated by weapons linked to sophisticated command, control, communications and intelligence systems. Whoever has the best C3i will win.'

According to the defence publication *Jane's* the 'gains in terms of efficiency, reliability and speed of decision making which can result from the proper use of modern C3 systems, have led to them being dubbed force multipliers'.

To oversimplify this somewhat, the 'force-multiplier' concept postulates that a commander can multiply the resources at his disposal by concentrating them in the key areas indicated by C3 systems. 'This may mean that a force which is numerically inferior and perhaps less well equipped in aspects other than C3 will nonetheless carry the day.'

Just as the adroit exploitation of C3 and C3i can act as a force multiplier and alter the balance of power in favour of the 'underdog', the destruction of that side's C3i could lead to a potentially disastrous 'force-divider' effect in which its limited military assets might be frozen by lack of communications. The West is more reliant on C3 than the Warsaw Pact and therefore places an inestimable importance on the secrecy of information concerning the weaknesses of its C3. What is not known is what action the West is prepared to take to guarantee that such knowledge does not fall into the hands of a potential enemy.

It is, perhaps, difficult to imagine how a possible future World War could be so strongly influenced by a technology which is discussed so little. None of the world leaders have ever expressed public concern about a build-up of C3i technology. Attention has always been focused on which side had the most tanks, missiles, aircraft, ships and submarines.

In reality, both sides are fighting a peacetime war to gain the upper hand in C3 and EW technologies. The West, in particular, relies heavily on C3 to counterbalance the numerical superiority of the Warsaw Pact countries.

According to publicity material, for example, UKAIR is designed to 'dramatically improve the strategy of Nato's air operations in times of hostility'. It will link up key United States Air Force bases in Britain with RAF sites, and is designed to interact with other command and control systems like ADCIS. UKAIR will also cover the vital air space between Western Scotland and Iceland, protecting the Atlantic supply route between the US and Europe. The consequent need to keep the West's secrets secret, is therefore imperative, although not an easy task in peacetime. Defence employees cannot be guaranteed to keep their knowledge to themselves, especially in the face of potential enemies hungry for information. As a book on C3 by lecturers at the Royal Military College of Science states: 'Although C3 is a potent force multiplier, particularly when linked to weapons systems, it does have weaknesses which, when exposed, can be exploited by a determined and knowledgeable enemy.' The 'weaknesses' referred to include the vulnerability of C3 systems to EW attack. The Royal Military College of Science lecturers continue:

'Recent advances in electronics have increased the versatility and capacity of field communications systems. As commanders and their staff have become more accustomed to these much improved facilities, their dependence on them has grown. Since a potential enemy will be well aware of this dependence, he can be expected to mount a considerable effort to turn this to his own advantage. In broad terms, communications EW is the exploitation or degradation of the enemy's use of the electromagnetic spectrum whilst protecting our own ability to use the same spectrum, as and how we wish.'

According to military sources some EW systems and projects carry a 'top secret' classification. EW is also big business. A recent GEC annual report had this to say about Marconi's EW involvement:

'Marconi Defence Systems Ltd continued to expand its international business with new products, an example being the Attack Drone, a multipurpose weapon which can destroy or jam enemy radars, armour and communications equipment over large areas of terrain ...

'The electronic warfare activity has good prospects for growth. The warner and jammer electronic warfare systems fitted to Tornado have been particularly successful and the radar homing and warning system, which automatically locates and identifies radar threats to Tornado, is a world leader.

'The Skyshadow jammer, which complements the warner, again beat all comers in recent Nato bombing competitions in the United States.

'Zeus, the next generation of warner/jammers (otherwise known as Integrated Defensive Aids) was successfully demonstrated during the year, and further orders for the installation in the British Harrier have been taken.

'Export prospects for this equipment are excellent, and several large contracts are currently being pursued. A new range of equipment to protect warships from attack by missiles such as Exocet has been developed and will be demonstrated this year.'

An intimate knowledge of such EW systems would be particularly useful to a country which wanted to build its own equipment to protect against missile attack. Armed with only simple technical information about the frequencies of Western EW equipment, the Soviet Union could, for example, build EW equipment to jam those frequencies. The military authorities who select such frequencies are not exactly spoilt for choice. The Royal Military College of Science lecturers state:

'Military users ... are restricted to certain frequency bands to fit in with the demands of civilian users. Even within the military bands there is intense competition between C3 systems and other users such as guided weapon systems, surveillance devices, ships and aircraft, for use of the limited number of frequencies available. The enemy also uses the same bands of the spectrum for his systems but additionally may use the spectrum to try to hinder our use of it. Thus frequency allocation is an increasingly difficult exercise.'

Another book, on guided weapons, again by the Royal Military College lecturers, contains a very short chapter on EW in which the lecturers state that frequencies 'must be kept secure'. The lecturers say that 'security classifications prevent discussion' of EW in depth.

A US book on EW states that the US Department of Defence defines the measures to be used against C3 systems thus: 'The integrated use of operations security, military deception, jamming and physical destruction supported by intelligence to deny information to, influence, degrade or destroy adversary C3 capabilities and to protect friendly C3 against such actions.' Timing is also regarded as an important part of any anti-C3 action since the idea is to disrupt hostile C3 systems when the enemy is relying on them.

The USSR largely excludes C3 systems from the inventory of defence equipment it is prepared to sell or donate to the developing world. The Soviets define their

Radio Electronic Combat strategy as 'the integration of EW with weapons of physical destruction to deny the enemy electronic control of its force'. Their plan, in the event of a conflict with Nato, is to destroy, by artillery and air attack, as large a portion of Nato as possible before the main battle. At the same time a large number of selected elements of Nato's command and control systems will be subjected to REC, leaving them confused and effectively neutralized. The remainder, if the plan succeeds, will be so weakened that they will be quickly overcome.

Clearly, the most sensitive part of a C3 system is not necessarily the equipment. Human know-how also needs to be protected. Furthermore, that know-how need not be technical. It can consist of knowledge, for example, of the location of a vital computer centre where intelligence information is stored. Or it might be knowledge of a particularly important link in a command and control chain.

One director of defence contracts at a large British C3 systems manufacturer, which is working on Star Wars command and control projects, put it like this: 'When you mention the word intelligence in defence circles, people can go very quiet. It is a very sensitive subject. For example a military establishment, as a whole, might decide that it is going to have secure computer systems installed. Knowing that they want to safeguard all their information might not be sensitive. But if there was a particular department that was installing a computer that was going to be used on intelligence, knowledge of that system and its use and application might well be very sensitive. At the Royal Aircraft Establishment there are about 26 computers of the same make. But the manufacturer knows the locations of only fourteen of them. Once you know of the existence of a computer you can get into the computer system. People can break the codes. Some employees can have genuine and correct access to computer systems, but if they then get into other databases on that computer which they shouldn't have access to, then there might be some concern.'

According to Royal Navy personnel, the UK has put particular effort into EW since the Falklands War in 1982. And the growing importance of the technology to the outcome of a future conflict has led to a tightening of the security measures surrounding EW work. One naval rating on security duty at the Royal Navy Equipment Exhibition in Portsmouth in 1987 revealed that he was working on EW and added: 'We are not only PV'd (positively vetted). It's constant vetting.'

Even a secretary could discover the weakest point of a C3i or EW system. As one defence industry observer put it: 'The magic in electronic warfare lies in knowing exactly where the enemy's weak point is.' A confidential report, leaked to the press, from the British computer company ICL makes it clear that even cleaners and catering staff can pick up sensitive or classified information by overhearing conversations or seeing sensitive documents. People can 'piece together the smallest scraps of information and create an overall picture of what we are doing', says the report. Despite controls and security, defence employees do discover information beyond their security clearance, often by accident. Usually this knowledge is no problem, if the person is loyal, stable and predictable.

Generally, the scientists who work on EW and C3i are oblivious to the secret war. They go home to their families after work without realizing the implications of their work and the potential dangers associated with the information that may be in their heads. They are mostly unaware that people have died in the peacetime pursuit of information relating to EW and command and control systems. The few who might ask themselves whether they could be of use to a foreign intelligence service probably conclude that they do not know enough. They assume, though they cannot be certain, that their knowledge does not provide the missing pieces to the jigsaw.

But the West knows what pieces are missing from the enemy's jigsaw and may be anxious, perhaps even paranoid, about ensuring that those pieces are not put in place.

The secret war is more important now than in the past when the relative simplicity of weaponry made it easier to calculate the odds in a possible conflict. Nowadays, it is the intangible technologies of C3 and EW which have the potential for being decisive. According to an article in the defence magazine *Navy International* in the summer of 1987, airborne EW of all types is now 'the most funded development and production area of the defence electronics industry'. In the US the heaviest funding 'is being poured into the electronic countermeasures sector, especially for active jamming systems'. The article continues: 'Some $7,800 million was allocated to the airborne EW market in 1985, more than double that of 1984, and although 1986 figures were not available at the time of writing it is certain that, despite Congress attempts to limit defence spending, the dollar value of the airborne EW programme will have increased again.'

Yet, even with enormous sums devoted to EW, uncertainties will always exist and it is these that provide the justification for the peacetime war. In the run up to a possible Third World War each side will plan large-scale electronic deceptions based on knowledge of the opponent's weaknesses. It means, in effect, that a hi-tech intelligence war must be fought today because, by the time hostilities break out, it will be too late to plan electronic countermeasures.

It is a conflict in which the protection of one's own

secrets is at least as important as discovering the enemy's weaknesses.

It would be comforting to believe that in peacetime the war is governed by a gentlemanly agreement which ensures nobody is killed. But there are few wars without casualties.

CHAPTER EIGHT

The Lady in the Lake

If there was any doubt that each case was being shrouded in a factual fog descending from officialdom then the proof, perhaps, lay in the most bizarre of the deaths. In the case of the 'lady in the lake', as it became known, the shortfall of forensic evidence was not only conspicuous, it was embarrassing. The search for the woman's murderer seemed to get little further than a dispute between the family and the authorities over whether indeed she was murdered.

Her death occurred on the night of Good Friday, 17 April 1987. At the time it seemed inconceivable that the lady in the lake would have known anything about C3i or EW.

It was an Easter bank holiday weekend and, for Thames Valley police, the beginning of what had seemed at first to be a routine murder investigation. It was an inquiry which would end inconclusively six months later, leaving behind a series of unanswered questions over not only the death but the direction of the subsequent investigation.

Early on the evening of Saturday, 18 April 1987, physiotherapist Marjorie Arnold, out walking her Alsatian dog, saw the body of a woman lying near the edge of Taplow Lake, a popular sailing and fishing spot close to the homes of celebrities such as Terry Wogan, Michael Parkinson, Ernie Wise and Frank Bough. It was also 150 yards from a manned police checkpoint on the

A4. Mrs Arnold stopped a motorist and together they pulled the body ashore. The dead woman seemed about 20-years-old and was wearing blue jeans, a red T-shirt and a quilted, sleeveless jacket. She had been gagged with a blue scarf, a noose was tied around her neck, her ankles were secured with a tow rope and her wrists were tied behind her back. She had been face down in eighteen inches of water for an indeterminate period.

Shani Warren's seemingly immaculate black Vauxhall Cavalier car was found parked in the lay-by adjoining the lake. It was later found to have a faulty gearbox which prevented it being driven away in first or second gear. Some of the car's contents were strewn around the grass, as if someone had been looking for something. Her handbag and some keys were missing.

Within a day of the body's discovery a high ranking police officer spoke of suicide. Six months later that view was officially confirmed. A pathologist employed by the Home Office declared that Shani had tried to strangle herself, gagged herself, bound her ankles, tied her hands behind her back and hopped in stiletto heels into the shallow water where she drowned. When police eventually closed down their incident room there were no material clues. And no murder suspects. If Shani was murdered, it was the perfect crime.

The night before her death Shani had gone out for dinner in Maidenhead with a boyfriend, Roger, and had seemed happy and relaxed. The two had arranged to meet again. Despite Shani's late night dinner with Roger she was up early that Good Friday morning and drove to her parents' house ten minutes away, in Stoke Poges. She had arranged to pick up an extension lead for her electric lawnmower from her father, Joe.

Her mother Elsie was away for the Easter weekend at the family flat in Bournemouth. Joe, who works from home, greeted Shani and gave her the lead, complete with a new plug. At the same time they confirmed arrangements for the following day, when Shani and her father were due to drive to Bournemouth to join her mother Elsie. As Shani, the youngest of three children, left her parents' house she asked her father who should do the driving to Bournemouth. He agreed to pick her up from her home. Shani blew him a kiss and said she would see him then.

It took Shani until the early afternoon to mow the front and back lawn at the house in Neville Close which she shared with two girlfriends. The three rented the house, then said to be worth about £70,000, from Shani's father for £130 a month. All three women pottered round that afternoon and Shani seemed to have no firm plans for the evening. At just after 6 p.m. one of Shani's friends, 26-year-old Fiona Oyston, was tidying her room upstairs when she looked out of the window and saw Shani loading the black sacks of grass cuttings into the boot of her 'A' registration car. She watched as the car drove off down the close. She did not notice Shani having any problems with the gearbox. Soon afterwards Elsie rang for Shani but it was too late. She would never get another chance.

Shani had been expected to take the grass clippings to the compost heap at her parents' house. 'My husband noticed she still hadn't arrived with the cuttings,' said Elsie. 'I remember thinking she must have gone to see a friend. It was a lovely sunny evening, it would have been a natural thing to do.'

Instead of arriving at her parents' house about two miles away she ended up seven miles in the opposite direction, at Taplow. At 6.50 p.m. a black car was seen in a lay-by just off the main A4 road at Taplow, five minutes from the centre of Maidenhead. Someone said the car appeared to be in difficulty. At about 1.30 a.m. on Easter Saturday morning a lorry driver, Donald Ward, pulled into the lay-by and saw the parked black Cavalier. 'I saw the car so I dipped my lights thinking it was a courting couple,' said Ward. 'I drove past it and reversed in behind it.' As Ward went to put the padlock on the back of his lorry he noticed the door of the Cavalier was open one or two inches. The next morning, when Ward returned to his trailer, he saw that the car was still there. He thought it was a little odd that the door of a relatively new car was still slightly open but it did not concern him and he drove away. Several hours later, at about 1.30 p.m. on Easter Saturday, the car was seen by horseriders who also noticed the door was slightly open. At about 6.30 p.m. on Saturday evening Marjorie Arnold spotted the body.

When police examined the Cavalier they found the driver's seat reclined, and a blank card in an envelope on the floor. Shani's lighter was on the passenger's seat. On the floor in front of the passenger's seat was her watch. Under the steering column was an Easter egg intended for Roger. Nearby in the undergrowth was Shani's credit card holder, her tow rope bag and a 'thank you' card to Roger for the dinner the previous evening. A policeman at Maidenhead said: 'Things were scattered as if someone had been looking for something.'

Dispersed loosely in the footwells of the driver's and passenger's seats were empty black sacks. The grass cuttings were nowhere to be found. It appeared that Shani, or someone else, had removed the sacks from the boot, emptied the grass cuttings, perhaps used the sacks for another purpose and left them in the front of the car. There was no reason for Shani to go to Taplow, in the opposite direction to her parents' house. Although the company that she worked for has a base nearby it is unlikely she would have wanted to visit the offices on a Good Friday evening.

Within hours of the body's discovery Thames Valley police, led by a Detective Superintendent Tony Miller, began a search of the area. Frogmen dragged the lake for clues, as a sailing club held their Easter Sunday regatta nearby. At first police speculated that she may have been unconscious when bound with rope and thrown into the lake. Although she had not been sexually assaulted, a Thames Valley police spokesman said there were injuries to the body, but it was not known how they were caused. The following day the tenor of the police investigation changed. The police began to suggest that Shani may have killed herself. Detective Superintendent Miller, said: 'For a person to commit suicide with their hands tied behind their back is not unknown. It would not be the first occasion I have come across it. The inquiries carried out so far have not given me any strong evidence to rule out the possibility of this being a murder or suicide.' He added that Shani had been depressed from time to time during the last few years, but that he was not attaching any importance to that. 'At times she had felt that life was not travelling the path she would necessarily want it to. However, it does not appear that there was an obsession.'

A police spokesman said: 'This is a most unusual case. It's 50/50 whether it's murder or suicide.' The initial police statements about 'injuries on the body' were forgotten and the newspapers spoke of 'no sign of injury or sexual assault'.

Unusually, forensic and medical evidence was scant. A Home Office pathologist who went to the lake and later carried out three post mortems on Shani said at first that it was too early to state the time of death. In fact the time was never established.

Possibly the body had been at the water's edge since the Friday evening, but it seems unlikely that it would have gone unnoticed for so long. Sailing enthusiasts and anglers use the lake and many people walk their dogs near the water's edge. Moreover the lay-by near the spot where the body was found lies adjacent to the busy A4. The lay-by, used frequently by motorists as a rest place and by lorry drivers as an overnight stop, is blocked off at one end, with a single entrance which also doubles as an exit.

The day after the police began suggesting suicide Shani's family began a long and ultimately unsuccessful campaign to persuade the authorities that suicide was, in their words, 'the last thing she would have done'.

Her 33-year-old brother Stephen Warren said: 'She was not the sort of girl who would have taken her own life. She was always extremely lively and extremely happy. She had lots of friends and was popular everywhere. We are a very strong family but we are gutted by Shani's death. She was not the sort to yield. But she might do as she was told if threatened with a gun or a knife.'

Stephen went on to describe his sister as intelligent and level-headed. 'Naturally like all ambitious people she got occasionally depressed, but not to the point of taking her own life. If it is suicide, and I can't accept that, then there must have been a third person involved. The logic of a situation where someone binds their own feet and then gags their mouth and ties their hands behind their back just escapes me.'

Fiona Oyston was bewildered by the death of her friend. 'I can't believe she would take her own life,' said Fiona. She also confirmed that Shani had no financial worries.

A note found in Shani's bedroom hardly reflected the mind of someone who was about to tie herself up and throw herself into a lake. 'Must book a good restaurant. Bottle of champagne. Bouquet of flowers for Mum.'

But the police and the Home Office pathologist gradually began to throw more weight behind the suicide theory. The fact that Shani had left no suicide note or led anyone to suspect she might be on the verge of killing herself became inconsequential. Detective Superintendent Miller said: 'The ropes binding her were tied in such a way that she could have done it herself.'

He added superfluously: 'This is a very bizarre case.'

Several days after the death, there was little new evidence emerging, except that tests had shown that Shani had been alive when she entered the water and that the cause of death was drowning. There was no suggestion that her death might have been linked to people who had died mysteriously in the defence industry. Indeed the idea was dismissed contemptuously by the authorities. Either they had no idea of the facts which were to emerge later, or, perhaps, they knew only too well. Why were the authorities so anxious to play down the possibility of murder? Surely there was nothing they wanted to hide?

Against a background of the family's vociferous rejections of the suicide theory, a noticeable lack of evidence, and growing disbelief among the public that Shani had killed herself, the police went on the BBC television programme *Crimewatch* and announced that they were treating the case as murder and to make an appeal for witnesses. Nick Ross, the show's presenter, introduced a Detective Superintendent John Childerley who, he said, was 'now' in charge of the case. Viewers were left to make the assumption that Detective Superintendent Tony Miller was now the former head of the Shani Warren investigation. Ross turned to Childerley and said: 'Let's get this clear. We are now talking about a murder inquiry, not a suicide.'

With unswerving conviction Childerley replied: 'We have always dealt with this as a murder inquiry from the very outset.'

Ross, who described Shani as 'young, blonde and photogenic', said that 'sometime' on that first day of the Easter Bank Holiday someone had murdered a young woman by drowning and left her in a lake just outside Maidenhead in Berkshire.

Detective Superintendent Childerley, having insisted

on *Crimewatch* that the police had always treated the case as murder, stated later in the programme: 'There is no injury to the body. There is no property that has been stolen. So there is no obvious murder.' Why was a ligature mark around Shani's neck not regarded as an injury, or the bruises on the back of her hand and on her thighs? Childerley's reference to the fact that no property had been stolen was also difficult to reconcile with previous police statements. Shani's handbag and car keys were missing. Did police have good reason to believe these had been taken but not stolen? If so, why were they keeping the reason secret? Clearly the authorities regarded the keys as important. Copies of the keyholder and keys were shown on *Crimewatch* and police made an appeal for the return of the originals. They did not make a similar appeal over the handbag. Neither did they say that the key-ring contained much more than Shani's car keys.

The police's attitude to the whole investigation was curious. It did not take a person of exceptional perception to notice they had no overwhelming desire to find a murderer. For example as soon as *Crimewatch* had finished, a reporter rang one of the numbers given and asked for further details of Shani's car. The reporter did not identify himself and, as far as the police were concerned, could have been an eyewitness. A policewoman answered the telephone politely, listened to the question, went away to find the answer and returned within two minutes with the information. After this there was an embarrassing silence while the reporter waited for the policewoman to ask why the information was being sought, who was seeking it and whether the caller had information about the murder. Nothing happened. So the reporter thanked her and put down the telephone. It was difficult to avoid the conclusion that, if the policewoman's approach was reflected elsewhere in the incident room, there was only an affectation of interest in investigating the death. Was it a case of a public display of resolve masking a secret policy of inertia?

Several months after the television appeal, no material eyewitnesses had come forward. This was despite the fact that Shani, according to Childerley was a 'very attractive young lady, a blonde 26-year-old driving a very smart car and the sort of person you would have looked at twice'. Police have no positive record of any sightings of Shani after 6 p.m. that Good Friday evening, even though thousands of cars had passed the black Vauxhall Cavalier parked just off the A4 on that first day of the Easter Bank Holiday. The lay-by was also clearly visible to passengers on trains on the main London to Bristol line. In fact more than 50 trains passed close to the lay-by between 6 p.m. and 9 p.m.

The BBC said that after its *Crimewatch* programme 100 viewers rang with possible leads. One was certain she saw Shani in the lay-by and also remembered seeing a well-dressed man and another car, possibly green, perhaps a BMW. Another woman had rung to say she had stopped in the lay-by on Good Friday evening, but would not say any more. Three hours after her call she telephoned Maidenhead police station, and the Leicester police station but refused to identify herself. Police were appealing to her to come forward again. 'She seemed too frightened to say anything,' said the BBC spokeswoman.

At a press conference about ten days after Shani's death, Childerley said the response from the *Crimewatch* programme had been disappointing. At the same conference he spoke of Shani's 'obsession' with the disease AIDS, saying: 'She was concerned about the current AIDS campaign and had told friends she had decided to give men a rest for a year.' He added: 'Shani tended to have one boyfriend at a time. Because of this pledge we think she had no current boyfriend when she was killed.' He did not know whether she had taken an

AIDS test, but the publicity campaign warning of the disease had apparently frightened her.

One might ask, at this stage, why the police were addressing an assembly of journalists on the subject of Shani's concern about AIDS. Were they suggesting in a round about way that she had killed herself because of a fear of AIDS? Or was the mention of AIDS a device to infer she was promiscuous and had therefore tied her wrists and legs together and hopped into the lake as part of a sexual experiment?

If the police remarks were supposed to clarify, their intention was well disguised. Childerley said: 'She was not promiscuous, but she was 26-years-old.' Several months later, in October 1987, when the murder incident room was closed, the police returned to the suicide theory. A Thames Valley police spokesman told journalists: 'There is not a shred of evidence to even suggest she was murdered.'

The investigation had taken on the shape of a tragicomedy, but with Shani's family as the real-life victims. Initially, police had considered murder a strong possibility. A day later they spoke of a possible suicide. A few days later they said it had been treated as a murder from the outset. And six months later they were deprecating the mere suggestion of a murder.

Mr and Mrs Warren looked to the inquest, at the end of October 1987, to resolve all the confusion. It must have been the final disappointment.

Shani Warren's inquest lasted several hours. It was supposed to be the culmination of a six month police investigation which had apparently involved 500 statements and scores of detectives. But the evidence produced at the inquest was hardly any more substantial than that which had been reported in the newspapers two days after the body was found. Most unusually, a video was shown of how Shani was bound, perhaps to show that the inquest was being entirely open.

The decision to show the video reportedly left Shani's family shaken. All except her brother Stephen left the court as the video showed Shani bound and gagged as she was pulled from the water. It began with a shot of Shani's car near the lake, with the seat in a reclining position. It moved on to show numerous stiletto heel marks around her car and at the edge of the water. And finally the cameras followed Shani's body into the mortuary. The Home Office pathologist, Dr Benjamin Davies, said he had decided early on that Shani had killed herself. Apart from two small bruises to each thigh and to the back of her left hand there were no marks on her body to suggest she had put up a struggle. The hand bonds had been loose and 'were not what you would use if you were trying to restrain an active young woman'.

There was no reiteration at the inquest of the police suggestion, made within hours of the body's discovery, that Shani may have been unconscious before being thrown into the water, even though the inquest heard that there was a ligature mark around her neck indicating that, before drowning, an attempt at strangulation had been made using the car jump lead. The inference at the inquest was that she had tried to strangle herself. Dr Davies said that he had carefully examined the body on three occasions and was convinced Shani could have applied the restraints around her hands and feet herself. He spoke of three previous cases where people had tried to strangle themselves and applied a gag before drowning in their baths. 'The more I hear, the more I believe this was suicide,' said Dr Davies. He added: 'But I am perfectly prepared to change my view.'

He said Shani's clothing was not torn, which therefore indicated that she had not been dragged through the barbed wire fence between the lake and her car. Her fingernails were undamaged and there were no marks on the body to suggest a struggle. Of the gag found wrapped around Shani's mouth and tied with a single knot at the side of her head, Dr Davies said: 'People do apply scarves so they do not cry out unintentionally and get saved.' And he said it was 'quite possible' that Shani had placed the black jump lead around her neck, complete with slip knot. He also believed she wound a length of car tow rope around her ankles before hopping into the lake. The red jump lead tying her wrists behind her back was loose enough for her to have wriggled free 'quite easily'. A former police inspector and knots expert agreed that it would have been possible for Shani to tie herself up. He said he had successfully managed to reconstruct the possible events. But he admitted that during the experiment his legs were not tied together. The inquest also heard that stiletto heel marks peppered the water's edge. No other footprints were found.

But Mrs Elsie Warren told the South Buckinghamshire coroner, John Roberts, that Shani had never shown any sign of contemplating death. She was a warm, affectionate girl who remained on friendly terms with her former boyfriends. Though she had vowed to give up men for a year because she was frightened of AIDS, she was happily planning her future. 'It was not a concern that she had AIDS,' said Mrs Warren. 'She just wanted to have a year off from men because of the possible danger.' She added that Shani had complained about her work as a secretary but had never talked of committing suicide. And, perhaps significantly, she explained:

'Shani would swim, but with her face up. She couldn't bear her face in the water, ever. There were twenty sleeping tablets at home that she could have used had she wanted to kill herself.'

And a friend of Shani said they had once spoken casually about suicide but she added: 'Shani said she would take an overdose if ever it got to that stage because all other methods were so ghastly.'

A consultant psychiatrist and medical director at the

Broadmoor high security hospital said he had examined diaries written by Shani over seven years along with other material and could find no evidence to suggest any mental disorder which could have precipitated suicide. 'The diaries she kept were of a very personal nature,' he said. 'If there was any serious abnormality I would expect to find it in those diaries. I found no trace of that. She appears to have been a well, socially integrated healthy young girl and not the sort of person one would expect to commit suicide.' He saw no reason to believe that Shani had committed suicide in such a bizarre and complicated way. It was 'very rare indeed' for someone to kill themselves and make it look like murder. He added that suicide was 'completely out of tune' with what he knew about Shani.

The only person believed to have seen a woman resembling Shani's description at the lakeside on Good Friday evening was nursing sister Mrs Sandra Organ from Kettering, Northamptonshire, who had responded to the police appeal on *Crimewatch*. She said her daughter had called 'hello' to a woman carrying dustbin liners. She said the woman turned, smiled and waved to them. Mrs Organ noticed a well-dressed man about 200 yards away. 'There was a man standing looking on, wearing a smart suit,' she said. 'He was in his late 30s or early 40s.' She said the man had been driving an expensive dark green car – probably a BMW. Police have been unable to trace the man or the car.

Mrs Marjorie Arnold, who found the body, had returned to the lake the following day to continue in a three day yachting event and saw a man 'half watching the police'.

Coroner John Roberts was faced with four main alternatives: suicide, accident, unlawful killing or an open verdict, which would suggest that there was insufficient evidence on which to give a ruling. Shani's family were in no doubt that she was murdered.

However, a coroner's court cannot indict anyone for a crime or bring in a verdict that suggests criminal guilt against any named person. These are matters to be decided by a court of law established for that purpose. The nearest verdict to murder is unlawful killing. But, in the end, the verdict of the coroner's inquest binds nobody. It is not even admissible as evidence in any subsequent proceedings.

Roberts made it clear he was not about to return a verdict of unlawful killing. He suggested he was persuaded against such a verdict by the police investigation. 'I am not satisfied on the evidence before me, particularly on the police inquiry, that there is evidence that I can properly bring in a verdict of unlawful killing. The evidence available to me does not fully or further disclose the means whereby the cause of death arose.' He returned an open verdict.

Why so little evidence of any consequence was unearthed by a six month police investigation is a mystery. It is a little unusual, perhaps even strange, that so little forensic evidence of any substance emerged.

Fortunately, during the investigation a sergeant in the Maidenhead police incident room had been willing to discuss the case, though he said he had to be careful what he said. It was his theory that Shani was meeting someone at the lay-by. It also appeared to him that someone had scattered her belongings while searching for something. But much of the evidence that might have been gained from tests of her clothing and body had been destroyed because she had been in the lake for so long before being spotted.

The police were particularly anxious to trace Shani's keys. She had carried a large bunch of keys. On it were keys for the house, the car, the burglar alarm. And a key to her office desk.

'We are very shocked and very surprised,' said the spokeswoman at Micro Scope, Shani Warren's employer. 'She always appeared cheerful and stable.' Shani had been with the computer company only a short time according to the spokeswoman, who volunteered the name of her previous employers. 'I believe they're something to do with oil,' said the spokeswoman. Shani had been a secretary to a divisional manager at Micro Scope. She was the equivalent of a personal assistant, agreed the spokeswoman. 'She was a very good secretary and a good organizer. Very efficient.'

Micro Scope specializes in the intelligent electronic systems which enable computers in different buildings or even in different countries to 'talk' to each other. According to a company press release dated 7 May 1987: 'Micro Scope have established a reputation as a leader in the supply of technology to the travel industry. The company's Micro Space system is installed for companies such as Intourist (Moscow) Limited, Panorama and Rainbow Mini holidays ...'

Micro Scope denied at the time that it was working on any defence projects and there was no reason to dispute this. But a series of events in the weeks following Shani's death are worth noting. On 27 April ICL announced that it had won a contract as part of the Nato command and control IUKADGE system. The following day a company called GEC Computers, part of the GEC group, announced that it had won a contract for Uniter, also a key element of the IUKADGE project, which in turn involves Marconi, British Telecom and Plessey Major Systems. And on 11 May 1987, GEC Computers announced that it was making its first acquisition for seven years. It was buying Micro Scope for about £16 million.

By September 1987 Micro Scope had been granted membership of the Defence Manufacturers Association. Micro Scope said at the time that membership would ensure that the company was given active support in supplying its networking expertise to the defence marketplace.

On the day of the acquisition, Rupert Soames, who was then general manager of GEC's Computers Applications Group, and son of the late Lord Soames, said his company had been collaborating with Micro Scope in the data communications market for about seven years. The two companies would be collaborating on the Uniter project for IUKADGE.

Micro Scope and GEC Computers are part of GPT Data Systems, a 'List X' contractor, which means that its staff are vetted to handle classified information. Soames made his views on staff security clear at a conference on security held in 1989. In his address he said: 'It is not enough just to change everybody's password when a trusted employee leaves; that ex-employee will meet all his or her colleagues down at the pub and will find out the new passwords over a pint of beer ...

'To my mind the worst threat from those who wish to spy or make money is in the potential to pervert members of staff, and we have to recognize that the types of people who are handling our information and our money have changed. Twenty years ago, the accounts department or document registry was run by loyal clerks who had been with the company or the department for thirty years and intended to stay there until retirement – the sort of people who were the incorruptible backbone of every organization.

'Today, the people who have the opportunity to steal are often highly mobile, ambitious, self confident and fiscally imprudent young people. How many of your programmers have been with you for more than five years? How many intend to be with you for another five years? How many of them want to drive sports cars? How many of them have small families and large mortgages? Such people have the combination of naivety and greed which makes them sitting targets for the skilled blackmailer.'

Of course, there was no evidence to link Shani Warren's work at Micro Scope with her drowning. But it was not inconceivable that Shani may have discovered something about the defence work of GEC Computers while it was collaborating with Micro Scope.

Nobody will ever know the true extent of Shani's knowledge, but in the area of C3 and EW, which could be decisive in a possible future war, any information may be regarded as highly sensitive. As defence specialist Antony Preston, in his book about a possible World War Three, points out: 'The magic of electronic warfare is knowing where the enemy's weak points lie.' And even a non-technical mind could grasp, for example, the names of key people in a project and if any of them had weaknesses which made them possible candidates for blackmail.

It seems an exaggeration to say that one person's knowledge could be much use to a potential enemy. But if that information is combined with what may be known already, to form a picture, the person assumes an importance that he or she may not realize.

In the peacetime war, both sides will do their utmost to obtain intelligence about the enemy and protect their own secrets. It is known that lives have been lost in peacetime in the acquisition of such intelligence. It is not known if lives are lost in the protection of such secrets.

CHAPTER NINE

Economical With the Truth

The independently-minded Dr Mary McHugh seemed on the point of resigning. She had shown a determination to treat an inquest as an inquiry, rather than a formality, and the novelty of her approach had led to criticism. A judge called her very stubborn and a 'mistress of discourtesy'.

What had been passed to her as an open and shut case that needed little investigation and even less publicity, slowly transformed into one of the biggest challenges of her career. She and her investigating officer found time after time that interested parties in the case, the Foreign Office, the dead man's employers, and even his widow, were telling the truth, but not all of it. In an attempt to ensure that witnesses could not hide behind the Official Secrets Act she sought to hear the evidence in secret in order to get at the full story. That bid was overturned after a High Court action and Dr McHugh, by her own admission, did not hear the full story.

She was presiding as coroner over an inquest at Croydon, Surrey, into the death of Dennis Skinner who had worked for the British computer company ICL at its office in Moscow. There he had met his future wife Lyudmilla Arianova. The inquest heard that both Dennis Skinner and his wife had 'longstanding' connections with the KGB, but that he was all the time reporting to British intelligence in London. He worked as the ICL representative in Moscow between 1968 and 1974 and after leaving the company was awarded the MBE for his services in Russia. He was in England between 1974 and 1976 during which time he trained as a banker and later went to work as the Midland Bank's Moscow representative.

Exactly how Dennis Skinner died will never be known. It emerged at the inquest, however, that in June 1983, two days before he died, he sent a note to the British embassy in Moscow in which he stated that his life was in danger and that he knew of a spy in the British security services. He pleaded to return home.

After the British embassy in Moscow received the note, Dennis was questioned in its secure room for three hours, but whether embassy staff offered him assistance is not clear. His sister Mrs Sheila Woodrow told the inquest: 'If the Foreign Office had got him out of there straight away he would still be alive.'

According to a report in the *Daily Mail*, whose reporter Stephen Lynas had spent many months investigating the case and had spoken at length to Lyudmilla, Dennis Skinner made a 'strange and frightening' telephone call from Moscow shortly before he died, when he warned his wife: 'We have a terrible enemy.' The *Daily Mail* named a man and said that during the phone call Skinner told his wife: 'He (the man) would do anything in the world to harm you.' The man, said the report, worked formerly at ICL and, at the time of the article, was head of the Eastern European operations of a computer and office systems supplier.

Three hours before he died Dennis made another telephone call, this time to the British embassy in Moscow. He apparently made it clear that he was going to be arrested by the Russians for espionage. And he asked enigmatically: 'Have you got the message?' Dennis's broken, barefoot body was found hundreds of feet beneath the open windows of his apartment, a tracksuit top over his head.

Dr McHugh directed the jury of six men and two women not to return a suicide verdict despite the fact that the Soviet authorities had said Dennis's flat was locked from the inside. 'This is a chilling story,' said Dr McHugh, 'all the more so when you consider that death should call upon him so short a time after the note was delivered (to the British embassy).'

She added that everything about Dennis Skinner pointed against suicide, including the medical evidence and the absence of a suicide note. She also dismissed the possibility of accidental death because of the difficulty in falling from the window and the way the tracksuit top had been pulled over his head. The jury, faced with the alternatives of an open verdict or one of unlawful killing, chose the latter.

Members of Parliament said the verdict had left the case open and, with ill-founded optimism, urged the authorities to investigate further.

The pressure that was brought to bear on the coroner in the Dennis Skinner case has implications for other coroners and other inquests. 'I can't say where the pressure is coming from,' Dr McHugh told the *Daily Mail* at the time of the inquest in 1984. 'Please don't ask. I will lose my job. So much pressure has been put on me from all quarters.' If this pressure had led either to a restriction on the amount and nature of information disclosed, or had discouraged Dr McHugh from pursuing certain lines of questioning, what hope was there that the inquests on Vimal Dajibhai, Arshad Sharif, Dr John Brittan, Peter Peapell and the others would get to the truth?

Forensic science could have provided critical evidence in some, if not all, of the cases. After all, the examination of microscopic evidence has been credited for decades with solving mysteries. Yet, in the investigations into the deaths of the defence employees, forensic scientists proved as useful as tribal rain dancers. It was particularly unfortunate, perhaps, that the times of death proved elusive. Such detail often provides critical answers in a police investigation, if answers are being sought with any degree of diligence. It was also unfortunate perhaps that there was no evidence from eyewitnesses.

Perhaps the shortfall in evidence accounted for the number of open verdicts where the coroner could not decide whether the deceased had committed suicide, had died accidentally or had been unlawfully killed. The Hampshire coroner, for example, recording an open verdict on David Sands, said: 'The evidence does not specifically reveal the facts of which any other verdict could be brought.'

And another coroner, John Roberts, said: 'I am not satisfied on the evidence before me, particularly on the police inquiry, that there is evidence that I can properly bring in a verdict of unlawful killing. The evidence available to me does not fully or further disclose the means whereby the cause of death arose.' When, as in Jonathan Wash's case, a post mortem in a foreign country had discovered suspicious injuries which were then mentioned in a report, the UK authorities failed, deliberately or because of incompetence, to list all of them in the translation.

Even in other cases where suicide or accidental death verdicts were returned, there was no conclusive evidence. Richard Pugh, a 26-year-old defence telecommunications expert who was found dead at his flat in Loughton, Essex on Wednesday, 14 January 1987, was assumed to have tied himself almost from head to foot with rope and wrapped it four times around his neck before or after placing a plastic bag over his head. Mark Wisner was also assumed to have died accidentally, having wrapped cling film around his face and having put his head in a plastic bag, apparently in an attempt to heighten sexual gratification. Dr Brittan and Robert Wilson were assumed to have died accidentally from carbon monoxide poisoning because they apparently forgot to open the garage doors when the engine was running.

In contrast to the lack of hard factual evidence, officials made a profusion of comments to journalists on a non-attributable basis, assuring them that the victim was either suicidal, depressed, suffering severe stress or had a history of medical, marital or sexual problems.

The comments from official spokespeople had the effect of confusing, deceiving or deterring journalists' inquiries. It was also made particularly clear that journalistic interest in the cases of the defence employees was not welcome. At its most innocuous level this meant a coroner refusing a police request to supply the dates of two inquests that had taken place some months earlier. His reason was that he knew the dates would be divulged to the press. At a more worrying level, there were anonymous threatening telephone calls.

There are some who feel that the disposition to silence on the part of the authorities is intuitive, that there is a natural disinclination among official information officers to impart information. There are others who feel that when there is a reason for believing disinformation is being applied systematically, there might be something, something serious perhaps, which is worth concealing. There are still others who argue that dissemination of misleading information can be defended where, for example, there are issues involved which may in some way impinge upon the defence of the realm.

For example, against the dictionary definition of 'junior' it is easy to verify the claim by the authorities that Arshad Sharif was a 'relatively junior programmer'. However, when the term is considered alongside the importance of the project he was working on, his special treatment at Marconi, his degree of responsibility, his university background, his subsequent work on missile systems, and the extreme sensitivity of EW in view of its direct association with intelligence, it was possible only to conclude that the use of the term 'junior' was intended to be misleading.

The outline of the facts surrounding Arshad's death became further blurred by the story that he had been having an affair in Bristol. When Mr Sharif, of his own volition, telephoned the Bristol police to ask where this story of his son's affair had originated, he was surprised to hear the source of the rumour given as a television reporter, when the fact of the matter was that the police themselves had been feeding reporters the story in the form of 'off the record' guidance. Mr Sharif, despite his doubts over the way the official investigation into his son's death had been handled, clearly continued to hold a deep-rooted respect for the police. They had, he said, 'shown a willingness to help'. He had therefore asked how to deal with all the enquiries from reporters. 'They said: "Don't tell them anything," ' said Mr Sharif. 'I said I had nothing to tell. Whatever story I had, I had told them.'

Information which fell short of the truth was also given out to newspapers investigating the case of Peter Peapell, who was found dead underneath his car inside his closed garage. Initial reports of his death had been uncoloured. Many had pointed out that 'police officers had been unable to reconstruct how Peter could have got underneath his car with the garage door closed or have closed it behind him when already underneath the car'.

Later, when Peter's death was discussed in the light of other bizarre incidents, a news agency report was sent to many newspapers which began: 'Colleagues of scientist Peter Peapell have ruled out a link with the defence deaths mystery centred on the Marconi electronics company.' The report continued: 'A colleague who worked closely with Mr Peapell said he could not believe the deaths were connected. The man, who did not want to be named, said: "None of his work had anything to do with electronics or computers. I think you could dig and dig but you would never find a link between him and Marconi or any of these men." '

The story and the remarks of the unnamed colleagues were bewildering. Far from having nothing to do with computers or electronics, Peter had written a book on computers. He had also published a technical paper on acoustic emissions in the journal *The Metallurgist and Materials Technologist*.

In fact the paper was written while Peter was a senior lecturer at the Royal Military College of Science and relates primarily to electronics and computers. On page one of the paper Peter refers to a computer controller, signal processing, oscilloscopes, energy and amplitude analysers and acoustic emission preamplifiers. On page three he continues: 'The frequency content of the signal is determined by ... passing it to a Tektronix 4051 table-top computer for analysis, utilizing built-in firmware and Fourier transforms. A reasonably comprehensive computer program enables all or any part of the captured signal to be plotted out and analyzed for frequency content in an attempt to characterize the signal source mechanism.'

At David Sands's inquest, although the seniority of his title was made clear, the nature of his work was discussed only in a circumlocutory manner. One newspaper quoted his company as saying that he had been involved in 'technical work'. Another said he had been dedicated to his work on 'communications, including satellites'. These descriptions were not incorrect but told only part of the story. Several months later a former senior employee at Marconi, who had left the company early in 1987 to work for another defence contractor, revealed that David had been involved in evaluating various command and control systems in other countries as part of his work on ADCIS. The former employee made a point of saying that David had written a paper on a C3 project which had been published about six months before his death. This turned out to be David's paper outlining his work on the ADCIS project. It was one of 64 papers published in the proceedings of a conference on military computers, and was in a subsection which specifically mentioned EW and which contained another paper on C3 by the superintendent of C3 at RARDE.

David Greenhalgh's fall from a bridge onto a main line railway was shrouded in secrecy and disinformation. The British Transport Police admitted that they had been instructed to make no mention to the press of David's name, address or occupation. One constable at the station which had investigated David's fall claimed that this news clampdown had followed a visit from Special Branch. When the news finally leaked out that David had worked at ICL Defence Systems, several journalists were told that he had been found with a slashed wrist and this had subsequently appeared in national newspapers. Later it emerged that this was untrue. No reason for his jump has ever been given and David's friends say he cannot remember exactly how or why it happened. As with other cases, the nature of David's job was referred to in abstruse or deceptive terms by the authorities. Journalists were told he was a salesman and this was the description which appeared in the newspapers. One quality daily newspaper even claimed: 'An unofficial police source said Mr Greenhalgh had been suffering from depression.' There was no evidence of this, say David's friends. And, far from being merely a salesman, he was a Nato contracts manager, in charge of a small team. Although not particularly technically qualified, his friends say he had been involved at a senior level with UKAIR and ADCIS.

In the case of System X designer Jonathan Wash who

fell from a hotel window in Abidjan on the Ivory Coast while working for British Telecom, there was a rumour that he had been taking drugs. It turned out that the rumour came from official sources and, according to his father John, its only foundation in fact was that Jonathan had been taking codeine for a sore throat. The suggestions that he was under stress and that his work had gone to pieces needed to be put into the context of the fear he had expressed for his life two days before his death and his secret booking of an early flight back to the UK. Furthermore the post mortem report by the Ivory Coast doctor, Dr Georges-Claude La Fontant, stated that Jonathan may have been the victim of an assault. The post mortem showed cuts to his forehead, eyeball, chin and hand. Six human scratch marks were also found on his chest. 'Given the severity and location of his wounds, the hypothesis of self inflicted injury or a fall is hard to accept. I thought it more a matter of assault, although I cannot confirm this categorically,' said the doctor. However, two post mortems in Britain conducted by the authorities contradicted these findings and found the injuries consistent with a fall.

In the Shani Warren case, the information emanating from official sources was particularly puzzling, with the police espousing first murder, then suicide, then murder, then suicide again. The relevancy of a police press conference which announced that Shani had a fear of the disease AIDS was unfathomable. Yet, surprisingly perhaps, only the *News of the World* found the Shani Warren suicide theory sufficiently bizarre to warrant detailed examination. It sent a reporter, Morven Kinlay, to the lake as part of a reconstruction. Morven was the same age and shape as Shani and wore similar jeans, a sleeveless jacket and stiletto heeled shoes. Accompanied by two colleagues as eyewitnesses she attempted, step by step, to bind and gag herself, tie a jump lead around her throat, bind her ankles, tie her hands behind her back and hop into the water. 'I tried to put my legs and feet through my arms to leave my hands tied behind me. It was physically impossible with both feet bound and wearing high heeled shoes,' said Morven. 'Even pulling up my knees as far as possible my arms were just not long enough. It would be difficult for a supple athlete with stilettos ... After being helped to get my hands behind my back I managed with great difficulty to lever myself to my feet. Then I tried to hop into the water. Several times I stumbled as my heels stuck in the ground and was unable to get back on my feet without help. I stood up to my knees in the murky water. Then, with a deep breath I plunged face down into the lake. Despite my colleagues being on hand to haul me out my immediate reaction was panic. As they pulled me clear I felt sure that anyone planning to kill herself in such a way would have to be deranged.'

The *News of the World* reconstruction unearthed one particularly pertinent piece of information. As Morven went down to the water's edge she found her stiletto heels left distinct prints in the earth, but her colleagues' shoes left no visible prints.

The coroner, in returning an open verdict, had taken into account the evidence that only Shani's footprints were found. Morven's colleagues, by doing nothing more complicated and scientific than walking by the lakeside had discovered potentially significant new evidence. Can we really believe that such a discovery was beyond forensic science?

The growing concern over the possibility of a link between the number of bizarre deaths and coincidences involving defence workers during the early months of 1987 was, in effect, gradually depressurized by three events: an inquest on a Marconi worker who had apparently committed suicide by way of a drugs overdose, a front page story in the now-defunct *Sunday Today*, attributing all the deaths to stress at work, and the timely discovery of Avtar Singh-Gida in Paris. If anyone felt that some of the deaths were linked and that there was an element of planning in the release of official information with the purpose of softening demands for a public inquiry, the timing of the events of those eight weeks of 1987 might have added some substance to their suspicions.

On 5 March 1987 *Computer News* broke the story of the mysterious deaths of Vimal and Arshad. On 30 March came the death of David Sands, when his car exploded into a fireball. On 10 April David Greenhalgh fell from a bridge and Stuart Gooding died mysteriously. By this time concern had reached a peak and MPs were asking a number of questions in the House of Commons. On the night of 17-18 April Shani Warren died, though there was no idea at the time that Shani's company Micro Scope had any connection with the employers of the defence scientists. Then came the stories which diffused public and parliamentary interest. The Sunday papers which first reported Shani's death also carried a short story on the inside pages of an inquest which had returned a verdict of suicide on a 46-year-old Marconi worker, Victor Moore, who had taken a drugs overdose. Although there was no suicide note it was the most conventional of all the deaths. And while the other inquests had been virtually destitute of hard evidence, Victor Moore's hearing was a factual oasis. His wife Margaret suggested that Victor had been suicidal. 'He did not agree with some of the things he was asked to do at Marconi,' said Margaret. Victor became unwell and sought early retirement. But he was turned down and after a long period of sick leave he was given three months notice. Shortly before the notice was due to expire he was found dead. It is most unlikely that Victor's death was linked to the others, but the timing of the inquest, whether deliberate or not, had the effect of diluting concern. At about the same time the *Sunday*

Today which had carried a front page leading article on 19 April stating that MI5 was investigating the deaths, carried in its next edition on 26 April another front page article declaring that 'Britain's top scientists are being driven to suicide because of unbearable work pressures'. Demands for a public inquiry were substituted unobtrusively with requests for Britain to stop working its scientists too hard. One MP had previously said publicly: 'It seems to be stretching credibility too far to say all these are isolated incidents. It is becoming more and more like a TV thriller.'

On 29 April, three days after the *Sunday Today* story, the same MP wrote to the defence procurement minister Lord Trefgarne and said: 'In some cases the classified nature of the work makes it difficult for scientists and technicians to talk to others about the problems they are experiencing. Some sort of counselling and support system might well reduce this problem.'

By early May 1987 the public clamour for answers to the deaths had ceased. Suddenly everything had been explained by the stress theory. David Sands's inquest in the third week of May was to produce an open verdict which threatened to reopen the controversy. But something happened two days before the inquest. A local paper carried the headline: 'We Find Missing Derby Scientist.' Acting on a tip-off from police the local paper found Avtar Singh-Gida working in a boutique in the red light district of Paris. His first reaction was to show anxiety that he might come to the attention of the UK authorities, and he apparently denied being the man the paper was seeking. But this did not destroy the story. It quoted the police as saying: 'We are confident we have got the right man.' Attention was subsequently distracted away from David Sands's inquest and onto a press conference to mark Avtar's return. During that conference he said, among other things: 'I didn't plan to disappear. I was just in a state of confusion. It's all a bit hazy now.' The line of questioning, however, focused on the fact that he had wasted police time. Nobody questioned how long the police had known of Avtar's whereabouts, despite the fact that in March the assistant chief constable of Avon and Somerset Police had said on television: 'As I see the issues now, we here will close the files on Mr Sharif and Mr Dajibhai and I feel that my colleagues in Derbyshire may be doing that in a few months time in relation to their case as well.'

In the wake of the publicity over Avtar being reunited with his wife, the many unanswered questions over David Sands's death were quickly forgotten. Several months later one Thames Television documentary editor summed up his feelings on the mysterious deaths with the words: 'That chap from Derby came back, didn't he.' To date, no British television company has transmitted a networked documentary investigation into the deaths, despite detailed programmes being broadcast in Australia, the USA, and Canada.

It is argued quietly in some circles of government that disinformation is a legitimate weapon in a war. Might it not also be regarded as a necessary tool in the peacetime war? The nature of the peacetime war is such that secrets must be protected and intelligence on potential enemies collected voraciously, well in advance of any possible conflict. By the time war breaks out, it might be too late.

CHAPTER TEN

Accident, Suicide or Murder?

Even taking into account the bizarre nature of the deaths, the lack of information about the circumstances surrounding them, the dubiousness of officially disseminated information, the lack of witnesses and suicide notes and other similarities, it remains perfectly possible that they were straightforward suicides and accidents connected by nothing more than coincidence.

Perhaps Arshad Sharif really did kill himself and had neglected to say why, despite the fact that he had recorded a message on a cassette and tape recorder purchased only hours earlier. The police may have been right in declaring unofficially that Arshad had been having an affair with a married woman in Bristol. He may have committed suicide because of the shame it would have brought on his family if the affair had been discovered. Perhaps Arshad considered that suicide, which is a religious crime under the Muslim faith, was less damaging to the reputation of his family than the revelation that he was having an affair. Although the police admitted that they had never known someone kill themselves in such a way, perhaps Arshad was punishing himself for some unknown reason. Perhaps there was no significance in the fact that the police suggested that the Sharif family should stay away from the inquest. There was no evidence that Arshad's death was linked to his avid interest in the simulation of technological developments or the fact that he was working in an area of signals technology which is, perhaps, the most sensitive in defence technology, an area involving stealth, EW and intelligence gathering.

Vimal Dajibhai, for reasons unknown, could have gone to Bristol unexpectedly to meet someone and, also for reasons unknown, jumped from a bridge. His reasons for going could have been entirely unrelated to his work. It may have been coincidental that both he and Arshad were Asian computer programmers who had worked at Marconi Underwater Systems and who had both driven from their London area homes to commit suicide within three months of each other more than 100 miles away in Bristol. There was no obvious significance in Vimal having known Avtar Singh-Gida, or in the fact that Vimal's house was only a few minutes drive from Arshad's main place of work. Perhaps it was also irrelevant that Vimal was working on the world's most advanced lightweight torpedo and was involved, in particular, with the simulation of signals technologies related to stealth and EW. Conceivably, the suspicions of the Dajibhai and Sharif families which prompted them, separately, to launch private investigations immediately after the deaths, were unfounded.

David Sands showed no signs of trying to avoid the derelict Little Chef café when he did a U-turn on a dual carriageway and crashed into it at high speed. The fact that there were two extra cans of petrol in the boot and that David was burned beyond recognition in the crash could have been irrelevant. Perhaps he was depressed about his father's chronic heart condition and did not leave a suicide note because the balance of his mind was disturbed. It may also have been irrelevant that he had just finished a major contract, had returned from holiday, was working for a sister company of Marconi and was working on the simulation of signals technologies and a secret application directly related to stealth, EW and intelligence gathering.

When Anthony Godley disappeared from the married quarters at the Royal Military College of Science there were reports that he was having an affair with a woman in the village. The fact that he never returned, by the 1987 deadline, to collect a large sum of money left to him in his father's estate, was not evidence that he was dead. His area of work was unknown and the Royal Military College of Science's concentrated expertise in the area of signals technology, stealth and EW may be irrelevant.

Perhaps Avtar Singh-Gida disappeared because of pressure of work. Or perhaps he was having marital problems even though he had bought his wife an anniversary present shortly before he went missing. His work for the Ministry of Defence in the field of signals technology almost certainly had nothing to do with his decision to leave the UK.

Perhaps Dr Brittan, the highly talented RARDE computer simulation expert and former Royal Military College of Science lecturer, had been genuinely remiss when he closed the side door of the garage and forgot to open the main door before starting his car engine on a particularly cold morning. After all, his son had suggested that he start the car to warm it up. Perhaps Dr Brittan was overcome so quickly by carbon monoxide that he did not have time to switch off the engine or open the car door and make towards the garage door. Or perhaps because of a persistent throat problem he decided to kill himself. There was no evidence that the mystery virus, which became a problem when he returned from the US, was relevant to his death. And there was no suggestion of a link between his death and the fact that the part of RARDE in which he worked was involved in signals technologies, stealth, EW and intelligence gathering.

Perhaps there was no connection between Dr Brittan and Peter Peapell although they had both worked at the Royal Military College of Science at the same time and had both died within a month of each other. It may have been due to nothing more than coincidence that both had recently returned from lecturing trips to the US and had both died of carbon monoxide poisoning. Peter Peapell had returned from a one year appointment at America's foremost naval establishment. Perhaps he used his exceptional powers of scientific understanding to devise a way nobody had thought of to close his garage door from the inside and end up in the position in which he was found, lying on his back under the car. Perhaps there was no connection in the fact that Peter's expertise was unparalleled anywhere at the Royal Military College of Science and that he was a simulation expert in an area directly related to stealth and electronic warfare.

Stuart Gooding could have lost concentration for some unknown reason when he wandered into the wrong lane of a quiet road in Cyprus and hit a lorry coming in the opposite direction. Such tragedies do occur and if he had not worked at the Royal Military College of Science the accident might have been of no wider interest. The fact that he was described as a student, then as an undergraduate and eventually as a scientific officer at a place of work which was not mentioned at the inquest may have been due to the usual reticence of the authorities. It must have been coincidental that David Greenhalgh fell from a bridge on the day that Stuart died and that Cyprus is a UK outpost for GCHQ, and EW related operations.

Although the reason for Michael Baker's BMW going across the central reservation of a dual carriageway was never established, perhaps he lost concentration for some reason while on his way to go fishing, and had the hideous misfortune to be the only one in his car to suffer a fatal injury. It was most unlikely that his death was linked to any of the others or that there was anything strange in the accident. All the peripheral issues, such as Michael's reluctance to go on that car journey, his part-time job in the SAS and his work on System X and digital communications could have been irrelevancies. It must have been coincidental that he was a signals expert.

Professor Keith Bowden could also have lost concentration, causing his BMW to cross the central reservation of a dual carriageway and go down a railway embankment in 1982. His wife Hilary said: 'No, he did not commit suicide. It is the last thing he would do. I just don't think that people commit suicide that way.' Hilary's grief turned to suspicion when the family solicitor said her husband's death involved foul play. An accident investigator hired by her solicitor says someone removed the new tyres on the car at some point before the crash and replaced them with worn out retreads. At the inquest the accident report was not brought up but Hilary has kept the wheels and tyres from her husband's wrecked car. The police claimed he had been drinking but Hilary said: 'We were very shocked by that because I had been told by a doctor that he had not been drinking, by a policeman that he had not been drinking and by the man who was with him all evening that he hadn't been drinking. I've only that information to go on. I've no other ways of knowing whether he did or didn't drink.' Although Hilary maintains doubts about her husband's death she finds the conspiracy theory implausible. 'If your husband commits suicide, it's the most hurtful thing in the world. There can't be anything worse, the guilt you feel is awful. So it's natural to reach for another explanation. But I don't believe in the conspiracy theory. I think it's a little far fetched.' It may be nothing more than coincidence that, like most of those who had died in unusual circumstances, Keith Bowden's work involved sophisticated, military computer simulations.

After Mark Wisner's death it was discovered that he was a transvestite, so perhaps he really was indulging in a sexual experiment which went fatally wrong. He was, after all, found with nine feet of cling film around his head with a hole cut out for his mouth, a bag tied around his neck with a tube of glue inside. There were suggestions that such an experiment was not uncommon among people wishing to achieve enhanced sexual satisfaction by restricting the oxygen supply to the brain. The long, unaccounted for period just before his death, the fact that he was not the only scientist to die in such bizarre circumstances and the timing of his death exactly a week after the bizarre drowning of Shani Warren might have been of no significance. It could also have been of no relevance that the Ministry of Defence's Aeroplane and Aircraft Experimental Establishment where he worked had unique EW testing equipment and was involved closely in the simulation of stealth technologies.

Richard Pugh could have been accidentally asphyxiated when he tied himself virtually from head to toe in rope. Like Mark Wisner it could have been a sexual experiment which went fatally wrong. The fact that, according to the police, very little evidence came out at the inquest could have been a genuine attempt to spare the family the embarrassment of publicity. It may have been coincidental that a company he had left recently was involved in digital networks and exchanges, C3i for Nato and associated EW equipment.

John Whiteman, a 31-year-old software engineer at British Aerospace, probably drowned himself in his bath because the stress of his job had made life intolerable.

He had worked all his professional life at British Aerospace's military aircraft establishment at Warton, Lancashire, and eventually became the leader of a team which was working on software for the European Fighter Aircraft, currently being developed by Britain, Germany, Italy and Spain. A software problem on the project had preoccupied John for nearly a year and he was taking mild sleeping tablets to ease the stress. His

36-year-old widow Dorothea said: 'He had been asked to make two software systems compatible – the British software system that he had previously worked on and also a German software system. He thought that it was an impossible task. He didn't think the two systems could ever be compatible.'

Dorothea found John lying face up in the bath. At the time she had no reason to suspect anything other than suicide. 'When the bathroom door was knocked down there was an empty bottle of the sleeping tablets that had been prescribed the night before, with the top off, just as if he had opened them up, swallowed them and thrown the bottle down on the floor. There were two bottles of whisky that had been full, one of them was lying empty on the floor and the other, with about an inch left of whisky, was lying on the side of the bath.' It seemed to Dorothea that John had swallowed all the tablets and had consumed nearly two bottles of whisky. In fact, according to a pathologist's report, he had only a small amount of alcohol in his blood – nothing like the quantity missing from the bottles. Moreover, the inquest heard that no trace of drugs was found in John's body.

'I thought this was very odd,' said Dorothea. 'At the inquest I asked questions like: "How would he be able to drown if he was not unconscious. Would he be able to drown himself consciously in a bath? The pathologist said he didn't think it would be possible. No matter what the state of mind is, the body would react to water entering the lungs and there would be an involuntary reaction. But the coroner did not really like this sort of question. He kept on trying to gloss over it." Also curious is the fact that, in the 90 minutes between the time that Dorothea last saw him alive and the time she found his body, John had reassembled a racing bike which had been packed away for the winter. 'He'd got some bills out to pay and his cheque book was open and a cheque was partly written. He'd also hidden a birthday card that my father had left for me. It seems as if something had disturbed him.'

With no suicide note, or any sign that John wanted to take his own life, the coroner returned an open verdict, leaving questions unanswered. Had John, for example, sought to cover up a suicide? Dorothea does not think so. 'I have been asked whether anyone was seen approaching the house. But I live next door to a sub post office and there are people coming and going and parking outside my house all day. It would never be noticed if there was a visitor.' British Aerospace told Australia's *60 Minutes* programme that the death was 'one of the mysteries of the world'. It may be nothing more than coincidence that the Warton site is being used by British Aerospace to coordinate the company's C3i programme.

Perhaps British Telecom employee Jonathan Wash jumped out of a hotel window because he was under stress because of his girlfriend's pregnancy. After all, his team leader at British Telecom had suggested it was suicide, and the UK authorities, by their reluctance to hold post mortems requested by the family and forgetting to mention all the injuries on the body, clearly felt that the death was not suspicious. If Jonathan was murdered, as his family insist, the death may have had nothing to do with the other scientists. It may have been coincidence that he had expressed a fear for his life and had died within hours of taking a British Telecom official into his confidence. The scratched messages on the wall of a room where his belongings were found may never be explained. There was no evidence that he was directly involved in defence work. Indeed his family believe his death may be linked to the fact that he knew, and was prepared to expose, corruption. It may have been nothing more than coincidence that he was a digital communications expert working on a project with profound military implications and had worked at both

GEC Telecommunications and British Telecom's Martlesham Heath research establishment, which is involved closely with signals intelligence and has close ties with GCHQ.

Although Robert Wilson shot himself accidentally the day after returning secret documents to Marconi, there was no evidence to suggest the two events were linked. Indeed a year later, when he was found dead from carbon monoxide poisoning, there was no reason to believe there were any suspicious circumstances. The coroner seemed to believe it was accidental and issued a warning about the dangers of running a car engine with the garage doors shut. It was perhaps coincidental that the part of Marconi in which he worked was deeply involved in signals technology and had close links with GCHQ.

Crime was quickly ruled out in the case of Gerard Darlow, a Marconi worker whose body was discovered on a bed in his second floor flat, with a knife wound in the chest and the front door ajar. Gerard's father, a serving RAF officer, explained that his son was having treatment for a 'slight manifestation of schizophrenia'. He was receiving drug treatment after a recent relapse, the inquest heard. The coroner seemed convinced that Gerard had stabbed himself to death and ruled that it was suicide. It may have been coincidental that Gerard's father told the inquest his son had deliberately stepped in front of a lorry in July the previous year, the same month that Robert Wilson accidentally shot himself.

The death of Marconi scientist Victor Moore was obviously a case of suicide, though he left no suicide note. There was clear evidence of stress at work and of psychological problems. His positive vetting and the sensitivity of his design work, which related directly to stealth and EW were, undoubtedly, irrelevancies. The involvement, again, of GCHQ in his work may have been a coincidence.

It is possible, even likely, that Trevor Knight died as a result of a combination of work and domestic pressures. Although on the day before he died he had telephoned his mother Rachael twice, and had sounded quite happy, saying he would see her over the weekend, the coroner, Dr Arnold Mendoza, made it fairly clear that Trevor had intended to take his own life. The contents of three notes found on a kitchen table which, said Dr Mendoza, gave 'a clear indication of his intention', were not disclosed, presumably to spare his family, close friends and employer any embarrassment. The fact that he had worked at Marconi Underwater Systems at Croxley Green, where Vimal Dajibhai had worked, and had later transferred to Marconi Defence Systems at Stanmore, where Arshad Sharif had worked, and which was deeply involved in a number of highly sensitive EW and stealth contracts involving GCHQ, may be immaterial. There is indeed a striking similarity with many other cases in that he had been involved in very sophisticated military simulations but there is no evidence linking this to his death.

Police investigating Shani Warren's death were uncertain whether she had been murdered or had taken her own life, but Benjamin Davies, a Home Office pathologist, did not hesitate to make clear his view that she committed suicide. Perhaps, for an unknown reason, she had wanted her death to look like a murder, though the absence of eyewitnesses remains as one of the most puzzling characteristics of the case. The lake is a local beauty spot, overlooking a main road and a main railway line. Moreover, she apparently died on a busy bank holiday weekend evening. Did nobody notice her tying a gag around her head, a noose around her neck, binding her hands behind her back, securing her ankles with a tow rope and hopping in her stiletto heels into eighteen inches of water? Shani's family believe she was murdered but they feel certain her death is not part of any larger conspiracy. Her company's involvement with a part of GEC which is deeply committed to C3 systems probably has no bearing on her death.

The fact that Jack Wolfenden and Ernest Brockway both worked at GCHQ and died in unusual circumstances within a few months of each other, prompted speculation that the cases may have been linked but this was strongly denied by the authorities. Some people, in particular, found it difficult to dismiss the fact that two deaths had coincided with a security purge at GCHQ in the months following the arrest on espionage charges of GCHQ signals specialist Geoffrey Prime. Jack, however, may have deliberately crashed his aircraft because he was under stress at work and was upset about his divorce settlement. His work in a highly classified EW related field and the fact that, like Peter Peapell and John Brittan, he apparently killed himself shortly after returning from work trips abroad, may not be relevant. Jack's colleague Ernest Brockway, who was found hanged, may have been unable to cope with his promotion at work. An inquest had been told that he had had to make new friends in a different department. His unexplained absence from work shortly before his death, the remarkable speed with which the police investigation was completed and the implications of his personal problems on the extreme sensitivity of his work, which related to EW, may add to the mystery but cannot be read as evidence of foul play.

GCHQ signals expert George Franks died as a result of a heart attack, according to the coroner and the police. The fact that some journalists had been convinced he had committed suicide by hanging may have been indicative, not of a conspiracy, but of the difficulty in obtaining accurate information in the days after the death. Even the Prime Minister Margaret Thatcher had been misinformed when she referred in the House of Commons to a suicide note. George's failure to summon medical help when he felt a heart attack coming on was, according to the pathologist, most unusual. Why the time of death could not be established was also a mystery. These anomalies, however, do not amount to evidence of foul play. Although there were suspicions that his death was, in some way, linked to his highly classified signals intelligence work at GCHQ, a connection was never firmly established.

Stephen Drinkwater, another GCHQ employee, may have died when a sexual experiment went wrong. Some people may point to the fact that restricting a person's oxygen supply by putting a plastic bag over his head and tightening it around the neck, is an established interrogation technique. A few weeks before Stephen's death, for example, it was reported in the national press that two people in Birmingham had made formal complaints against the police, claiming they had been tortured by having black plastic bags put over their heads. In Stephen's case, however, no evidence of foul play emerged at the inquest and the coroner seemed convinced it was a tragic accident. It may be nothing more than coincidence that Stephen worked in the one section of GCHQ that was allowed to take print-outs of signals intelligence information.

The coroner inquiring into Stephen Oke's death said there was no evidence of suicide but speculated that Stephen may have died accidentally after tying his hands together and hanging himself from a beam. Perhaps this was yet another experiment that went wrong or a planned suicide for reasons which did not emerge at the inquest. Privately, local police were not convinced of either the suicide or accident theories but, without any evidence of foul play or any motive for murder, they found it difficult to treat Stephen's case as a possible suspicious death. Police, however, remain intrigued by the death in the light of the extreme sensitivity of his work in signals intelligence.

Many people have tried to establish coincidence or conspiracy by plundering official figures on occupational mortality but, as George Bernard Shaw said, the 'man in the street knows that you can prove anything by figures, though he forgets this the moment figures are used to prove anything he wants to believe'. If an organization has an uncommonly high or low suicide rate in a given period it could be a statistical fluke. In the last six months, for example, nobody has apparently taken their lives while working in the defence industry. Indeed this may be the case, or it could be that details of professions are not being mentioned at the dozens of inquests held every week in Britain. Another explanation is that suspicious deaths may have gone unreported in the papers. Even murder victims sometimes rate only a few paragraphs in their local papers. Of the 685 murders in Britain in 1986 the BBC cuttings library discovered that only 300 made the national press.

Even if an organization's suicide rate were significantly lower or higher than the national average, what would that prove? If the rate were lower, how would that diminish the likelihood that any of the deaths were suspicious? A doctor does not assume that a patient complaining of chest pains is probably suffering from indigestion because heart disease in the hospital's catchment area is generally on the decrease. Only a close and timely examination of each death will yield any clues to the truth.

But if these 25 deaths were connected by anything more than coincidence, what could be the connection?

In March and April 1987, in the wake of the initial publicity about the bizarre deaths of Vimal Dajibhai and Arshad Sharif, several newspapers and television programmes quoted specialists speculating on the subject.

Several US newspapers quoted Andres Finguerut, a

defence economist at the International Institute for Strategic Studies in London, who said: 'Some of the top computer programmers in the UK happen to be people of Indian descent. They have specialized in it and are very good.' He added: 'I'm not saying they're a security risk but maybe somebody somewhere thought they were.'

The American magazine *Newsweek* said there were no end of theories as to who might have been behind the mysterious deaths. These theories pointed the finger at, among others, 'the KGB and even the dirty tricks department of Britain's own security service'. Another American magazine, *Time*, carried the following somewhat curious quote from an unnamed intelligence source: 'We do not have any evidence to suggest that the men took their own lives to escape British security or some foreign spymaster.' The *Guardian* reported the police as saying that the deaths were coincidences. The *Sunday Mirror* likened the cases to an episode of the Avengers television series, first shown in 1965, in which scientists apparently killed themselves in a bizarre way but were later shown to have been brainwashed. In contrast the *Sunday Today* revealed that there was no plot. 'As the *Sunday Today* reveals, the suicides were caused by the appalling pressures of work faced by defence scientists.' The *Sunday Sport* reported in a front page article that the Kremlin had given instructions to 'wipe out Britain's top space spy scientists'. On a more serious note, *The Sunday Times*, which expended considerable resources examining the cases, pointed out some of the unanswered questions and concluded that the prospect of completely unravelling the bizarre incidents was remote.

The Financial Times, referring to four of the scientists, said each was concerned with advanced computer software and signals processing, which it described as a fast moving scientific area 'vitally important both in the military and in commercial applications'. In a television documentary, also on four of the cases, Rupert Pengelley, of *International Defense Review* said of Vimal's work on underwater systems: 'It's a matter of great sensitivity as far as the Russians are concerned. In many ways the British are the most expert potential adversary they have in the underwater field so they will be wanting to know what we have done to improve Sting Ray. They will want to know what we plan to do with the next generation of torpedoes. It is perfectly possible that the Russians would have targeted, that is to say sent somebody to look for information on, a particular project from a particular factory but whether this is the case in point is up to the police to divine.' One foreign correspondent wrote of four of the cases: 'Even considered individually, the mysterious and brutal deaths cry out for attention.' When six cases had come to light an Associated Press correspondent wrote: 'All the deaths look like suicides, but only two have been ruled that officially. In no case has a convincing motive for suicide been made known. Three of the scientists worked for Marconi, one of a handful of European companies directly involved in the Reagan administration's Strategic Defense Initiative... But officials of the government and Marconi alike insist that none of the victims were directly involved in the program.' The *Los Angeles Times*, in a front page article, asked: 'British Scientists Deaths – Suicides or Conspiracy?' It pointed out that Vimal Dajibhai, Arshad Sharif and David Sands had died in violent and mysterious circumstances. All were apparent suicides but there were no witnesses to any of the deaths. It quoted a UK government minister as confirming the men worked on defence projects and saying that the 'matter would be kept under review' but that there was 'no need for a formal investigation'.

In 1988 and 1989 the US television news organizations

NBC and ABC, and the Australian documentary programme *60 Minutes* showed the contrasting views of some families and the authorities. The *60 Minutes* programme, for example, quoted one widow as expressing her belief that her husband may have been murdered. In the same programme the then Secretary of State for Defence George Younger said: 'If you've got many thousands of people working on a project, sadly quite a number of them are likely to die or go to other jobs or change their circumstances during the course of a long project. Although it is sad if anyone dies, I don't see any particularly sinister aspect of that.'

Younger was asked if he thought there were too many coincidences. He told the Australian reporter: 'That is your interpretation and not necessarily mine. If you've been going into particular cases and particular instances there are strange things that happen. I do not know anything about the deaths. You are the expert on the deaths, you must look into that for yourself.' The reporter went on to ask whether there would be an inquiry. Younger replied: 'No. I am concerned with the provision of the aircraft and the matter of unfortunate employees who may have difficulties of one sort or another is a matter for the companies concerned who employ them.' Henry Champ of NBC News, however, thought the implications of the deaths went beyond the concern of the companies. 'Washington and the American people are fully aware of the fact that many of the projects that these scientists were involved in were ones that were funded, partially funded or would inevitably be sold to America.' He added that, if the deaths had happened in the US, there would have been a public hearing.

In Britain, the *Observer* focused on Marconi's Cosmos project which had implications for Star Wars research and which was discovered by journalists investigating the deaths of Vimal and Arshad. The

Observer said: 'Hopes for the entire Star Wars project depend heavily on simulation techniques ... The Americans emphasize the importance of "extraordinary security" for computer programmers – the heart of the SDI project – to prevent sabotage and the leaking of information.' Since the *Observer* article, it has been discovered that most of those who died mysteriously were indeed involved in computer simulation. The *Mail on Sunday*, which examined Peter Peapell's case in particular declared: 'Suicide, accident or murder? Police rule out the first two ...'

But for conspiracy and coincidence theorists alike, there seemed an insurmountable gap between speculation and proof. Those who believed in suicide and coincidence needed only to look to the authorities for supportive comments. Those who wanted to believe in coincidence but also sought the facts to ensure there was no foul play, were left wondering if the reticence of the authorities was an automatic response to questions about a sensitive subject, or was a conspiratorial suppression of important information.

In private conversations theories ranged from the pressure of work in defence to a military author's suggestion that the Soviets were coming ashore from trawlers moored off Scotland, torturing key defence personnel to obtain information and killing them in ways to make the deaths look like suicide. Further speculation converged on the possibility that the employees could have been involved in an espionage ring and the Soviets were moving to close it down. A more plausible theory was that those who died had known something about illicit sales of advanced military weapons to Eastern Bloc or Third World countries. This theory, like the others, was not substantiated but it added to the concern of those who wanted an inquiry.

One senior Marconi employee who disclosed details of David Sands's work would not give a theory but felt the deaths needed investigating. He described David's work as 'particularly sensitive' and actively sought information on the other cases. Another senior member of staff working for a defence contractor said: 'I can't believe in suicide. I have been in programming all my working life, in many different companies. I've never known anyone commit suicide. If people don't like the job they can get another job. Companies are crying out for people with their skills.'

There were yet others who said that the stress of working in an environment where security requirements prevented employees from airing their work problems at home, could drive people to suicide. But stress was not proved to be the cause of the deaths. In fact, in many of the cases there was evidence that the employees were looking forward to their future. Vimal, for instance, had bought a new suit, new shoes and a book on the financial sector in preparation for his new job in the City when he fell from a bridge. Others, such as David Sands, had recently successfully completed projects when they died. The stress theory leapfrogged over the unanswered questions. It also discounted the more likely possibility that the individual could have had a transfer to another job rather than commit suicide. With the acute shortage of skills in the computer industry, with thousands of vacancies, even people in their sixties have been able to find new jobs.

In the end, two theories predominated. The first was that suicide, accident and/or coincidence lay at the root of all the deaths. This was the most believable of the two possibilities. The second theory, that at least some of the scientists had been the victims of foul play, was particularly distasteful. But it needed to be examined.

It was inconceivable, in fact, that each of the employees had been killed systematically in such a way as to fool the families and the public into believing there were no grounds for suspicion. Some of the cases must have been genuine suicides or accidents. At the same time it was difficult to accept, without questioning, the view put forward vigorously by the authorities that, while the similarities were odd, there were no grounds for concern. Too many defence industry employees working in particularly sensitive areas had died in unusual circumstances, without satisfactory explanations, with minimal evidence, with no eyewitnesses and no suicide notes, to enable observers to discount totally the possibility that there was more to the deaths than met the eye.

If, however, murder was an explanation for some of the deaths, who could have been culpable and what were the methods used? Some of the possible explanations put forward were as bizarre as the deaths. There were suggestions, for instance, of externally applied pressure. Techniques suggested included threats being made to individuals about their children or the application of toxins which were indiscernible by the time a post mortem was carried out, if one was performed at all. There was also the suggestion that aspects of psychological warfare were being applied, whereby stress was deliberately induced in a victim over a period of time.

Such explanations could have been dismissed out of hand but for the fact that the wife of one of the scientists said she had been told by a professional medical adviser to the family that there was a possibility that a toxin may have been applied without her husband's knowledge. And at least one individual was being treated at the Medical Foundation for the Care of Torture Victims in London for what he claimed was psychological abuse shortly before the mysterious deaths came to light in March 1987.

It was also curious that the few known facts were sometimes arranged by the authorities in such a way as to accentuate irrelevancies or trivia while not mentioning or giving little attention to possible clues. For example, the police stressed that only Shani Warren's stiletto heel marks were found by the lakeside. But journalists found later that ordinary shoes made no impression. At a police press conference, a detective said, somewhat curiously, that Shani 'was not promiscuous but she was 26-years-old'. This led to speculation of questionable relevancy that, although she had had only one boyfriend at a time, there had been a succession of them. One Sunday paper subsequently quoted a friend of Shani's as saying: 'She fell for wealthy, good-looking older guys ...' Little attention was paid to the disclosure, several days after Shani's death, that marks had been found on her neck which indicated an attempt at strangulation before drowning. Police remarks about Shani's supposed dread of AIDS were also curious, even more so when she had apparently not even mentioned this fear in her personal diaries.

At the police conference about the deaths of Vimal and Arshad, much detail emerged about the religious cult that Vimal had, on only one occasion, visited with his family. Yet no explanation was given for the spanner found in the driver's footwell of Arshad's car, or why his automatic Audi had come to a rest only a few yards from the tree to which he had apparently tied himself. No explanation was given for why there were smoked cigars found in his car when there was a no smoking sign on the dashboard and he had complained to the owner of the guest house where he spent his last night that he had a sore throat. No explanation was given of what he was doing in Bristol more than 100 miles from his home, or who he had seen in the twenty hours before his death, or why, hours before his death, he had produced a bundle of high denomination notes tied in a rubber band when he went to settle his account at the guest house. On the last point, no notes were recovered from the body, yet the anomaly was not even mentioned at the full inquest.

Arshad's father received only the few pennies that the police say they found in his son's pockets. What happened to the bundle of notes? If he was murdered for the money, why did the inquest return a verdict of suicide?

In Vimal's case the authorities had remarked that the death was likely to have been a tragic suicide. Unencumbered by facts, this conclusion had an appealing simplicity. It was easy to forget that there was not so much as a fragment of evidence which suggested that Vimal had intended to take his own life.

It seemed unlikely at first that a blanket of secrecy could be thrown around evidence which raised awkward questions, but it became clear that the system of coroners' inquests lent itself to such obfuscation. In fact the suitability of UK coroners inquests as a forum for investigating deaths in mysterious or controversial circumstances has been questioned for several years. After the unsatisfactory outcome of such cases as those of Helen Smith, Blair Peach and Roberto Calvi, repeated calls were made in Parliament for the setting up of a new tribunal of inquiry under a High Court judge with normal rules of evidence and procedure to investigate such deaths. The problem is that coroners' courts rarely pinpoint the blame for a death. They are inquiries, not trials, and while they will determine the cause of death, and where, when and how it occurred, they will not necessarily say why. Furthermore the coroner exercises a formidable control over what evidence is heard. The coroner decides what evidence to call, which witnesses should be called and he asks them the questions he feels are relevant. No interested party is normally allowed to see the statements of the witnesses, usually prepared by the police for the coroner's use, either to show that certain witnesses have been overlooked and should be called to identify inconsistencies or to cross examine witnesses about them.

In cases which touch on national security issues, it is not inconceivable that the coroners and the police may not receive all the information that is necessary to complete their inquiries. Coroners who become too questioning in such cases could find themselves under pressure. The coroner in the Dennis Skinner case took the unusual step of complaining of such pressure saying: 'I can't say where the pressure is coming from. Please don't ask. I will lose my job. So much pressure has been put on me from all quarters.' In May 1988, it was reported that the coroner conducting the inquest into the shooting of three IRA suspects in Gibraltar, allegedly by British special forces, was 'under an awful lot of pressure over this business'.

Were unseen influences the reason for the lack of evidence in some of, possibly all, the deaths? At David Sands's hearing, for instance, the coroner recorded an open verdict with the comment: 'The evidence does not specifically reveal the facts of which any other verdict could be brought.' And at Shani Warren's inquest, the coroner said: 'I am not satisfied on the evidence before me, particularly on the police inquiry, that there is evidence that I can properly bring in a verdict of unlawful killing. The evidence available to me does not fully or further disclose the means whereby the cause of death arose.' After Stephen Oke was found hanged, with his hands tied in front of him, the coroner said: 'It could have been an accident but there is insufficient evidence for me to be certain.' Murder does not seem to have been considered in earnest by most of the coroners.

A jury may perhaps have considered the evidence in a different light and expected to see far more evidence than was read out at most of the inquests. But we shall never know because in all the cases, except in that of Jack Wolfenden's apparently accidental glider crash, the coroner exercised his power not to appoint a jury.

One of the few insights into the British government's

attitude to mysterious deaths in the defence industry comes from 1956 when an underwater EW expert called Buster Crabbe disappeared while diving in Portsmouth harbour. Apparently his task had been to investigate the propeller of a Soviet ship, the *Ordzhonikidze*, which was docked at Portsmouth during an official visit to Britain by the Soviet leaders Khrushchev and Bulganin. Even though the Soviets complained publicly about illicit diving the British authorities at first denied any knowledge. In response the Soviets leaked a diplomatic message which showed contradictions in official statements about the affair. Soon, some embarrassing facts began to emerge. According to Peter Wright in his book *Spycatcher*, the security services telephoned police at Portsmouth and arranged for a hotel register to be sanitized. Crabbe and an accomplice had booked into the hotel in their own names but the relevant pages were removed. It was also discovered that the police had told the hotel proprietor not to speak to journalists. In reply to questions in the House of Commons the then Prime Minister Anthony Eden said: 'It would not be in the public interest to disclose the circumstances of Mr Crabbe's presumed death.'

The magic in EW is knowing the enemy's weakest point. That point could, for example, be the location of a critical digital communications centre or a computer site which holds high grade intelligence information. Even knowledge of a high ranking official on a particular project, who perhaps might have character weaknesses, might be useful information for a potential enemy. Such knowledge is hardly technical but it might be highly sensitive.

The importance of security in a project such as Uniter could not be overestimated. Said to be the most innovative project of its kind in the world, Uniter will provide communication links, designed to withstand the effects of a nuclear explosion in the atmosphere, to at least 100 military sites and support both IUKADGE and UKAIR. It will carry some of the most classified Nato information on Britain's air defences which are responsible for supporting operations in the Greenland-Iceland-UK gap, a choke point through which Soviet submarines must pass when entering the Atlantic to threaten the US and the supply lines from the US to Europe in time of war. The supremacy of the oceans is meaningless without air supremacy. Yet much of the hardware and software will be based on commercial products from companies such as Plessey, GEC and Micro Scope to reduce costs. British Telecom's director of customer marketing Nick Kane said of Uniter: 'It is one of our largest defence contracts yet.' BT will manage the installation and commissioning of 90 digital exchanges and 14,000 telephones. GEC, as prime contractor, gave BT the deal after a competitive tender.

Was it easy to ignore the fact that many of the companies and establishments where the dead defence employees worked were involved in some capacity with Uniter?

In most, if not all, the cases there was a period before death occurred which could not be explained. Mark Wisner was apparently in a room in the house which he shared with two friends for more than twenty-four hours before his body was found. In David Sands's case he disappeared for more than six hours on a Saturday two days before his death. With Vimal Dajibhai and Arshad Sharif there were long unexplained gaps between the time they were last seen alive and the time their bodies were recovered. In Peter Peapell's case he went to put away the car at about 3 a.m. and was not found until about 9.30 a.m. An unexplained period also preceded most of the other deaths, in particular those of Shani Warren and Jonathan Wash. And nothing is known about what happened in the hours that led up to David Greenhalgh's fall.

Also, in some of the cases, the nature of the death itself had apparently destroyed forensic evidence. In David Sands's case, evidence was lost in the fireball that followed his crash. In Shani Warren's case police said forensic evidence had been destroyed by the length of time her body had apparently been in the water. With Vimal Dajibhai the 240 foot fall onto solid ground had apparently destroyed much of the forensic evidence except the puncture mark on his buttock, which was later dismissed as one of his multiple injuries.

Furthermore, the possibility of sabotage could not be ruled out in some of the cases involving car accidents. Some of the scientists experienced mysterious car accidents in the weeks before they subsequently died of other causes.

It is difficult to discount the possibility of murder in at least some of the cases. But if murder was committed, who were the murderers? There seemed no good reason for the Soviets to murder Nato scientists who would have been more use to them alive, unless, perhaps, they had been closing down a spy ring. Yet there was not even the suspicion of any evidence that these people were involved in espionage.

Is, then, the West capable of murdering its own citizens? It seems most improbable, not least because of the difficulty in extrapolating a motive. But it cannot be ruled out.

After the death of GCHQ employee Ernest Brockway there were suggestions that he had been depressed. These rumours in turn gave rise to questions about the vetting of defence employees for character weaknesses. In fact *The Sunday Times*, after investigating Ernest Brockway's death, made the point that the vetting procedures that all GCHQ employees go through are supposed to detect 'personal weaknesses that might make them security risks'. Furthermore, a personal weakness such as depression was considered enough to make somebody a security risk. GCHQ employee Geoffrey Prime who was jailed for 35 years for espionage was found to have been suffering from acute depression and in 1988 GCHQ introduced new vetting procedures to give government security investigators access to the medical records of GCHQ's 7,000 staff providing that individuals gave their consent. Staff were also asked to sign a health declaration as part of their positive vetting clearance which asked them whether they had ever suffered from 'severe depression, mental illness, nervous breakdown or nervous debility'. The *Guardian* newspaper commented at the time: 'The measure is the latest in a series first proposed by the Security Commission in 1983 after the Geoffrey Prime spy affair.'

There had been many suggestions privately and publicly that the defence company employees may have been seen as security risks. The Americans and the British are anxious to the point of paranoia about Western technology ending up in the hands of the Eastern Bloc. Dealers of second hand computers have in the past been jailed for selling equipment which was commercially obsolete yet deemed still to have a military use to the Soviet Union. They have stood accused of aiding the Soviet effort to improve its command and control systems. In one crown court hearing a senior official from the Royal Military College of Science appeared for the prosecution and emphasized the importance of C3. He testified that Nato was able to counteract the superior resources of the Eastern Bloc by keeping a 'four to five year lead in the field of command and control'. Russia's own computers had apparently proved unreliable in this respect and the acquisition of a Dec Vax 11/780 US-built computer would have been a real asset to the Russians. The dealer concerned in this particular case had been arrested and charged after UK officials had been tipped off by US intelligence staff.

In comparison with the penalties for smuggling Western technology products to destinations in the Eastern Bloc, little is said about the penalties for exporting the knowledge of those who work in critical areas of C3 to Warsaw Pact intelligence services. In a democracy, little can be done to stop someone of questionable loyalty leaving the defence field and working, either in the UK or abroad, for technology firms which may have Eastern Bloc connections. In some cases the Soviets might attach considerable importance simply to discovering the location of a critical computer site or the name of someone who is vulnerable to blackmail. Is it possible that UK civilians could die prematurely because of something they know? Peter Wright in his book *Spycatcher* describes how the CIA plotted assassinations. In fact the Americans apparently told Wright that they were 'in the market for the requisite expertise'. Wright also speaks of the need by the West to practise strategic deception on the Soviets. Perhaps, for example, the West's C3, which would be a decisive factor in any war, is not as advanced as it is claimed to be. If such a deception has been perpetrated by the West, any of those who died might have known about it. The assurance of deterrence could be devalued, even undermined, if the Soviets found out for certain that they stood every chance of success in a conventional war.

In the UK, MI6 is known to have investigated how far the hallucinatory drug lysergic acid diethylamide (LSD) could be used in interrogations. Wright says: 'Both MI5 and MI6 also wanted to know a lot more about the advanced poisons then being developed at Porton, though for different reasons ... MI6 wanted to use the poisons for operations abroad.' He later mentions a demonstration by a UK research laboratory of a dart tipped with poison. Curiously, Wright also refers to some mysterious deaths of people who were suspected of being possible security risks. 'Three deaths, two of which were suicides, in such a small group of people, at a time when we were actively investigating them, seemed far more than bad luck. MI5 was terrified that it would be linked publicly with the deaths.'

There are other stories which suggest that the British secret services are not whiter than white. In 1985 a front page story in the *Sunday Telegraph* said: 'Police hunting the killer of Hilda Murrell who died mysteriously in March last year, are examining the theory that her murderer was a private detective under contract to MI5 or another security service.' The article told of a bungled surveillance operation and how police had interviewed two private detectives and the widow of Barrie Peachman, a Norfolk based investigator who committed suicide soon after Hilda Murrell was killed. One private detective who was interviewed by police said later that he knew that Hilda, whose nephew Rob Green, a former naval commander, worked in naval intelligence, had been under surveillance by a private detective agency. The private detective, a former provost in the RAF's intelligence branch, was quoted as saying, 'It's quite normal for the security services to recruit people like myself to do all kinds of jobs, dirty or otherwise.' Another of the detectives was quoted as saying: 'Something went badly wrong and it involved officialdom. Now everyone is running around in ever decreasing circles trying to plug gaps.' Mrs Peachman, herself a private investigator in her husband's firm, said his suicide had been linked with 'private and personal matters'. It was admitted that, acting on the instructions of a confidential client, her company had organized surveillance of a number of people.

A pathologist, Dr Don Arnott, who personally investigated Hilda's death, believed she may have been drugged or poisoned before she died. He spoke of a suspicious wound on her arm which could have been the mark of a hypodermic needle used to inject poison. There were suggestions that Hilda, who was a prominent anti-nuclear campaigner, may have received naval intelligence. Dr Arnott said: 'I cannot rule out the possibility of a state crime or that Hilda was a victim of big business.'

Both Labour and Tory governments have acquiesced in the seemingly strengthening resolve of the military and intelligence authorities to protect their secrets. The current government, however, has shown that it is prepared to go to extraordinary lengths to throw a shroud around information pertaining to intelligence, as demonstrated by the unprecedented raid on the BBC over its series of programmes *Secret Society*, which included one on the Zircon spy satellite, and the campaign to prevent the publication of Peter Wright's book. Action was taken even in cases where national security was not an issue as in the injunction against the BBC Radio Four programme entitled *My Country Right or Wrong* which carried interviews with former intelligence officers. When the BBC eventually broadcast the programme, Fred Holroyd, who had worked for military intelligence in Northern Ireland in the 1970s said, in a discussion over whether the security services should be accountable to Parliament, that they should be 'brought back into the democratic world'. He went on: 'If they are not brought back, then we will end up being as bad as the other side, if we haven't already ended up that way.'

In 1987 the government took action to repress support for a Private Member's Bill which made what many regarded as responsible proposals to alter the all encompassing nature of the Official Secrets Act. In January 1988 the *Independent* newspaper reported that the discretionary power of the Royal Prerogative gave British governments the right to circumvent the law in the execution of certain Crown duties. 'Officers of the security services could even be empowered to kill their fellow citizens,' said the paper.

The vast majority of the deaths examined here were tinged with the suspicion that there were those in a position of authority who knew far more about them than was divulged at their inquests. In all large businesses which are heavily reliant on computers, key staff are watched closely. One US-based commercial company which employs several thousand people in the UK, is reported to discourage personal relationships among staff because of the fear of a collusion in crime. Indeed, in one company, two senior computer staff had formed a close working and social relationship until the woman was found dead in unexplained circumstances. At the inquest it was said that the company had frowned upon the woman's relationship with a male colleague. The coroner returned an open verdict.

In commercial companies, where large sums of money or sensitive information is processed by computers, the important operators and their supervisors are watched closely for signs of stress, depression or financial problems or indeed anything which could make them behave unpredictably. Some data processing managers who work in the banking field are advised by their professional bodies to do regular checks on the bank balances of critical computer staff. The implication is that those falling into debt may turn to electronic crime to supplement their income. It would be hard to imagine that security personnel do not keep a close eye on defence employees for similar reasons. After all, a depressed employee, or one who is disgruntled or is under stress, could be susceptible to offers from the Soviets who would be particularly grateful for certain information, especially relating to EW.

Jonathan Wash's pregnant girlfriend or his undisclosed 'terrible secret' might have made him a security risk. Arshad Sharif's supposed affair might have made him a security risk. Vimal Dajibhai's association with a religious cult, even though casual, could have been interpreted as posing a security risk. Richard Pugh's sexual practices, Mark Wisner's transvestism, Stephen Drinkwater's sexual proclivities and Ernest Brockway's depression might have been regarded as personal weaknesses and therefore potential security problems. Lieutenant Colonel Godley's apparent obsession with a woman in the village may have made him a security risk. Gerard Darlow's schizophrenia, Jack Wolfenden's unpredictable behaviour on returning from the US, Dr Brittan's absences from work and Brigadier Ferry's car accident which changed his personality may have made them all security risks.

One of the most potentially dangerous security risks in the eyes of the authorities is that posed by disgruntled members of staff who have, by accident or lack of security precautions, or perhaps as a normal part of their work, acquired particularly sensitive information.

In a survey conducted by the British computer firm ICL, 62 per cent of commercial businesses saw the most serious threat to security coming from trusted insiders. Only five per cent considered that outsiders such as hackers represented a threat. In defence companies, the risk of trusted insiders turning into security risks is a virtually insoluble problem. Someone who left a company without the determination to honour the terms of the Official Secrets Act might be seen as a particular risk. The acquisition of highly classified information could arise simply by a member of staff seeing something on someone's desk. The wife of one of the defence employees referred to one member of staff she knew at a defence contractors who had caught sight of 'something he wished he hadn't seen'. A highly intelligent person, even without the highest security clearance, could piece together a picture of a project by talking to others or being given greater responsibility than might be the case if there were sufficient members of staff with the appropriate skills.

Shani Warren's diaries revealed she was disgruntled at work. One of the last people to have seen Arshad Sharif alive said: 'For some reason there was a lot that didn't come out at his inquest. It seemed strange that he would commit suicide when he was looking forward to getting married and leaving defence to set up his own business.' Vimal Dajibhai was also about to leave Marconi, George Franks was in dispute with his GCHQ employers, Trevor Knight and Ernest Brockway were disgruntled at work, David Sands was considering getting out of the 'rat race', David Greenhalgh had been working on UKAIR which was awarded to his company at about the same time as his near fatal fall, Victor Moore had been disgruntled and had just left his job, Richard Pugh had recently changed his job and Jonathan Wash was in dispute with British Telecom and was fearful of his life. Alistair Beckham was disenchanted and John Whiteman had been unhappy to the point of making his feelings known to top Nato officials. The case of Robert Wilson, who had handed in secret documents to Marconi the day before accidentally shooting himself, is a mystery. The private lives and relationships at work are not known in the cases of Dr Brittan, Peter Peapell, Stuart Gooding, Michael Baker, Stephen Oke and Keith Bowden.

Defence scientists are generally sensible, level-headed types who do not like making a fuss. Most would probably be astonished that anyone could even contemplate that the West would murder its own civilians in the name of national security. When one such scientist was questioned about the death of his colleague and next door neighbour who had been working on a top secret project, he was philosophical, even unconcerned. Then, after an hour or so, he suddenly became angry.

'People die round here and you never ask why,' he said. 'It does you no good asking questions.' There was no reason to doubt that he was telling the truth. 'Look,' said the man, 'there's very little I can say. You often hear things that sound odd. For example, there was a man who died when these huge double doors in the basement closed. I think it was an industrial accident.' He shrugged and lowered his voice. 'I never figured out why he wasn't able to get out of the way. The doors are electrical. They close very, very slowly.'

Despite further questioning, he refused to elaborate. His neighbour had been found hanging from a beam in his loft in late 1987. No eyewitnesses. No suicide note.

'If you worked there you'd understand why I have to be so careful. There are some bastards around. That's all I can say. These things happen.'

Epilogue

'It's a rather bizarre story so I won't go into detail initially,' said the soft spoken engineer Joe Vialls.

He was ringing in March 1987 with an account of how he had been unwittingly subjected to psychological abuse, what many of us might regard as clandestine brainwashing. The subject matter could have been tailor made for rejection. Computer journalists are not usually predisposed to writing stories about psychological engineering. Even worse for Joe, the *Computer News* newsdesk had become a magnet for the deranged after the paper broke the story on the strange deaths of two Marconi scientists. It seemed that we had stirred from apathy anyone of questionable sanity who had ever thought of ringing a newspaper. This did not make us particularly receptive to Joe's contention that psychological modification had become a military science which was not only researched but regularly practised, that someone could be persuaded to believe they were a stunt driver driving through a building made of cardboard or that they could be a victim of deliberately induced stress which was sufficient to disturb the balance of their minds. The idea, at best, was outlandishly implausible. The temptation to dismiss Joe's personal experiences as more imaginary than real was almost overpowering. Nevertheless, it was too easy to be disparaging without considering all the facts. Joe had put his case with an articulate and apparently disinterested honesty that was difficult to discount.

David Sands's death, said Joe, 'rung so many alarm bells'. He was particularly concerned about the way David had turned off a main road on his way to work and for no apparent reason driven his car at high speed into the side of a café. Joe, a former Air Force engineer, went on to describe an incident in January 1986 when his three litre Ford Capri went into a spin at high speed. The dual carriageway was dry and visibility was good. The car hit dense brush on the central reservation and came to a halt, facing in approximately the right direction. When he realized, with some surprise, that he was unhurt, apart from a minor whiplash injury, he tried to move the car and found that the handbrake was on. He had no recollection of what had happened but assumed that for some reason he had attempted a handbrake turn at high speed. He felt his life was still in danger.

At a time when journalists were looking for an explanation of how or why scientists were killing themselves in such bizarre ways, Joe's theory was no more eccentric than some of the deaths. It also drew attention to the clandestine partnership between the military and the psychologists.

It was agreed that Joe would come into the *Computer News* offices a few days later and discuss his experiences with myself and the editorial director Ron Condon. He arrived a few days later with his wife Marilyn and bundles of documents. The experiences he recounted all that afternoon were almost unbelievable. When he enlarged on events he had mentioned only briefly during the telephone call his story remained consistent and he answered most questions in impressive detail. Yet the exact nature of the alleged psychological abuse remained the subject of speculation. At no point was Joe able to say, with any degree of certainty, how or why the abuse occurred. He felt his life was still threatened, perhaps by another allegedly subconscious action. Approaching a newspaper gave him a feeling of security, though at that stage, curiously, Joe did not seem to want publicity.

I am not a psychologist and cannot make claims about Joe's sanity or the credibility of his story, though I feel that neither he nor his experiences should be dismissed summarily. Of course, much is against him. His story stands or falls on his credibility. The onus is on him, therefore, to provide cogent evidence that his sanity is beyond reproach, a test that none of us, if put on the spot, would find particularly easy.

Counting against him is the ease with which his story can be ridiculed. It is difficult, if not impossible, for Joe to prove that he has been subjected to what he terms behavioural modification so it is easy to write off his experiences by simply branding him a paranoid. Nevertheless, I have seen documents which confirm that the police have made inquiries into his assertions, the results of which were 'inconclusive'. I have also seen reports from specialists which clear Joe of any mental illness. In fact one psychologist in his report suggests that in terms of mental agility Joe may be among the top two per cent of the population. The view of psychologists is that Joe's assertions cannot be dismissed. None doubt his sincerity. But neither the letters from the police nor the psychological reports prove the veracity of what he says has happened to him.

Inevitably, Joe's assertions are one-sided. They cannot be checked with the alleged perpetrators because no concrete evidence of wrongdoing exists against any named individuals. Joe's argument is that he is uncertain about the exact nature of the psychological abuse because it took place without his knowledge, at a level deep in his subconscious. Under hypnosis, though, Joe has apparently recalled aspects of his treatment. However, despite the coherence of his story and the meticulously maintained documentary evidence, I find it all difficult to believe. It might be easier to ascribe his alarm to a lively imagination or an excessive suspiciousness of others. On the other hand, it is tempting to feel that there is no smoke without fire. Joe certainly believes that he has been subjected to stress which has been deliberately induced. This conviction is fully supported by Marilyn who is clearly concerned that the uncertainties over his treatment will affect her two children, both of school age. It is also not easy to ignore the fact that his case has attracted more than the passing interest of the police and the London-based charity, the Medical Foundation for the Care of Torture Victims. The charity, based in the National Temperance Hospital in London, has an information leaflet which states: 'The Medical Foundation is an independent charity which cares for people who have been tortured; it provides information on the existence of torture and the work currently being done by health professionals is designed to relieve the physical and psychological suffering of its victims.' The leaflet also makes the point that sophisticated torture techniques can leave few, if any, physical signs.

Joe believes that psychology has reached the stage where it is 'every bit as much of a science as acoustics or metallurgy'. It is possible, he says, for the subconscious to be clandestinely influenced to such a degree that people can be 'tricked' into killing themselves. Such a system, he asserts, provides the perfect solution for a democracy wanting to remove a small number of people who are predisposed to endanger national security. The system is inherently safe because the public would be unable to comprehend that it was possible. He goes on to say that, from talking to many psychologists, it appears that psychological 'engineering' can be achieved by preconditioning a subject without their knowledge and giving appropriate specific instructions shortly before their deaths. Joe speculates that this may explain the 'missing' periods before David Sands's crash and the carbon monoxide poisoning of Peter Peapell. At the time that Joe first made contact he was unaware, in fact, of the details of the other deaths, but, perhaps coincidentally, the police had been unable to explain the last hours of Arshad Sharif, Vimal Dajibhai and several of the others. This may not necessarily be suspicious, though. There may be simple explanations for these missing periods of which we are unaware.

It is now more than two years since Joe rang me up and we have spoken on many occasions, mostly on the telephone but sometimes over lunch. He is an intelligent, fluent, wittily negative talker. But he seems to see a conspiracy with virtually every turn of his head. It is not for me to judge whether this is confusion, paranoia or a direct result of his experiences, but I owe it to him to relate what he says happened.

His story begins in 1983 when Joe, aged 46, born in Australia and living with his family in Ipswich, Suffolk, says he was assigned to supervise a sensitive oil drilling operation on an inland rig in India, just outside Calcutta. His wage slips show that he was paid about $3,000 net per month, plus expenses. The operation, which was being carried out on behalf of the Indian Government, was using an advanced drilling fluid system, developed by a large US defence contractor, which 'while not revolutionary' was considered too sensitive to be exported to the USSR. It had the potential for significantly improving oil production in India. Joe was told that a high level of discretion would be needed because several Soviet advisers from the Moscow Institute of Drilling would be at the site.

In July 1983 he arrived at Calcutta and was booked into the city's only five star hotel, though he spent more time at a caravan at the rigsite. He found he was one of only two Westerners on the Soviet dominated site.

All went well at first and Joe was even able to take a month's holiday. He wrote a series of 'handover' notes to a colleague, the style of which provides a flavour of his personality.

'Food stocks – in cupboard near door with plates, cutlery, cooking utensils and most other things. You will need some more coffee and probably 10 packets of Maggi instant noodles – a real asset as you can shovel them down your gullet after 2 minutes cooking.

'Hygiene – what hygiene??? You have sink + bucket + water bottles + water purifier in food cupboard. For bath proceed as follows: get water from well by office, heat, strip, add 30% vol Dettol and have a stand up bath. My dog will lick you dry if you run out of towels.

'Refrigerator – ho ho ... promised but not yet in sight.

'My dog – is a black and white mongrel bitch with an excessive amount of fleas and is about to give birth to six or seven puppies ... please feed at my expense. Disperse intruding USSR dogs with housebricks stacked outside trailer. Forget the fleas as we also have mosquitoes and bed bugs – she is probably the best company I've had at the rig and doesn't talk back as the rest of them do!'

In the notes Joe also records that the rigsite had been visited recently by the USSR consul to Calcutta and the senior adviser from the Russian embassy in New Delhi. He noted that they had arrived with 'much pomp and ceremony' in an air-conditioned Mercedes with USSR pennants. 'Much bowing and scraping took place and all areas of the rig were looked at,' wrote Joe. He remembers being interested in seeing certain members of the Indian State-owned Oil and Natural Gas Commission (ONGC) 'standing rigidly to attention, for all the world as though they were considering a tour of duty in the Red Army'. On Monday, 21 November 1983 he wrote that, after the visit by the Russians, the Soviet interest in the rig 'intensified' and the Indian authorities began a twenty-four hour guard on the well.

While on holiday in October 1983, Joe's only contact with his company was to inquire how preparations were going for the displacement part of the fluid operation which was scheduled to take place a week before his return. He learnt that a minor set-back meant the displacement proper would probably not happen until the time of his arrival back in Calcutta.

Soon after his return Joe found that his inexperienced colleague had used an incorrect fluid in the preparation procedure which ultimately caused interruptions in the oil flow. The colleague had by this time gone back to the US.

'The result of the displacement was unpredictable and disastrous,' said Joe.

What happened in the next few months is detailed in reams of documents. To summarize, Joe suspects the rig was sabotaged, though he is not certain why. He believes this may have been to prevent the Indian government and the Soviets realizing the true benefits of the US company's advanced 'invert' family of drilling fluids. Why the US authorities allowed the fluid to be sent to India in the first place is not clear. Joe assumes it was a mistake.

The effect of the alleged sabotage was to attempt to discredit the fluid system. Evidence of problems at the rigsite was contained in a confidential letter written by a senior member of the US oil company to Joe and two other employees connected with the project. 'Gentlemen ... I don't think any of us, in the course of our careers, will ever find ourselves associated with a more awkward situation as we find ourselves in on the current well we are attempting to run for the ONGC.' His views were echoed by Joe who wrote in a letter to his superiors: 'I have seen some tough ones but after this everything else will seem like gopher digging.' Joe was sent a telex by his supervisors suggesting a way to overcome the problems but says that following their advice would have compounded the difficulties. He therefore went ahead on his own initiative and devised an alternative method which was 'extremely hazardous, but it worked'.

Joe now believes that the American authorities had wanted the system to be seen by the Indians and the Soviets as ineffective and regarded his tenacious efforts to prove its qualities as a nuisance.

In February 1984, while on a holiday in Sydney, Australia, he says he received an anonymous telephone call warning him that if he attempted to return to India he would be found to be carrying drugs. 'I attempted to extend the conversation but the caller hung up quite rapidly.' On his return to India Joe took the precaution of having his luggage sealed 'just in case anyone was contemplating having a go at me'. At Calcutta his baggage was opened, subjected to a very thorough search, but he was allowed entry without further hindrance. Little of any significance happened after that until April 1984 when Joe says that he was subjected to 'harassment' while staying at the hotel in Calcutta. He received 'erratically timed telephone calls to destinations that I had not booked, early calls that I had not ordered, supposed inventory checks on the room at point blank notice and much more, all of which served to break up my sleep pattern most effectively'. Also, technical difficulties at the rigsite increased, adding to Joe's latent stress problem. On a later trip to India, Joe asked his company if he could be relocated to a different hotel which was 'considerably cheaper and still quite acceptable'. He says he was told to remain at the original hotel. It was made clear that if he did not like the hotel he could always quit the job.

In Joe's version of events the following is, perhaps, the most controversial. He says he noticed unusual sounds emanating from his telephone and fixed bedside cabinet.

In a lengthy document which Joe compiled about the events in India he wrote: 'In an attempt to gather data of the audio effects, almost always administered while I was falling asleep, I placed a tape recorder on the bed with freshly demagnetised heads and a tape fresh out of the packet. In the morning I played it back and was considerably alarmed to find an electronic noise on the tape, impossible to describe in writing, which seemed at the time to keep pace with the sound of my breathing. As I gradually fell asleep, so the electronic noise (or pulse) also slowed down, always maintaining exactly the same rate as the breathing itself. This tape I carefully packed away.'

Joe says he approached the US consulate but was told the problem was all in his mind. 'By this time I was clearly feeling (and probably showing) the strain but was determined to follow through with the job. I had no intention of walking out either then or later. My problem seemed to be whether I could keep on an even keel for long enough to outwit them, whoever 'they' actually were. I myself went from bad to worse in that my subconscious mind was almost certainly telling me to go, get out of India, stay away from the rig, while my conscious mind was telling me to attend to my duties, look after the rig, do NOT go home and so on. The result was a level of personal stress that even I cannot find the words to describe.'

During a holiday in July 1984, Joe went to England and discussed his problems with an 'old boss', a retired group captain whose name Joe supplied. Through the group captain Joe was referred to the police in East Anglia. 'I was interviewed by a Sergeant Bowron of Special Branch at Ipswich police station. Sergeant Bowron listened to the suspect tape and said he would take it away for analysis.' Sergeant Bowron also took another cassette which Joe had used to test his tape recorder in his hotel room.

Joe was reassigned to Egypt but did not go. Subsequently, he resigned in a short letter to his company, dated 6 October 1984, which read: 'Suffice to say that I have always in the past provided the best possible service to customers by way of my own knowledge backed up, if required, by service and equipment support from the corporation for whom I have been working. The latter item appeared to be missing during the recent contract in India which was, as you know, quite sensitive not only in pure technical terms but also due to the delicate situation existing with the Soviet crews at the rigsite.' In a reply dated 14 October 1984, Joe's company 'regretfully acknowledged' his resignation, said his final cheque would be deposited in his account, thanked him for his contribution and wished him good luck.

Joe began a new job in the UK with another large oil company, on a salary of $2,900 a month, but says that the psychological pressure continued to be applied. He says he was told that there were complaints about him, but these were not specified and Joe could not see what was wrong. He also says he was sent a chemistry paper by his company to assess his areas of weakness for further training. 'So complex was the paper that I had a Ph.D. Chemistry friend of mine complete it for me. His main comment was that he had personally had to research some of the answers. In his opinion it was quite ridiculous as a "training" chemistry paper.' By this time, he says, his stress level was so high that it came close to 'finishing him off'. It was while working for this company that Joe was involved in the car incident. 'There was something wrong about the crash but I could not put my finger on it at that time. I had had a very strong thought the night before that I was going to crash the car, specifically the three litre Ghia, and this I found strange, I do not believe in premonitions.'

After the incident, Joe went to see a psychologist in his home town of Ipswich. The psychologist, Raymond Seal B.Sc. used hypnosis to attempt to establish what had happened in the crash. Apparently Joe had pressed the accelerator pedal fully down to the floor and shortly afterwards pulled on the handbrake while at the same time turning the steering wheel sharply. 'I then went on to try to recover the car from the situation.' Joe's story was backed up by Seal who said that no psychologist could dismiss his claims.

In June 1986, Joe rang Suffolk police about the cassette tapes he had handed over more than two years before. The tapes, however, were not returned and no explanation was offered. In September 1986 Joe decided to have his own analysis carried out on the tapes. He contacted his solicitors who wrote to Suffolk police.

On 22 October 1986, Suffolk Constabulary's detective chief superintendent responded by saying that he was able to confirm the following:

'1. The notes taken by the officer during his interview with Mr Vialls were only "rough form" and taken as an aide-memoire of the conversation. These notes have since been destroyed.

2. The photographic and taped items referred to are now held at Felixstowe Police Station and are available for return to Mr Vialls. Perhaps you could arrange for him to contact Detective Sergeant Bowron on Felixstowe 282178 when some mutual arrangements can be reached for their return.

3. The material referred to above was not forwarded to any other department and it is not intended to take any further police action in respect of this matter.'

On 30 October Joe wrote to Sergeant Bowron at the Felixstowe police station, asking that the material be released into the custody of Mrs Marilyn Vialls who would produce identification on request. A few days later Marilyn went to collect the tapes at Felixstowe but they were not there. After a long wait Marilyn was told the tapes would be at another station, Martlesham Heath, later in the day. A detective constable explained that an appointment should have been made to collect the tapes.

But Joe wrote later: 'I can think of no good reason why an appointment should be required to recover personal property from a manned police unit.' After a brief inspection of the cassette in the reception area of Martlesham Heath police station, Joe says it 'became rapidly obvious that the cassette in question appeared to have been modified electronically'. After a professional investigation which showed that the tape had 'suffered heavy, though possibly accidental, damage with respect to the recording', Joe wrote to the Suffolk police and to the Police Complaints Authority.

In one of the letters he wrote:

'The first tape showed a recording level of +1 to +3dB which is perfectly normal for the equipment in use. The second tape to which considerable importance had later been attached was found to have suffered a reduction in recording level to minus 20dB – which is close to total erasure. Expert examination showed no splices in the tape itself but did show a completely uniform reduction in recording level for the entire tape run. Thus it could not have been caused, for example, by accidental exposure to a random magnetic field.'

Joe also wrote that if the police had performed a technical analysis on the tape they would have taken a copy to guard against possible damage to the original. He asked for the copy to be made available to him.

In a reply dated 5 January 1987, the chief constable of Suffolk Constabulary states:

'I regret the inconvenience your wife experienced when she called at Felixstowe police station. Due to other commitments, Detective Sergeant Bowron was unavailable and, it appears, was unfortunately not aware of your wife's intended visit.

'I am unable to shed any light on the apparent reduction in audible quality of the tape you refer to, other than by natural deterioration. While in our possession both cassettes were secured in a metal cabinet at Force Headquarters and were not the subject of any copying or indeed technical examination. I would reiterate that neither tape was forwarded to any other agency.

'I trust this explanation meets with your satisfaction.'

Joe observes that the police had offered two different accounts of where the tapes had been stored. Originally it was stated that the cassettes were 'now at Felixstowe Police Station'. Less than three months later the chief constable declared that 'while in our possession both cassettes were secured in a metal cabinet at Force Headquarters', which is at Martlesham Heath.

Joe also questions the assertion that the tapes were not subject to any copying or technical examination. He wrote: 'It does occur to me that detective sergeants in Special Branch do not take material away for examination and then hold it in safe keeping for more than two years if they think it is worthless.' On the subject of the police's suggestion that the tape may have suffered natural deterioration Joe says: 'I am advised by experts that since both cassettes were of an identical make, used on identical equipment and on the same date, it is ludicrous to imply that just one of them would undergo a sort of metamorphic change while its twin retained an almost perfect level of 1-3dB in the same police metal cabinet.'

In July 1987 the Police Complaints Authority reported the results of its investigation. It acknowledged that the police statement that the tapes were at Felixstowe was 'factually incorrect'. It said they were technically in the possession of the detective sergeant who worked there. More significantly, perhaps, the Authority wrote: 'The investigation has failed to confirm how or when the damage occurred to the tape. However, if it did occur whilst in the possession of the Suffolk Constabulary they state that the damage must have happened accidentally.' It went on: 'The investigation has shown that the detective sergeant failed to communicate with you and should have informed you of the outcome and returned the tapes.' However, Joe was still no nearer finding an explanation for his strange experiences in India.

On 6 August 1987, Suffolk Constabulary's deputy chief constable acknowledged that 'enquiries' had been made at the time Joe handed over the tapes to the police, but it 'could not be established whether or not any criminal offence had occurred'. His letter went on: 'Whilst the outcome was inconclusive, you should have been appraised of it and the tapes returned. I very much regret the concern this matter has obviously caused you and hope you will accept my apologies as set out in the Police Complaints Authority letter of 29 July 1987.'

It is not difficult to understand why the police investigation into Joe's case proved 'inconclusive'. It is not an easy task to prove or dismiss allegations of psychological abuse. Yet Joe's frustration at not getting to the bottom of what he firmly believes happened in India is also understandable. It is his contention that psychological engineering is a 'safe solution' because nobody believes it possible.

In addition, simply to write off Joe as a lunatic is to debase the immense support he has received from his wife Marilyn who had listened to the original cassette tape and remembers that she was 'horrified to hear quite clearly a metronome, beating time perfectly with the sound of breathing. The timing slowed, as though the beat of the metronome was controlling the rate of my husband's respiration. There was an enormous "Why?" in my mind but it seemed rather sinister and for that reason I actively encouraged his visit to Special Branch.'

Her statement continues:

'I drove my husband to Ipswich police station for the interview with Special Branch where the tapes were left in police custody. It was a little odd that at no time was there an offer either to return the tapes or to provide an explanation. I put it down to a long drawn out inquiry and that in time all answers would be revealed. It was upon my husband's request two years later that the tapes were returned after a lengthy delay, as they were not where they were originally said to be. Upon the return of the tapes, the tape was played by my husband before providing a signature. I could not hear the metronome but thought that it must have been on another part of the tape. However upon returning home and playing the tape through I could no longer hear the metronome and the breathing was barely audible.

'Since no explanation was offered by the police as to the reasons for the obvious alteration I was, and still am, deeply disturbed about the conclusions reached by whoever had listened to, perhaps analyzed and then altered the tape. My faith in the police remains, but an explanation is in order from someone somewhere.'

The Medical Foundation for the Care of Torture Victims has taken much interest in Joe's experiences. Apparently a video was taken of Joe answering questions under hypnosis and 181 folios of documents compiled. The Foundation also referred him to several psychologists for assessment. I have seen one psychological report and a summary of another. The summary, by a Dr Oliver Briscoe, concluded that although Joe was currently mentally well he might, in the past, have suffered a 'paranoid confusional state'. Nevertheless, he stated that no psychiatrist could dismiss Joe's findings.

The report by Professor Lionel Haward, a doctor of psychology, formerly at Surrey University, is a six page document on Joe's mental health written for the Medical Foundation's director Helen Bamber. The report's findings touch on subjects which most people feel have an overwhelming sense of unreality, post hypnotic suggestion and post hypnotic amnesia. In Joe's case, at least, the effects of these techniques, if they have been used, seem to have been to produce a susceptibility to have a suggested action implanted under hypnosis which Joe would then carry out to the best of his ability when a trigger signal was given. Afterwards, the suggestion would be erased from his mind as if it had never existed.

This might seem the stuff of science fiction but to psychologists it is a subject which is well documented. In fact Professor Haward's references to post hypnotic suggestion have an air of professional disinterest that shame the lay person into wondering how such a long established phenomenon could have escaped one's attention for so long. The Professor's report is based in part on Medical Foundation documents, Joe's behaviour during investigative hypnosis, a telephone discussion with one of Joe's recent colleagues, interviews with Joe and Marilyn and data derived from 'psychometric and psycho-physiological testing'.

The Professor writes that his examination was part of the Foundation's investigation of 'complaints made by Mr Vialls to the effect that for some years he has been persecuted and victimized, and subjected to various psychological techniques applied in a clandestine way to the detriment of his mental and physical well-being'. Without remarking on whether such techniques could in fact be applied clandestinely, the Professor describes Joe as a man of 'high intelligence with unusually good powers of concentration'. He continues: 'His memory is extremely efficient; his long term memory, with intervening distractions, is above average and his short term memory is appropriate to the top 2 per cent of the population.

'He is not a natural risk taker but in emergencies will accept risks and take responsibility for them after assessing the probabilities and consequences. He is not by nature a critical or orally aggressive person and prefers to achieve results by reason rather than direction. He values co-workers who are law abiding, trustworthy and patriotic, concepts which rank high in his list of human attributes.'

In conclusion Professor Haward finds that he is intelligent, 'basically normal' and of stable personality. No evidence exists of psychiatric disorder such as a paranoid condition. He adds: 'He is particularly susceptible to hypnotic induction and to all other hypnotic techniques, and would be a facile victim of any of the methods described in his statement of complaint. Despite his assurances of being free from any psychological sequelae from his recent experiences, he nevertheless appears to be suffering a considerable degree of emotional turbulence of relatively recent onset which is probably out of his awareness.'

If there was any doubt that post-hypnotic suggestion is possible, the Professor states in the body of his report that Joe could be 'quickly and deeply hypnotized, could be induced to hallucinate under hypnosis with vivid imagery, obeys post-hypnotic suggestions accurately and immediately upon presentation of the trigger sign, and develops complete amnesia for selected experiences which are resistant to probing, even by the hypnotist creating the amnesia, until the correct release sign is given'. In fact the Professor says he has 'no hesitation in declaring that Mr Vialls would be extremely susceptible to clandestine hypnosis and to post-hypnotic suggestions of the kinds described in his statements'. He adds: 'It should be noted that evidence has been given under oath in court that post-hypnotic suggestions can persist for well over one year.'

In the light of the documents relating to Joe's experiences, I decided to take a wider look at the relationship between the military and the psychologists. It was Professor Haward's belief, which he expressed in a letter to Joe, that those involved in the military and security fields will have 'studied the psychological aspects of clandestine activity – brainwashing, deliberately induced stress and other examples of man's inhumanity to man'. The Professor added that the USA provides 'excellent career prospects in these highly specialized fields and so provides a considerable range of talent available for consultation'.

The Soviets, too, have developed the use of psychiatric treatment mainly, it seems, to suppress political dissent. Vladimir Titov, an inmate at a 'special' hospital near Smolensk, told journalists in October 1987 of his punishment for revealing details of the use of forced labour from prison camps for projects such as the Siberian gas pipeline. Titov was injected three times a day with mind-altering drugs such as Aminazine and Galoperidol. At times, he 'couldn't sleep, lie down or even walk'. In the summer of 1987, the Soviet press acknowledged for the first time the existence of psychiatric abuse, in the words of Izvestia, 'here as everywhere else'.

Most of the research in the UK, however, is innocuous and often has benefits extending into the civil world. For example, psychologists expend much research time making it easier for people to understand and use computers. And at the Royal Air Force Institute of Aviation Medicine in Hampshire stress in pilots is investigated. The Institute advises the Armed Services, the Civil Aviation Authority, airlines and industry. Studies are also directed towards the effects of drugs or heat and cold on flying performance.

According to a Ministry of Defence brochure, the Army Personnel Research Establishment, also in Hampshire, has a civilian staff of about 75, more than half of which are scientific staff including medical officers and psychologists. The brochure states that it will investigate, for example, a tank gunner's performance with various sight systems. It adds that 'experimental psychological research' is carried out on 'advanced military systems'. Psychology is also a specialism within the Institute of Naval Medicine and the Admiralty Research Establishment at Teddington which 'covers the broader aspects of applied psychology, physiology and diving'. The main Ministry of Defence building in London also requires in its recruitment advertisements 'scientists from a wide range of disciplines, engineers and psychologists'.

Undoubtedly, some of the research in the West will involve studies of psychological warfare, though much of it is secret. More than 70 classified documents on the subject were made available to Peter Watson, former assistant editor of *The Sunday Times*, who wrote a book on the uses and abuses of military psychology called *War on the Mind*, published in 1980. In it, he lists some examples of documents which were classified 'secret', 'confidential', or 'for official use only'. Document titles include 'Exploratory Efforts Concerned with a Study of the Interrogation Process' and 'Use of Hypnosis in Intelligence and Related Military Subjects'. He also notes that details of British psychological operations in Ulster were 'top secret' in Britain but were 'not impossible to come by in Washington'. However, he states in parenthesis that the 'Ministry of Defence does not even acknowledge that the army has any psychological operations'.

It is hard to conceive of Western governments using sinister psychological techniques but there seems little doubt that they keep abreast of them, even if only to adhere to the military adage 'know the enemy'. Nevertheless, some observers go as far as to suggest that the British and American authorities are well informed on Soviet policy on 'finding answers to the eternal question of the perfect murder'.

One highly regarded book on this subject is *Spy* by Richard Deacon and Nigel West, the nom de plume of Tory MP Rupert Allason. The book refers to a nerve gas called GB which is apparently colourless and tasteless and was developed from a formula which the Russians had been experimenting with in the last war. It can kill a human being in four minutes. When the vapour from as little as three drops is inhaled it paralyses the nerve centres. 'The secret has since been discovered in the Western world,' say the authors. They add later: 'The Western world has also experimented in seeking what might be the perfect killer drug.' The authors go on to name a specialist who told thirty 'scientific intelligence officers' at a meeting at Cambridge that one could commit the perfect murder with a minute quantity of a gas called FAE, a highly complex compound which can be made only in laboratories equipped for experiments in obscure poisons.

They also quote an unnamed expert who says: 'You could put the gas in a person's drink in liquid form and he wouldn't know the difference, as it is odourless, colourless and tasteless. There is a delayed action of twenty minutes and then, after a slight convulsion, the person is dead. A post mortem would show no unusual chemicals present in the body. A doctor would suppose the victim had died of respiratory failure. This is as near as you can get to the perfect murder.' The authors of *Spy* also describe a method of luring intended victims into a tightly sealed room containing a block of ice which is thought to be impregnated with carbon dioxide fumes. 'Once this was done, they would probably die fairly soon, leaving no clues as to what killed them.'

They add: 'There have been numerous efforts in recent years both by the KGB and CIA to improve on murder techniques. The CIA seem to have gone to the absolute limit in this respect by asking members to put forward plans for the perfect murder.'

Are such methods really used? Forensic experts say that the notion of killing someone without leaving any clues as to the cause is far-fetched. One cannot easily forget, however, the well publicized death in London of the Bulgarian defector Georgi Markov. He had suddenly felt very ill and had developed a temperature of 104°. His wife called the doctor who thought Markov was suffering from flu and advised that he should be kept as cool as possible. But that night Markov told his wife: 'I have a horrible suspicion that it might be connected with something that happened today. I was waiting for a bus on the south side of Waterloo Bridge when I felt a jab in the back of my right thigh. I looked around and saw a man drop his umbrella. He said he was sorry and I got the impression that he was trying to cover his face as he rushed off and hailed a taxi.' At Markov's inquest it was said that he had been killed by a metal pellet containing poison twice as deadly as cobra venom. The pellet was fractionally larger than a pinhead. It is assumed, though never proven, that his death was the work of Eastern Bloc agents. It may not be surprising to learn that Eastern Bloc countries have used such methods.

What is particularly disconcerting, however, is the evidence which suggests that psychological methods have reached advanced stages of deployment in the West. Indeed, according to Philip Agee who worked for the CIA for twelve years, its structure as long ago as 1959 contained an 'organization of the Deputy Director, Plans (Clandestine Services)', which had a division headed 'Psychological Warfare and Paramilitary Staff'.

In 1988, the *Sunday Telegraph* carried a 'Brainwashing Challenge to CIA' story which reported that former patients of British born psychiatrist Dr Ewen Cameron were seeking damages, claiming that he had used them as unwitting guinea pigs in a secret research project funded by the CIA. The story stated: 'The case ... will embarrass the agency, threaten Cameron's outstanding reputation and call into question the whole practice of psychiatric medicine.' Eight people who had attended Dr Cameron's hospital in Montreal between 1957 and 1960 were claiming $1 million damages from the CIA. Among the alleged 'treatments' was the use of sleep inducing drugs coupled with repetitive tape recordings of the patients' own or Cameron's voice. One patient claimed he had suffered loss of memory after he said the CIA had 'programmed', 'unprogrammed' and then 'reprogrammed us'. The agency was alleged by the patients to have been testing brainwashing methods.

Documents released under the US Freedom of Information Act show that between 1953 and 1963, the CIA had authorized 149 projects attempting to control man's mind in one way or another, involving 80 institutions and 183 research workers, many of them in independent colleges and universities. Public interest in these particular documents was provoked by a disclosure in 1976 before a US Congressional Committee that a Dr Frank Olson had been given, without his knowledge, the mind altering drug LSD in a drink and as a result had thrown himself from a tenth storey window. Until the disclosure Dr Olson's family had been left to believe that he had committed an insane suicide. Dr Olson's death occurred in 1953. If it can be correctly assumed that in the past 35 years research on such drugs has not been stopped, techniques for their use would by now be at an advanced stage indeed.

Other psychological techniques, which do not involve any physical invasion of the subject's body with mind altering drugs have also been developed. For example, the British are alleged to have used techniques such as sensory and sleep deprivation in Northern Ireland to elicit information quickly from internees. According to observers, these techniques can produce symptoms such as hallucinations, profound apprehension, depression and suicidal fantasies. In his book *Spycatcher*, Peter Wright refers to a Ministry of Defence establishment which gave him a demonstration of a poisoned dart fired from a cigarette packet. He also refers to a 'mysterious car accident in Spain', and to unexplained suicides.

* * *

I am often asked whether I think the scientists' deaths are part of a conspiracy or are entirely coincidental. The answer is I don't know.

My feeling is that it is highly unlikely that all the deaths are connected. Some must have committed suicide for personal reasons unknown to us. Others must have died in genuine accidents. Still, however, my suspicions remain in some of the cases. Vimal Dajibhai's death in Bristol is particularly odd. And why did Arshad Sharif die in an apparently unprecedented fashion? Even a police officer I spoke to was sceptical about Stephen Oke's death. He found it difficult to accept that Stephen had put on a record and was about to have a meal, when he suddenly decided to tie his hands in front of him and hang himself from a beam.

In investigating the work of the deceased, and whether there was a motive for murder, I came across much information about electronic warfare. The more I discovered about EW, the more fascinating the subject became. EW relies heavily on knowledge of the enemy's systems. Both sides put much effort into discovering each others' secrets. The capability of computer simulation in providing a wide view of the weaknesses and strengths of friendly and enemy systems is vital. EW can be a decisive factor in a war.

In the context of the peacetime war, which is taken so seriously by both Nato and the Warsaw Pact, it is more difficult to treat the deaths in isolation. Although the individuals may not have had an overview of their projects, both sides have shown their concern at the ease with which the other can piece together scraps of information. And, in EW, the enemy need only discover its weakest point.

Despite the introduction of the Security Service Act in December 1989, the secret services are still far removed from public accountability. Some observers have pointed out that intelligence personnel could, for example, under the powers granted by 'Royal Prerogative', murder their fellow citizens in the interests of national security. It is perhaps also worth mentioning that, if the secret services are indeed involved in actions as sinister as murder, the recent reform of the Official Secrets Act will further secure their anonymity.

Criminologists say there are three criteria for proving a murder: opportunity, motive and method.

With most of those mentioned in the book, the opportunity certainly existed. In the majority of cases there were no eyewitnesses and the periods before their deaths could not be explained. In the same cases, a motive also existed. They could have been regarded, in varying degrees, as security risks. As for the methods, Joe Vialls has at least one suggestion.

Tony Collins

Glossary

A & AEE – Aeroplane and Armament Experimental Establishment.

ADCIS – Air Defence Command Information System. *C3* system due to be in service with the British Army in Germany in the early 1990s. David Sands was working on ADCIS before his death. See also EASAMS.

ASMA – Air Staff Management Aid, a *C3* system developed by *ICL* for the RAF.

AUTOMATIC TEST EQUIPMENT (ATE) – electronic equipment used to check the operation of printed circuit boards and other components before and after final assembly. Can also be used to simulate the effects of operational conditions on electronic equipment in service on a regular basis.

BRITISH AEROSPACE (BAe) – the UK's largest aerospace company, employing 70,000 on aerospace production with annual sales of nearly £4bn. Manufactures missiles, components and both civil and military aircraft. Many of its products, including Airbus, Harrier and *Tornado*, are developed as part of joint ventures.

BRITISH TELECOM (BT) – public telecommunications network provider, large buyer of *System X* exchanges. Privatized in 1984, although the UK government still holds a 49 per cent stake in the company. Employs more than 240,000 producing annual sales of over £11 billion. Jonathan Wash was working for British Telecom's Telconsult subsidiary in Abidjan when he died.

C3, C3i – see COMMAND AND CONTROL SYSTEMS.

CID – Criminal Investigation Department of the UK police employing plain clothed detectives.

COMMAND AND CONTROL SYSTEMS – the intelligence behind sensors and weapons, command and control systems use computers and communications to support and deploy resources such as troops, missiles and *weapons platforms* with some degree of automation. Examples of military command and control systems include *ADCIS*, *ASMA*, and *UKAIR*. Such technology is often referred to as C3 (Command, Control and Communications), or C3i (Command, Control, Communications and Intelligence).

CORONER – local official, often a solicitor or medical practitioner, responsible for holding inquests on the bodies of persons who have died in sudden or inexplicable circumstances.

COSMOS – large scale *simulator* developed by *Marconi* for underwater weapons systems, tactics and software. It has been implied that the techniques developed for Cosmos could be used to simulate aspects of the US *SDI* project.

EW – Electronic Warfare. EW is a covert and critical adjunct to every modern conflict. In broad terms it comprises three distinct areas: Electronic Support Measures (ESM), which in essence involves intercepting enemy *signals* and analyzing the information contained in them; Electronic Countermeasures (ECM) which includes jamming and electronic deception designed to counteract enemy missiles and confuse communications; and, the most secret element of all, Electronic Counter Countermeasures (ECCM), the protection of computers, electronic equipment, communications, *C3*, missiles and *weapons platforms* from enemy EW actions. ECCM includes *stealth*.

EASAMS – subsidiary of the *GEC* group, Easams employs around 900 people, mainly on software consultancy work. Conducted feasibility study for *ADCIS* along with *Software Sciences* and also did some of the original design work for *UKAIR*. David Sands was employed by Easams.

ELECTRONIC COUNTERMEASURES (ECM) – see EW.

FORTRAN – scientific computer language used extensively at *Marconi* and other defence firms.

GCHQ – Government Communications Headquarters. The UK government's electronic listening post, based in Cheltenham. Part of GCHQ's work includes the analysis of electronic and *signals* intelligence which can be built into *simulators*, *EW* equipment and *C3* systems.

GEC – the General Electric Company of Great Britain, not connected with General Electric (GE) of the US. The UK's largest manufacturing company, employing around 100,000 people with an annual turnover of £6 billion. Manufactures everything from lightbulbs and washing machines to defence systems. In 1989 GEC, in a consortium with West German electronics company Siemens, bought rival firm *Plessey*. GEC's subsidiaries include *Marconi* and *Easams*.

ICL – International Computers Limited. The UK's largest indigenous computer manufacturer. Chief subsidiary of the British STC (Standard Telephones and Cables) group. Employs around 20,000 people with an annual turnover of almost £1.4 billion. Many government departments, including those concerned with intelligence, use ICL computers. The company also has a large defence division which specializes in the development and installation of *C3* systems.

IFF – Identification Friend or Foe. Electronic system which enables missiles, weapons systems and *C3* systems to distinguish between friendly and hostile targets.

IUKADGE – Improved UK Air Defence Ground Environment. System aimed at providing early warning of air attacks and a clear picture of the progress of a conflict as it unfolds. Expected to cost up to £7 billion and take UK defence into the 21st century, IUKADGE has been delayed by computer software problems. The prime contractors for the *C3* element of IUKADGE are *Marconi*, *Plessey* and the American aerospace and defence company Hughes. *Uniter* and *UKAIR* will form integral parts of IUKADGE.

MI5 – department of British secret service concerned with home affairs, roughly equivalent to the American FBI. The MI stands for Military Intelligence.

MI6 – department of British secret service concerned with foreign affairs, similar to the American CIA.

MARCONI – subsidiary of *GEC*. There are eleven companies within the GEC-Marconi group, which employs a total of 47,000 people and has annual sales of £2 billion. Marconi divisions include: Marconi Command and Control Systems, Frimley, Surrey; Marconi Defence Systems, Stanmore, Middlesex; Marconi Radar Systems, Chelmsford, Essex; Marconi Space Systems, Portsmouth, Hampshire; Marconi Underwater Systems, Portsmouth, Hampshire. These five Marconi divisions employ around 16,500 people. Marconi became part of GEC following a takeover in 1968. In February 1989, four men, including the former head of Marconi Space and Defence Systems Major General John Sturge, were arrested on charges relating to alleged fraud after a lengthy investigation at a number of Marconi divisions. Three Marconi companies, including the holding company, Marconi Space and Defence, and Marconi Secure Radio Systems, were also charged.

MICRO SCOPE – Maidenhead based computer communications company where Shani Warren was employed at the time of her death. Micro Scope, which employs around 130 people, was bought by *GEC* Computers for £16 million in 1987.

PLESSEY – UK electronics company specializing in telecommunications. Prior to its takeover by *GEC* and Siemens in 1989, Plessey was a rival to *GEC* and *MARCONI* on a number of defence projects, although it had collaborated with them on others. Jointly owned GPT (GEC Plessey Telecommunications) with GEC. Employed 26,000 and had annual sales of £1.3 billion.

PTARMIGAN – in simple terms a communications system developed by *Plessey*, described as a military version of the *System X* digital telecommunications exchange. Ptarmigan, which will be linked to *ADCIS*, has so far cost more than £1 billion at current prices.

RARDE – Royal Armament Research and Development Establishment.

REC – Radio Electronic Combat. Soviet *EW* strategy planned to take effect during a conflict with Nato.

RAPIER – ground to air missile system with

sophisticated *EW* capability. Manufactured by *British Aerospace*, Rapier will work in conjunction with *ADCIS*.

ROYAL MILITARY COLLEGE OF SCIENCE – the UK's foremost defence technology training establishment, based at Shrivenham, Wiltshire. The college has unique facilities and runs courses on a variety of technical defence topics, mainly for army officers, but also to a lesser degree for RAF and Royal Navy personnel. Peter Peapell was employed by the college at the time of his death.

SAS – Special Air Service. Highly secretive unit of the UK army formed in 1941, renowned worldwide for its anti-terrorist techniques, but primarily trained for raids and sabotage behind enemy lines in times of war. Also has an intelligence gathering role.

SDI – Strategic Defence Initiative, otherwise known as Star Wars. US defence project initiated by President Reagan in 1983 and aimed at deploying a highly automated defensive shield of lasers and other high technology weapons against nuclear attack.

STC – see ICL.

SIGNAL PROCESSING – technical term for the electronic process of transforming electrical impulses, sound waves or radio waves ('signals') generated by equipment such as radar and satellites into a form that can be e.g. displayed on a monitor or interpreted by a weapons guidance system. A technology used extensively in highly sensitive fields of defence electronics, including *C3* and *EW*. The process of gathering signals generated by enemy equipment is known as signals intelligence ('sigint').

SIMULATORS – in the military context, computer systems used by defence electronics firms and Ministry of Defence establishments to provide a secure and economic means for the development and testing of electronic equipment including *EW* systems, weapons systems, and *C3*.

SOFTWARE SCIENCES – subsidiary of the UK's Thorn EMI group, a large electronics conglomerate with defence interests similar to those of *GEC*.

SPEARFISH – Marconi Underwater Systems' heavyweight, wire-guided torpedo which incorporates a secret propulsion system, enabling it to attain higher speeds than previous torpedoes. Uses similar electronics technology to *Sting Ray*.

SPECIAL BRANCH – branch of the UK police which deals with political security. Liaises with *MI5* and *MI6*.

STAR WARS – see SDI.

STEALTH – evasion of detection by enemy sensors by the use of e.g. radar absorbing materials. See also *EW*.

STING RAY – Marconi Underwater Systems' self-guiding torpedo, claimed to be the most advanced lightweight anti-submarine torpedo in the world. Can be launched from surface vessels and aircraft. Designed to counter the Soviet submarine threat for the next 20 years. Vimal Dajibhai worked on Sting Ray from early 1986 until his death. According to Ministry of Defence figures published in 1988 nearly £2 billion has been spent on Sting Ray's development and production. Despite teething problems, the Royal Navy ordered 2,000 Sting Rays in 1986 at a cost of £200,000 each.

SUPERCOMPUTERS – advanced computers which can perform millions of calculations per second. Supercomputers are frequently at the heart of *simulators*.

SYSTEM X – digital telecommunications exchange jointly developed by *GEC* and *Plessey*. *British Telecom* is currently replacing its old, electro-mechanical telephone exchanges with System X exchanges. Adaptations of System X also have a military role as a key component of *Uniter* and other defence systems.

TIGERFISH – Wire-guided, heavyweight torpedo in service with the Royal Navy. Vimal Dajibhai worked on modifications to Tigerfish at Marconi Underwater Systems between 1983 and 1986.

TORNADO – fighter/bomber aircraft jointly developed by the UK, Italy and West Germany at a cost of nearly £3 billion. Designed to work in conjunction with *IUKADGE*, Tornado relies heavily on electronics developed by *GEC* to detect targets in a severe *EW* environment. 700 have so far been delivered to the RAF, German Air Force, German Navy, Italian Air Force and Royal Saudi Air Force. See also *British Aerospace*.

UKAIR – command and control system designed to support the strategic air defence of the UK, expected to be operational well into the 21st century. The contract for the design and implementation of UKAIR was awarded to *ICL* in the early part of 1987. David Greenhalgh had been involved with UKAIR. See also *Uniter* and *IUKADGE*.

UNITER – communications system which will link at least 100 RAF and United States Air Force sites around the UK, including operational bases. The backbone for both *IUKADGE* and *UKAIR*, Uniter is designed to withstand the effects of a nuclear war. Final stage due for completion in 1991. *GEC* is prime contractor, although *British Telecom, Plessey* and *Micro Scope* are also involved. Cost not fully disclosed.

WP – Warsaw Pact.

WEAPONS PLATFORM – military vehicle, such as an

aircraft, tank or ship, capable of carrying weapons.

ZEUS – Marconi Defence Systems' air defence *EW* system, worked on by Arshad Sharif. Designed for the Harrier jump jet, Zeus is a joint project with American defence contractor Northrop.

Results of Marconi Internal Inquiry

In 1988, following intense press coverage of the deaths, GEC's managing director Lord Weinstock commissioned an internal inquiry to look specifically into the deaths of the Marconi employees. Brian Worth, formerly a high ranking officer at New Scotland Yard, was appointed to conduct the inquiry, which took three months to complete. Although the full report was not published, in February 1989 Marconi allowed a small number of journalists who had shown a particular interest in the story to have access to a summary of the inquiry's results. The summary is published here in full.

FROM THE OFFICE OF BRIAN WORTH O.B.E.

1. Lord Weinstock asked me to look into the deaths of a number of GEC/Marconi employees. These deaths, although ostensibly suicides, nevertheless attracted considerable media attention and comment.

2. Having already prepared and submitted a comprehensive report on my inquiries so far, this is a synopsis of the approach I adopted and of my conclusions.

3. The deaths had already been individually investigated by Police Forces with the locus in quo and by Coroners' inquests. I did not therefore attempt an investigation from first principles but looked at the sequence of deaths collectively to establish whether:

   a. the deaths were credible as suicides on their own facts,
   b. there were any common or linking factors,
   c. the deaths as suicides appeared unusual when looked at in the wider or national perspective.

4. I therefore visited all the Police Forces concerned, where I discussed individual cases with Senior Officers, and whenever possible with the officers who had carried out the investigations. This enabled me, given excellent co-operation, to review the facts elicited and to conclude that against the normal parameters of inquiries into suicides and unusual deaths, the investigations were rigorous and objective.

5. An added impetus was given to some of the investigations by the spur of media interest.

6. The highlighting of these deaths in isolation from comparable or national suicide profiles can be misleading, and with this in mind I attempted to set the sequence in context. The numbers concerned, however, seem too small to permit firm conclusions; for one or two deaths either way will produce a disproportionate effect on calculations.

7. The suicides if viewed against a backdrop of cultivated suspicion or mystery, generated by speculation rather than evidence, look a little odd. But when a ratio of just over 3 suicides each year in a work force of 35,000 is looked at against a national yearly average of 10 suicides per 100,000 of population, a different view may be taken, even accepting that the comparison can only be a rough guide.

8. It may also reasonably be said that when the GEC experience is compared with other similar industries, the suicide profile appears less unusual.

9. The methods adopted in some of the cases although bizarre are not unique.

10. I had no remit to look at deaths of those persons in the defence industry, not employed by GEC, who were included by the newspapers in an overall aura of suspicion. I nevertheless kept them in focus. On the facts available their inclusion did not, in my view, further support a conspiracy theory.

11. It is pertinent to state that the newspapers alluded to the victims as 'scientists' whereas on any reasonable definition of the term most were not. And where it was claimed they were involved in highly classified work this was almost invariably not the case.

12. I concluded on the evidence available that the suicide verdicts reached were credible on their own facts, and in the four cases where open verdicts were returned the probability is that each victim took his own life. Whether the incidents are looked at singly, collectively or in any groupings, there is no evidence of a commonality of purpose or design; nor indeed a pattern of deliberate outside influence.

Brian Worth
Formerly Deputy Assistant Commissioner
New Scotland Yard

Bibliography

Arms and Artificial Intelligence. Edited by Allan Din, Oxford University Press, 1987.

CIA Diary. Philip Agee, Penguin Books, 1975.

'Command, Control and Communications.' A.M. Wilcox *et al* of Royal Military College of Science, *Brassey's Battlefield Weapons Systems and Technology Series Volume VI*, Brassey's Publishers Ltd, 1983.

Electronic Intelligence – The Interception of Radar Signals. Richard Wiley, Artech House, 1982.

GCHQ – The Secret Wireless War. Nigel West, Coronet Books, 1987.

'Guided Weapons.' R.G. Lee *et al* of Royal Military College of Science, *Brassey's Battlefield Weapons Systems and Technology Series Volume VI*, Brassey's Publishers Ltd, 1983.

Introduction to Electronic Warfare. D. Curtis Schleher PhD, Artech House, 1986.

Milcomp Military Computers, Graphics and Software Conference Proceedings, Wembley Conference Centre, London, 23-25 September 1986. Microwave Exhibitions and Publishers Ltd, 1986.

Milcomp Military Computers, Graphics and Software Conference Proceedings, Wembley Conference Centre, London, 29 September – 1 October 1987. Microwave Exhibitions and Publishers Ltd, 1987.

Milcomp Military Computers, Graphics and Software Conference Proceedings, Wembley Conference

Centre, London 27-29 September 1988. Microwave Exhibitions and Publishers Ltd, 1988.

Military Microwaves Conference Proceedings, The Metropole Hotel, Brighton, 24-26 June 1986. Microwave Exhibitions and Publishers Ltd, 1986.

'Naval Electronic Warfare.' Dr D.G. Kiely, *Brassey's Seapower Naval Vessels, Weapons Systems and Technology Series Volume V*, Brassey's Publishers Ltd, 1988.

Navies of World War 3. Antony Preston, Bison Books Corp, 1984.

Official Secrets Act – The Use and Abuse of the Act. David Hooper, Coronet Books, 1988.

Space Weapons. Rip Bulkeley and Graham Spinardi, Polity Press, 1986.

Spy. Richard Deacon with Nigel West, Grafton Books, 1988.

Spycatcher. Peter Wright, Viking Penguin Inc, 1987.

'Surveillance and Target Acquisition Systems.' A.L. Rogers *et al* of Royal Military College of Science, *Brassey's Battlefield Weapons Systems and Technology Series Volume VII*, Brassey's Publishers Ltd, 1983.

Task Force – The Falklands War 1982. Martin Middlebrook, Penguin Books, 1987.

The Search for the 'Manchurian Candidate' – the Secret History of the Behavioral Sciences. John Marks, Dell Publishing, 1979.

The Second Oldest Profession. Phillip Knightley, Pan Books, 1987.

War on the Mind – the Military Uses and Abuses of Psychology. Peter Watson, Hutchinson and Co Ltd, 1978.

Index